BEVANISM
Labour's High Tide

BEVANISM
Labour's High Tide

The Cold War and the Democratic Mass Movement

Mark Jenkins

SPOKESMAN

First published in 1979 by:
Spokesman
Bertrand Russell House
Gamble Street
Nottingham

Printed in Great Britain by
Bristol Typesetting Co. Ltd.
Barton Manor
Bristol

ISBN 0 85124 273 1

This book is dedicated to the Soviet Union's 'Tolpuddle pioneers': Vladimir Klebanov, Valeria Novodvorskaya, Vladimir Borisov, who, during 1977-79 underwent imprisonment and psychiatric internment for attempting to form genuine, free trade unions in the USSR. Their cause shall be embraced by millions.

Acknowledgements

The author acknowledges the assistance of the following people and organisations.

Professor Philip Bagwell
Professor Ralph Miliband
The British Library
The Transport House Library
The London University Library
The London School of Economics Library
The Library of the Polytechnic of Central London
The Modern Records Centre, University of Warwick
The South Thames College Library
The Willesden Library
The Tribune Library and Archives
The Marx Memorial Library
The Audit Bureau of Circulation
The Hendon Newspaper Library (British Library)
The TUC Library
Michael Foot, MP
Ian Mikardo, MP
Lord Castle
Lord Leek
Lord Brockway
Jo Richardson, MP
Andrew Roth (for whom special thanks for access to extremely valuable archive material)
Richard Clements, Editor of Tribune
Robin Blick
John Archer
Hilary Jenkins
Pauline Jenkins
Megan and Emily Jenkins

Contents

Contents

Diagrams

Glossary

Trade Unions

AEU (now AUEW) Amalgamated Engineering Union
AFL American Federation of Labour
ASSET (now ASTMS) Supervisory Staff Association
ASW Associated Society of Woodworkers
AScW Association of Scientific Workers
Bisakta Union for Iron, Steel and Kindred Trades Workers
CEU Constructional Engineering Union
CGT Confedération Général de Travail (French Communist Union Centre)
CIO Congress of Industrial Organisations (USA)
ETU Electrical Trades Union
FBU Fire Brigades Union
FO Force Ouvrière (French Trade Union Centre)
ICFTU International Confederation of Free Trade Unions (Non-Communist)
IFTU International Federation of Trade Unions
ITS International Trade Secretariat
NASD National Amalgamated Stevedores and Dockers (Blue union card)
NUFTO National Union of Furniture Trades Operatives
NUGMW (now MGWU) Municipal and General Workers Union
NUR National Union of Railwaymen
NUTGW National Union of Tailors and Garment Workers
PTU Plumbing Trades Union
TGWU Transport and General Workers Union ('White' union card)
TU Trade Union
TUC Trade Union Congress
UPW Union of Post Office Workers
USDAW Union of Shop Distributive and Allied Workers
WFTU World Federation of Trade Unions (Communist)

Labour Party
CLP Constituency Labour Party
'The Club' Trotskyist entrist group in Labour party
GMC General Management Committee (local Labour party)
KL Keep Left
Labour Independents Group of pro-Moscow expelled Labour MPs
LLOY Labour League of Youth
LP Labour Party
LPACR Labour Party Annual Conference Report
NALSO National Association of Labour Students
NEC National Executive Committee
NULO National Union of Labour Organisers
PLP Parliamentary Labour Party
SF Socialist Fellowship
SO Socialist Outlook
VFS Victory for Socialism

Other Socialist
Comisco Committee for International Socialist Co-operation (or Second International or Socialist International)
PSF French Socialist Party
PSI Italian Socialist Party (Nennist)
PSIUP United Italian Socialist Party
PSLI Italian Socialist Party (Saragat)
SPD German Social Democratic Party

Communist
Cominform Communist Information Bureau
KPD German (now West German) Communist Party
'National Fronts' Alliances of East European parties under communist control
PCF French Communist Party
PCI Italian Communist Party
SED Socialist Unity Party (Communist) of Eastern Germany
NKVD Soviet state police (now KGB)

Other
CENTO Central Treaty Organisation (formerly Baghdad Pact)
CIGS Chief of the Imperial General Staff (UK)
MEA Ministry of Economic Affairs (UK)
NATO North Atlantic Treaty Organisation
SEATO South East Asia Treaty Organisation

Chapter One

The World of Bevanism

The last quarter of a century has witnessed the crystallisation of a mythology about the Bevanite movement which has gained wide currency. This contemporary mythology denies the movement its full historic credit as the broadest, most popular Labour current this century and, simultaneously, attributes to it weak, and purely parliamentary, organisational forms, and neglect of trade union struggles. But, above all, contemporary mythology largely ignores the greatest single deficiency of the Bevanites—their inability to develop and proffer a coherent and consistent characterisation of the states of Eastern Europe and their agencies, and their role in world politics.

This study is intended as a contribution to the re-evaluation of the Bevanite movement, so often overlooked and unfavourably compared with a highly idealised view of the left in the thirties. This popular approach is typified in the following selected comments on Bevanism by David Coates[1],

> 'This was no "grass roots" mass working class movement of the ILP kind'.

> '. . . the Bevanites had no organised working class roots'.

> 'For Bevanism did not operate, as had the ILP and the Socialist League, against a backcloth of mass working class discontent'.

Such unsupported assertions have been possible only because hitherto, no detailed study had been made of the Bevanite movement.

The student of the Bevanite movement will find, to begin with, one refreshing difference with the nostalgia-ridden thirties—a confident, assertive working class, re-invigorated after the brutal symmetrical oppressions of Stalinism and fascism which had alighted on Europe in the days of the ILP and the Socialist League, a working class determined not to be anybody's 'backcloth'.

The great victory of 1945 represented the overwhelming desire of the working class movement and its supporters to place behind them the years of Chamberlain and Churchill, of unemployment, poverty and war, to place Labour in office to secure some fundamental changes in the conditions of life. The Bevanite movement was the differentiating out of the more determined elements in the Labour movement, encouraged but not satisfied with the achievements of the Attlee government in foreign and domestic policy.

The beginnings of left discontent were already in evidence as early as 1947 in the *Keep Left* revolt. Among the fifteen MPs who put their signature to this policy document[2] were many who were to become leading Bevanites. Its three authors, Richard Crossman, Michael Foot and Ian Mikardo played almost as important a role as Bevan himself in determining the course of the Bevanite movement later in the fifties—Foot as the editor of Tribune, Mikardo widely regarded as the organiser, and Crossman first as a theoretician and then as the Bevanites most illustrious defector. Keep Left has established for itself the reputation of the most short-lived of all Labour left revolts, being over almost as soon as it had started. For this reason the Keep Left group has never received the attention it deserved. On examination it proves a remarkably resilient grouping with a continuity which enabled it to absorb the Bevanite rebels four years later. But before examining it, we need to survey the international political issues to which the group addressed itself and which presented such obstacles to its development prior to 1951.

Why could the Keep Left signatories play a leading part in the Bevanite movement in the fifties *but not succeed between 1947–50*? This question is doubly perplexing given the assumption of Miliband that the public ownership programme of *Keeping Left*, published in 1950, had conceded ground to the 'consolidators' of the Labour establishment.[3] For this would have made them a less attractive proposition to any emergent left wing dissent in the Labour party than they had been three years earlier.

To some degree the answer is to be found in the mood of organised Labour. There was a very real surge of loyalty to Labour, of which the voluntary wage freeze of 1948–50 was one expression, during a period of severe economic crisis. But this economic crisis itself was no mere British phenomenon. The causes of it, and the remedies applied to it, were international to the core. And the political problems arising from these 'remedies' which the Keep Left group encountered in 1947 became more intractable in 1948 and 1949. It is this *international dimension of the problems of the British Left* that provides the key to the understanding of the course of its development, not only in the period of the prehistory of Bevanism (1947–51) but also in the period of its zenith (1951–54) and decline (1954–57).

Pre-occupation with the left's parliamentarism and its assumed shortcomings in the sphere of cohesive organisation,[4] popular among the contemporary radical left, can detract from an examination of the far more profound problem of Bevanism's inability to present a rounded out analysis of the world into which it was born—the world of the two 'camps'[5]—of 'western' capitalism and imperialism, and 'eastern' Stalinism, and of developments within and relations between the two in the post war period.

The Bevanites and their predecessors in Keep Left were impressionistic with regard both to the United States and the USSR, the twin leaders of the two 'camps'. Henry Pelling has demarcated three distinct phases in the evolution of the British Left's attitude to the USA in the space of five years.[6] In 1945–47 Keep Left asserted that 'America has swung right when the rest of the world is going left'. In the Marshall Aid period from 1947–49 they discovered a proximity between Truman's policy 'and the principles of Democratic Socialism'. By 1950 the honeymoon was ended by the Korean war and the left recoiled from the American embrace.

In regard to Russia the record is hardly more encouraging. Fond recollections of the Grand Alliance gave way after 1947 to shock and horror at Stalin's consolidation of Eastern Europe, which in turn was superseded by a heady optimism about the emergence of more liberal Soviet leaders after Stalin's death.

Although the Bevanites were members of a party which was affiliated to the Socialist International we seek in vain in their pronouncements for a truly international perspective of socialism. They behaved as if the establishment of Socialism was a task to be achieved within a fundamentally British perspective. Whilst they approached some economic and political questions from a global standpoint (in particular the relationship between the third world and the metropolitan countries), they never approached an understanding of the essential political interdependence of the class struggle in eastern and western Europe. Imperceptibly but surely they fell foul of the theory of the two 'camps'.

The first signs of problems to come lay in the way Keep Left retreated before the first shots of the Cold War. It is with the Cold War[7] then, that we must begin.

Some of the international political problems to which 'Keep Left' addressed itself re-emerged more acutely in 1950–51. 'One World, not hostile blocs,' said the Left's manifesto '. . . prevent . . . the division of Europe into an American and a Russian sphere of influence'.[8] What Keep Left sought to avoid, events ran to meet between 1947–50. The Bevanites spent the fifties bidding to unravel the Gordian knot that Washington and Moscow had tied across the face of Europe and the world.

How did the Grand Alliance become the Great Schism? At first sight the division of the world into Soviet and American spheres of influence, sanctified by the threat of mutual nuclear annihilation, appears to be a negation of Teheran, Yalta and Potsdam, whereas it is, in actuality, the *realisation* of those agreements. *It is harmony underlined by discord.* The *strategic* agreement to divide Europe took the form of a *practical* disagreement as to how it should be done. To juxtapose detente to cold war as mutually exclusive is to perpetuate mystery. The antagonism of the Cold War was the form in which the agreements were concretised.[9]

The collapse of Nazi power on the continent of Europe had unleashed powerful forces of social revolt from below. Each party to the end of war agreements feared that the other might possibly seek to harness these forces to secure additional advantage. The two spheres of influence became transformed, by a series of miscalculations, into two armed camps. Each side over-reacted to the over-reaction of the other, so that an antagonistic collaboration supplanted the Grand Alliance. *But the agreements are intact to this day.*[10] All the Cold War did was to crystallise them. A clue to the meaning of the Cold War is to be found in the following . . .

> 'Thus individuals and even entire classes can be driven into actions not as a direct reflex of a real and clearly comprehended economic, social or political stimulus, but at varying degrees of a tangent to these material forces. To say otherwise is to believe that all human beings act at all times with a total consciousness of what they are doing. "Over-reaction" to an imagined or exaggerated threat is as much a part of history as "under-reaction" by classes or individuals to warnings of dangers that were all too real.'[11]

As an example of this over reaction, we may cite the example of Greece. Both Stalin and Churchill had been agreed that, after the war, Greece was to remain a 'western' sphere of influence. Stalin even went to the length of ordering the Greek communists' uprising to be wound up,[12] so faithful was he to these agreements. President Truman's declaration on Greek and Turkish independence on 12th March 1947[13] was a direct response to the challenge of the Greek Communists to British hegemony *and the Stalin-Churchill agreement.*

Truman felt forced to issue this declaration since the declining power of Britain both in the Balkans and in Palestine obliged the United States to take on the policing role she had previously performed.

Yet the Greek uprising produced great tensions in the 'eastern' camp, foreshadowing a rift between Stalinist Russia and Tito's Yugoslavia, whose sympathy and aid to the native Greek Communist cause seemed to strengthen the prospect of a Balkan Federation of non-capitalist states, in which Yugoslavia might have the dominant voice.

To whom then was the Truman declaration directed? To Stalin and Russia who had given their solemn pledge on Greece and who, on Churchill's own testimony, stood by that pledge? Can we detect in this instance the first signs of an over-reaction to an event which was *beyond Stalin's control*? Stalin was no more keen on revolution in Greece than he was on revolution in China.[14] The class struggle in Greece, in China, and in Rumania where violent strikes erupted in the summer of 1947, was upsetting the carefully laid stratagems of Teheran, Yalta and Potsdam. For these had been agreements between governments, not agreements between the contending classes whose line of battle ran laterally *across 'east' and 'west'*.

A sympathetic idea, but one which does not lead its author to the same conclusion, is expressed in the following . . .

> 'The momentum of change over this quinquennium (*1945–50 MJ*) and the fact that the world was so far *outside the expectation and, even more, the intention,* of statesmen pose in an unusually clear form one of the recurrent problems involved in interpreting political change. Should not the events of these five years be seen as the outcome of forces over which men could not hope to exercise any real control?'[15]
>
> (*my emphasis—MJ*)

Frustrated by the failure to exercise the necessary degree of control over the process and momentum of change (whether one calls it 'the class struggle' or not) did the leaders of 'east' and 'west' begin to construe in the Rumanian strikes and the Greek and Chinese revolutions, the handiwork of their erstwhile allies? Disturbances in the 'east' could thus be seen as the work of western governments; disturbances in the 'west' the work of 'eastern' ones. Daniel Yergin, in a recent publication,[16] has uncovered a curious aspect of this contradictory view of each of the antagonistic 'camps' towards each other. It would appear that there were two groups advising Truman with regard to Russia. One group held to the view that Russia was a world revolutionary state with whom co-existence was impossible. This view, the 'Riga axiom', was for unrelenting ideological warfare. The other group held that the Soviet Union was like any traditional great power, part of the international status quo. This latter view, the 'Yalta axiom' was in the ascendancy in the period of Roosevelt, but gradually gave way to the tougher 'Riga' conception in the counsels of Truman after 1947. Unable to arrive at a view of the USSR which could reconcile the essentially conservative regime of Stalin with the revolutionary historical foundations upon which it rested,

American administrations were prey to *two mutually contradictory views* as to what constituted the Soviet Union and Soviet world strategy at different periods in the immediate post war world.

A parallel dualism is evident too, in the utterings of Khrushchev, and other Soviet leaders, who have gravitated from denunciations of the tendency to war inherent in the capitalist system, to affirmations of the practicality of different social systems living harmoniously together. Only quite recently have the Kremlin and the White House begun to trust each other[17] in a new detente. After the Truman declaration the process of escalation to two 'camps' was rapid. In June 1947 heavy fighting broke out in Greece. By the winter atrocities against the Communists were being reported[18] and a rival Communist government had been established. To the strategists of the Pentagon and Whitehall it may well have appeared that the Greek uprising was part of a global revolutionary strategy. At the same time, the strikes in Rumania were the first since 1935. The strikers' targets were the Communist Party's counter-inflation policy, Communist officials and police.[19] To the Kremlin's advisers might not this be seen as part of a global strategy of 'counter revolution'—for propaganda purposes if for nothing else? In September at Szklarska Poreba, in Poland, the Cominform was established. Its role as a policing organisation for the Kremlin was highlighted by the fact that membership was confined to the Soviet and East European Communist parties with the addition of the French and Italian purely out of considerations of prestige.[20] That it was not the old Comintern reborn for the purpose of promoting world revolution was clearly misconstrued by Yugoslavia. At its first session, her delegate, Kardelj, severely censured the French and Italian Communist parties for failing to take power at the end of the war.[21] Within months Yugoslavia was expelled from the Cominform for failing to submit to the economic dictates of the Soviet Union and for its clandestine encouragement of the Communist rising in Greece.

The intransigent rhetoric of Zhdanov was less to do with revolution than with the consolidation of the grip of the Kremlin oligarchy on a Europe being wooed with General Marshall's dollar aid. Zhdanov's policy required not only the sealing off of the Eastern economies into autarchic subservience but, above all, the elimination of all possible channels for independent working class and peasant organisation[22] and expression within the Stalinist camp. This meant the elimination of independent, genuine Social Democratic parties through forcible 'fusion', and the creation of 'national fronts' with remaining parties under Stalinist domination. These new states were to be called 'Peoples Democracies'. The process of forcible fusions, mergers, trials and executions of those who opposed them was already well under way in 1947, the year the Cominform was established.[23] In Czechoslovakia the steam rollering process took longer due to difficulties with the Social Democratic Party, which announced its preference to remain independent in October, 1947. Desperate to complete the consolidation the Stalinists engineered a coup in the Spring of 1948. Masaryk died in mysterious circumstances and the General Secretary of the Czechoslovak Social Democratic Party was removed from parliament and forced into exile.[24] The new President of Czechoslovakia, Gottwald, was elected on a show of hands![25]

Throughout Eastern Europe there was forcible collectivisation,[26] target setting in industry, the removal of 'moderate' Stalinists like Gomulka in Poland and a multiplying series of terror trials.

As an inverse and bloodless counterpart to this in the 'west', the French and Italian Communist Parties were excluded from the coalition governments into which they had entered at Moscow's command at the end of the war.

The 'microcosm' of this crystallisation of Europe and the world into two 'camps' was the partition of the German nation. Even within Germany the nucleus itself, Berlin, was divided. The *prelude* to this historic dismemberment was the splitting of *the German working class movement.* In this process the Russians showed greater initiative than their former allies, and, as always, the split was engineered under the banner of 'unity', with the sudden and surprise formation of the 'Socialist Unity Party' (SED) under Stalinist domination throughout Eastern Germany. The Social Democratic party leaders' decision to accede to Soviet pressure for a merger marked an abrupt reversal of their previous position. The merger was announced in Das Volk in April, but on 1st March in Berlin, the central committee's resolution to merge had been defeated 5 to 1 by 2,000 delegates, who shouted Grotewohl down into the bargain.[27] But it was of no avail. Henceforth genuine Social Democrats could exist independently only in the West. But Moscow's fear of independent parties did not extend to bourgeois ones. These parties continued. Unlike genuine working class parties for whom national unity was a pre-condition of class unity, the bourgeois parties could apparently be relied upon not to obstruct the Kremlin's design for a divided Germany.

It is instructive that this offensive was undertaken in the Soviet zone on 22nd April, 1946 *in the middle of the Grand Alliance* period, almost a full year before the official opening of the Cold War, lending credence to the view that the partition of Germany was a necessary consequence of the division of the Labour movement. The reason for the Russian initiative and the process of the partition of Germany is too complex to be dealt with at this point.[28] But a little needs to be said about the intentions of the great powers in this respect.

The division of Germany was discussed at Teheran by the 'big three' in December, 1943. At Yalta, after intermediate committee work, the *temporary* division of Germany was agreed after 'the idea of partitioning Germany into a number of states was dropped.'[29] Unless evidence is produced of a secret agreement to divide Germany permanently, it must be assumed that the Soviet and western powers' public pronouncements on the need for a unified Germany were, at least in the period of the Grand Alliance, genuine. Yet Germany *was* divided, and it would appear that the over-riding need to weaken Germany and its reborn Labour movement (particularly on the part of Russia) was the salient consideration.[30] That the intentions of statesmen once more failed to square with eventualities is noted by one commentator in the following manner . . .

> 'The morals of the twentieth century, the commitment, at least on the part of Britain and America, to principles of good order and good conduct in international affairs prevented their agreeing to the partition of Germany in a cold blooded manner . . . but the partition was inevitable nonetheless.'[31]

The fragmentation of the German Labour movement radiated outwards in a chain reaction to encompass the German nation itself, Europe, the world trade union movement and the Socialist International, all fracturing along the boundary line of the two 'camps'.

No other single event shaped the political environment of the Bevanite period to anything like the extent of the partition of Germany. The Berlin airlift signalled a dramatic and dangerous new low in the climate of relations between 'east' and 'west'. Berlin has come to symbolise the Cold War. From the Cold War derived the oppressive atmosphere of McCarthyism which penetrated right to the heart of the Labour movement in the period of the inquisition of the Bevanites.

Likewise in the deliberations and political disputes, divided Germany placed itself highest on the Bevanite agenda, irrespective of their own subjective priorities. The issue of German rearmament, and West Germany's inclusion in the 'western' alliance, for a period, eclipsed all else.

It is possible to take issue with the manner in which Keep Left and the Bevanites conducted the debate on Germany and the Cold War prior to 1951, and the German rearmament debate after 1951, in particular the political conceptions and attitudes of the various *tendencies* within the Keep Left Bevanite *current*.[32] But one cannot with great justification deny that the issue which underlay these debates—divided Germany —was *the* issue of the day, not only for Europe, but for the international and British Labour movement. 'Preoccupation with questions of foreign policy'[33] expressed a proper sense of priority.

Indeed preoccupation with home policy, and the narrowing down of horizons to 'shopping lists'[34] of interests to be nationalised, seemed to grow as the left current declined after the mid fifties. The Left has no reason, therefore, to apologise to radical historians for its preoccupation with international politics in the Bevanite period. International politics, and Germany in particular, commanded their attentions.

Henceforth any aspiring left current needed an international conception that would offer some escape from the paralysing polarisation whereby association with one 'camp' was viewed as akin to contamination by supporters of the opposing one.

What was needed was an approach which might make possible a rational critique of *world* politics and *world* economics with all its contradictions, antagonisms and interdependencies. The 'third way' represented only the modest beginnings of such an approach. But as the temperature of the Cold War dropped ever lower, the theory of the 'third way' met the full force of the Kremlin international propaganda machine.

The Third Way

The Keep Left manifesto wanted a Britain that would be 'friends not satellites of America' and that would 'undermine Russian suspicion of Social Democracy' by repudiating President Truman's proposals for 'Collective security against Communism'. This was an ambitious task. But the MPs who undertook it could hardly have anticipated the hostility they were to arouse from both 'camps'. Ironically the brutal policies of the Stalinists in Eastern Europe drove some well-meaning Lefts into a de facto acceptance of the other camp. This caused serious disagreements within Keep Left.[35] Indeed there would have been little reason, prior to the iron curtain's falling in Europe, for the Left to curry favour with anti-Russian sentiment amongst the mass of the British people at all. The Soviets were still regarded widely as the former allies in the struggle against fascist totalitarianism and were in any case economically exhausted by the war. Tribune was well aware of the weakness of the Soviet economy and for this reason argued that the prospect of a Russian attack in Europe was absurd.[36]

It was even argued that Labour should become instrumental in securing a loan to assist the Russian grain famine[37] and shortage of machinery. But this did not prevent Tribune from concluding that *American presence in Europe* was basic to the achievement of a Social Democratic 'Middle Way' in that continent.[38] The power political conception involved in this reasoning is vividly illustrated by an equation which read 'America plus Western Europe plus Britain and the empire can halt Russia; Russia plus Western Europe plus Britain and the empire can halt America.'[39] The Russians and their co-thinkers in the CPGB (and the Labour Party) had little difficulty in persuading their followers that the 'middle way' was a sophisticated Social Democratic apology for Washington's way.

Konni Zilliacus, the maverick of the neo Stalinist left[40] denounced it as 'innocent prattle about anti-American cum anti-Soviet power'.[41] Bevin, he alleged, was more realistic. Bevin realised there were two camps and he was in one of them. Presumably this argument applied equally to Zilliacus himself —at least until Tito was expelled from the Cominform, at which point a 'third way' appeared to have arrived even for Zilliacus. But the resilience of the prospect of a 'third way' was not so easily to be disposed of. The problem was that it could not be achieved except by resolute struggle against both 'camps', by asserting in other words, that the class struggle was international and that socialism required the ending of both capitalist and Stalinist domination in western and eastern Europe respectively. To take the third way to its logical conclusion would have led to a conception not very different from the idea outlined by Trotsky in the Transitional Programme of the Fourth International—a combined political and social revolution east and west. Indeed the Stalinists themselves sensed this in a distorted way when they (falsely) accused Tito, Rajk and others in Eastern Europe of being 'Trotskyists'.

Every move that Stalin made to hermetically seal his sphere of influence brought forth an escalating countermove by Washington which was further reciprocated by Moscow. The division of Europe, which Tribune had warned would mean 'the greatest calamity for its people' was achieved.[42]

What underlay the political crises of the immediate post war years were serious economic problems, arising from the war itself and its accentuation of the uneven development of the world economy.[43] If the American economy was on its feet after the armaments boom of the war years,[44] the British economy was relatively speaking, on its knees, and continental Europe on its back. The full extent of the unevenness did not fully dawn on western leaders until it found expression in chronic payments imbalances and, consequently, currency instability.

Differential investment, productivity and growth rates combined to produce very unequal trading partners in the post 1945 era. This expressed itself in an acute shortage of dollars —the 'dollar gap'. The devaluation of sterling on 18th September, 1949, touched off a wholesale re-adjustment of exchange rates in the sterling area and western Europe.

> 'It was "the most extensive re-alignment of exchange rates ever carried out in a short period of time".'

and represented

> 'an attempt to close the dollar gap by the deficit countries "adjusting their exchange rates in order to lower the prices of their goods and increase their sales to the western hemisphere".'[45]

Although the British devaluation (30 per cent) was greater than that of Germany (20 per cent), France (22 per cent), Italy (8 per cent) and Belgium (13 per cent), nonetheless living standards in the UK were generally higher than those prevailing on the continent. This may go part of the way to explaining why British Social Democracy fared better than its continental sister parties between 1945–51.

The political implications of the acute dollar shortage in Britain in 1947 were clearly grasped by Crossman commenting on Bevin's victory over the Keep Lefters at the Margate conference of the Labour Party in the summer of 1947.

> 'What he (Bevin) achieved at Margate was enthusiastic endorsement of his view that we should go on behaving as one of the Big Three at least until the dollars run out; and that we should not prepare preventive measures to meet the crisis in advance but run slap into it in the middle of our way through.'[46]

In Crossman's view the only way to prevent widespread unemployment resulting from the dollar shortage would have been through another dollar loan or forcing drastic measures on the TUC leaders. In the event both ensued.

Crossman had not long to wait. The first convertibility crisis erupted in July 1947 and the attempt to make sterling convertible into gold or dollars, which had been one of the conditions of earlier loans, had to be suspended after five weeks.[47] With Britain and continental Europe in such a weak economic position the United States had now to press ahead with the plan outlined by Secretary of State, Marshall in his

Harvard speech, as much to prevent a slump in the US economy as to consolidate West European capitalism. Tribune commented that the Marshall plan was a firm and swift response of the US to Communist consolidation in Eastern Europe. Initially the Russians were to have been invited to participate, but dissatisfaction with the terms ruled this out. This placed Czechoslovakia in a difficult position. The Czechs' consent to attend the planning conference on Marshall Aid was announced and renounced within a fortnight that July! The Soviet Union moved to insulate the East from the dollar lubrication of the world market.

The period of Marshall Aid in Britain lasted from July 1948 to December 1950. In that period there was something of a recovery in the British economy and its payments position, though this did not prevent a second convertibility crisis and devaluation in 1949. During these same two years of Marshall Aid Labour was able to secure the collaboration of the TUC in a wage freeze. There was a consolidation of support for the government in difficult times. But Marshall Aid had placed Labour firmly in the American 'camp'.

The organic unity of the world economy ensured that eastern Europe would not escape these troubles. Eastern Europe was less developed than the west. It had, if anything, suffered greater economic dislocation.[48] It had no vast economic resources to fall back upon. If the foundation of the western bloc was the bounteous industry of the United States, that of the eastern bloc was the thriving industry of Soviet military-police-bureaucratic control. Only in this 'industry' did the Soviets have the advantage over the United States.[49]

Marshall Aid was offered to Eastern Europe and had some enthusiastic supporters amongst East European communists. Stalin did send Molotov and a team of experts to examine the proposals, but recoiled from the terms which would have involved submitting an inventory of Soviet resources.[50] Apart from the violent disturbances in Rumania in 1947, famine and food shortages were reported in Poland in the same year. In Germany famine resulted partly from the policy of dismantling factories and partly from the lack of co-ordination between occupying zones.[51]

The failure of an aid programme to materialise in Eastern

Europe ensured a truly grim economic era for its peoples. But this failure was aggravated by the 'strategic embargo placed by the "west" on its trade with the Sino-Soviet bloc'.[52] East European exports to America and the west fell from 40 per cent of the total to 15 per cent between 1948–53.

Impressive growth rates in Eastern Europe in the post war era were due to concentration of resources on heavy industry investment, all of this at enormous sacrifice, suffering and shortages of even basic consumer goods. The revolts in East Germany and Hungary in 1953 and 1956 were intimately connected with this economic hardship, and became concentrated in the demand for sovereignty, autonomy and freedom from Soviet suzerainty. The Russians recognised this full well, and from somewhere, summoned up their version of Marshall Aid, some time later . . .

> 'Russia undertook new loan commitments in the early 1950's although the death of Stalin and the Berlin uprising that followed it led to the granting of a loan of $128 million to East Germany in August 1953, and the annulment of $3,200 million of war reparations owing to the Soviet Union. 1956, however, saw the introduction of a massive Soviet aid programme following the Polish and Hungarian uprisings of that year.[53]

Stalin's rejection of the Marshall Aid offer, then, led to a sharp 'leftward' lurch on the part of all the parties under his control in eastern and western Europe. A continental campaign began against the Marshall plan and against the integration of the west European economies under dollar hegemony.[54] The British Communist Party was a little late in adapting to the new line. Their MP's actually voted *for* the US loan to Britain.[55] But these errors were quickly recanted. Conditional CPGB support for the Labour government ended abruptly in October 1947,[56] for Labour was now seen to be an active partner in the imperialist 'camp'.[57]

Tribune warned that western CP's could now be relied upon to slither into sectarianism and adventure.[58] Dock strikes in 1948 and 1949 are held by Pelling to have been part of a plan of disruption of the European Recovery Programme.[59] On both occasions the invocation of the Emergency Powers Act brought them to a speedy end. At the time Tribune was concerned that socialists could find themselves becoming a progressive wing of one 'camp', 'rather than an independent third entity trying to mediate between the forces of West and East'.[60]

The CP's hostility was not reserved for Attlee, Morrison and Bevin. It was equally directed against those who *opposed* 'collective security against communism'—Keep Left, and the supporters of the third way.

> 'All the "leftism" of the "Keep Left Group" of which Crossman, Mikardo and Foot are the chief spokesmen, has revealed itself as nothing but a group in open support of the reactionaries of both parties and as providing the leading spokesmen against the CP.'[61]

But the efforts of the British party were entirely modest compared with the adventures unleashed by their monolithic continental Cominform sister parties. Whereas in France the PCF, as part of the coalition government of the immediate post war years, had opposed strikes initiated by popular working class discontent, in the November strike wave 'armed communist pickets compelled workers to stay out . . .'[62] The purpose of these strikes, which had their counterparts in Italy also, was to put pressure on governments who collaborated in the Marshall Aid plan. The effect was threefold. Such tactics alienated social-democratic workers and strengthened working class loyalty to their social democratic leaders, creating serious problems for the left socialists. Secondly, in the long run they split workers' organisations at national and international level. In France the CGT split against the wishes of Jouhaux, who had been instrumental in amalgamating the CGT and the Communist CGTU eleven years earlier in the popular front period.[63] As a result the Force Ouvrière came into being. Over a million swelled into its ranks within months. The FO then applied to affiliate to the World Federation of Trades Unions which promptly split the following year (1949).

That this splitting of the world trade union movement was *primarily* the result of Cominform policy is evidenced by the events of the immediate post war period. The old international

Federation of Trades Unions (IFTU) had been smashed by Hitler. The TUC provided offices for its exiled staff. It still retained for a time the allegiance of the AFL, TUC, the Swiss and Swedish national union centres. But so anxious were the European trade unionists to achieve unity with their East European allies that the TUC ditched the IFTU in 1943 because its rules would have prevented the attendance of Soviet Trades Unions from a conference to unite the world trade union movement. When the conference finally took place on 6th February, 1945, the American CIO and the Soviet unions were in attendance, but the American Federation of Labour absented itself in protest at the TUC's winding up of the old IFTU *without a conference*. The AFL boycotted the second conference of the new World Federation of Trades Unions (WFTU) in Paris in October the same year, but 56 other national union centres were present. Since *only one* national centre was permitted to affiliate, the AFL and the Christian union centres were disallowed. All of this amounted to extraordinary and even unwise 'generosity' on the part of the TUC to appease the Soviet trades unions.[64] But severe tensions developed nonetheless after 1947. Arthur Deakin protested at the misuse of the WFTU in the campaign against the Marshall plan, and the split came at the WFTU bureau in Paris between January 17–21, 1949, when the TUC and the CIO walked out in protest. The Soviet, French and Italian unions appeared to have controlled the propaganda organs of the federation, from whence the anti-Marshall campaign was conducted. They were also anxious to terminate the autonomy of the International Trade Secretariats (ITS) and to bring them under tight central control. These secretariats co-ordinated the activities of workers in the same industries. Control of them would have prevented scrutiny of wages and working conditions in the east and would have secured a valuable additional implement in the anti-Marshall campaign. It was the ITS's that led the way to the formation of the International Confederation of Free Trades Unions (ICFTU). The WFTU promptly labelled them 'splitters of the working class'.[65]

The adventurism and sectarianism of the Moscow-based Communist Parties, and the unions, and union centres in which they had influence provided the best possible pretext for those in the western 'camps' who may have wished to split the world trade union movement. But this was not the only victim of the new 'third period'. A further achievement of Moscow's sharp ultra-left turn against the Marshall plan was the splitting of the international socialist movement. Independent Social Democratic parties that had existed in eastern Europe were affiliated to Comisco (the Committee of International Socialist Conferences),[66] the embryonic Socialist International established after the war on the initiative of the British Labour Party.

Initially some east European Socialist parties, notably the Czechs, had viewed Marshall Aid favourably but a change of line was engineered as a result of Soviet pressure and at a Socialist International Conference in December 1947, these parties submitted their own draft on economic aid. This was rejected, whilst a resolution accepting American aid 'without strings' was accepted with the East European parties abstaining. Following a meeting of Comisco on January 10th, 1948 a conference of all socialist parties was called for 21–22 March, to discuss Marshall Aid. But before the conference assembled, the Czech coup had been executed in February. The Socialist international was effectively split as a consequence. No East European parties were present.

The Kremlin could not have allowed the Czech Socialists to be present at that conference because their known predilection for American aid might become a 'pole of attraction' for the wavering Stalinist apparatus in Prague.

> 'the Marshall Plan affair confirmed the view of Stalin and his advisers not only that Dr. Eduard Benes and the National Front system were unreliable, but that the Gottwald group at the head of the Communist Party was not wholly reliable either. Klement Gottwald and other Communist members of the Czechoslovak cabinet had, of course, originally voted in favour of their country's participation in the Marshall Plan'.[67]

Those Social Democrats who had attempted to ingratiate themselves with the Kremlin by moderating their enthusiasm to the Marshall plan were not spared when the axe fell after the coup, even though Social Democrats rejected the merger with the Communist Party by 2–1.

On March 3rd, 1948, the Socialist International issued a statement which declared,

> 'Communists cannot achieve their aims without support from a minority from within the camp of Democratic Socialism. As in Czechoslovakia, so in Hungary, Rumania, and Bulgaria, individual Socialists, by permitting or abetting Communist attacks on democracy, have connived at their own destruction.'[68]

On March 20th a further meeting of Comisco made clear the issue of the split . . .

> '(The Committee) is fully aware that the Communist Parties have been ordered to destroy democratic socialism. The Committee has consistently tried to maintain cordial relations between Socialist Parties of all countries, but it notes that many of them have been forced to submit to Communist control or to disappear altogether. The responsibility for the split thus caused inside the European Socialist movement rests wholly with the Cominform and with the policies through which the Cominform has tried exclusively to serve the interests of the Soviet Union.'[69]

In the same month that this statement was issued, the remnants of Eastern European Social Democracy, now absorbed into the Stalinist machine, were participating in an anti-Marshall plan conference as the Socialist International was duly endorsing the draft Labour Party statement accepting it. So now the trade union movement and the international socialist movement[70] had been split . . . Henceforth each union and party 'camp' came increasingly under the sway of either Soviet or American world economic and political gravity in one or the other of the blocs—WFTU or ICFTU, Cominform or Comisco. But those who remained in the 'western camp', and those lucky Stalinists who were fortunate enough to live in the 'west' whilst remaining in 'eastern camp' organisations were able to retain organisational independence and a varying degree of responsibility to the working class membership that elected them. In the East the 'parties' and 'unions' of the

Kremlin became hunting-grounds in the bloody purges of the late 1940's. Those Social Democrats who voluntarily accepted the mergers[71] of their parties with Kremlin-controlled Communist Parties, at best, could hope to become transformed into harmless mouthpieces as state functionaries, although one or two became ardent Stalinists. At worst they could enjoy the fate of Rajk and Slansky. The charge of 'wreckers' and 'splitters', so often hurled at the Trotskyists by supporters of Stalin could, once again, with complete justification be levelled at the Cominform. In Germany, with the assistance of the western allies, they had split the unions, the workers' parties, the nation and the capital. The temporary partition had become a permanent one. *The partition of the German Labour movement was then visited upon the whole of Europe, just as the fate of the German Labour movement in the thirties anticipated the fate of the entire continent.* Germany in the thirties and the forties mirrored and expressed in its most acute form the condition of the continent at whose heart she lay.

Amongst those wide layers of the population not directly in association with organised Labour, Moscow's adventurist policies were a catalyst in driving the middle class to the right and compounding the problems of the Social Democrats. De Gaulle, not surprisingly, made sensational gains in the French municipal elections in the late autumn of 1947 and began his famous 'tours'. Commenting on the General's accession to the leadership of the French right, Tribune rejected the false choice between American monopoly capitalism and Russian communism, De Gaulle, and Thorez, 'Scylla and Charybdis'.[72] But the relentless recoil from left wing parties continued.[73] In 1949 the Social Democrats were defeated in the West German elections. Social Democracy lost to the Catholic Peoples' Party in Austria. Even in Australia the Labour government fell to a Conservative coalition. The world of Bevanism was largely shaped by relationship of the American and Soviet superpowers, how they reacted to the class struggle and to each other. The only means available of gauging the level of the class struggle are the figures for strikes, and voting for working class parties. The latter figures are likely to be less dramatic than the former, since parliamentary elections filter the militancy of organised labour through the voting behaviour of the entire population. Nonetheless there is a correlation between the two. The countries chosen are the four largest—Britain, France, West Germany and Italy, with the addition of Norway and Sweden for comparative purposes, since these two countries like Britain at the time, were Social Democratic in temperament and, unlike Italy and France, their Communist Parties did not carry enormous weight.

The strike figures reveal that the tempo of the class struggle expressed at the level of industrial disputes built up from the end of the war to a peak of over 6 million days in 1947–8, and remained at a high level into 1950–51, thereafter falling to within 2–3 million days up to 1957 (See Figure 1). Of course it must be borne in mind that to some extent the Kremlin-directed strike wave of 1947 exaggerates the picture, but it does not distort the general trend of a fall in this main index of the class struggle between the forties and fifties. This can be tested by examining the strike figures for Britain, Sweden and Norway where the Kremlin's strike initiatives were less likely to show up in the figures (See Figure 2). In Britain the pattern is consistent with the average trend although there is a *higher* peak in 1955–57. Sweden's figures also peak in 1947–48 but, again, in 1951 and 1953 they peak at a higher level. Norway's peak comes a little later in 1948–49, and this too, is superseded by a new higher peak in 1956.

In fact these figures indicate a possible distorting effect of the influence of pro-Kremlin parties without negating the objective trend of the class struggle, because in Italy and France where the union centres exhibit marked Communist domination, the 1947–48 peak *is not capped at any time during 1951–57*, whereas in Britain, Sweden and Norway, they *are.* Perhaps the anxiety of the Kremlin to better relations with the 'west' after Stalin's death is revealed in the French and Italian figures. Just as Italy and France greatly *exceeded* the average strike rate in 1947–48, they are shamed into second and third place by the more 'conservative' British trades unionists by 1957!

As with strikes, so with voting in parliamentary elections. The percentage votes for working class parties show a very steep decline in Italy and France where the disruptive effect

Figure 1
Average and Individual Strike Rates in Selected European States, 1944–57.

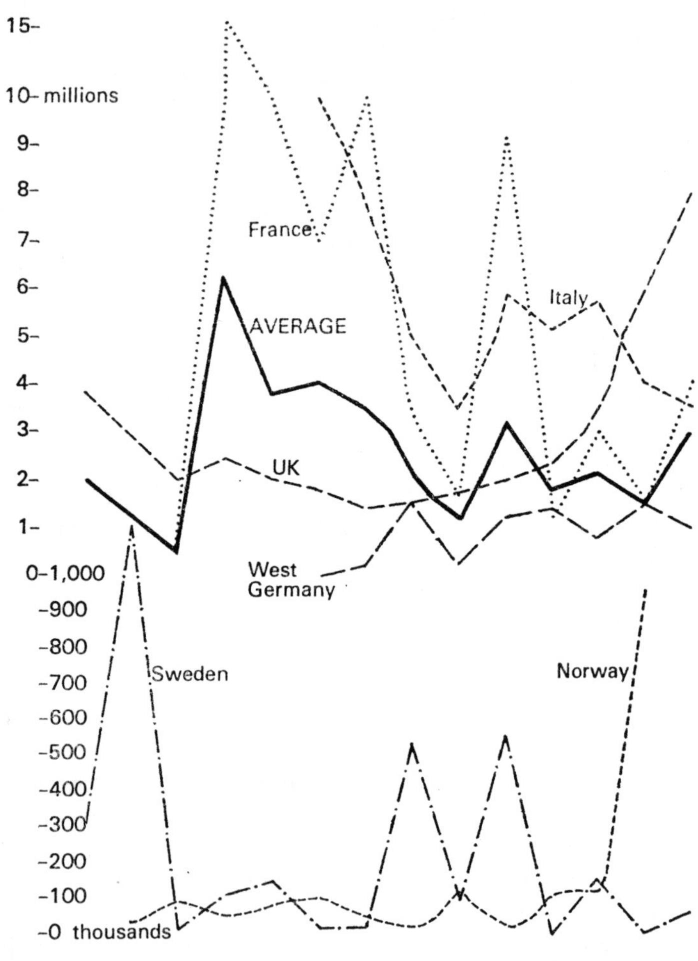

The strike figures and percentage votes for working class parties in selected European states from which this diagram is constructed are taken from *European Political Facts* (pp. 123–63), by Cook and Saxton, Macmillan London, 1975.

Figure 2
Average Strike Rate and Voting for Working Class Parties in Selected European States, 1944–57.

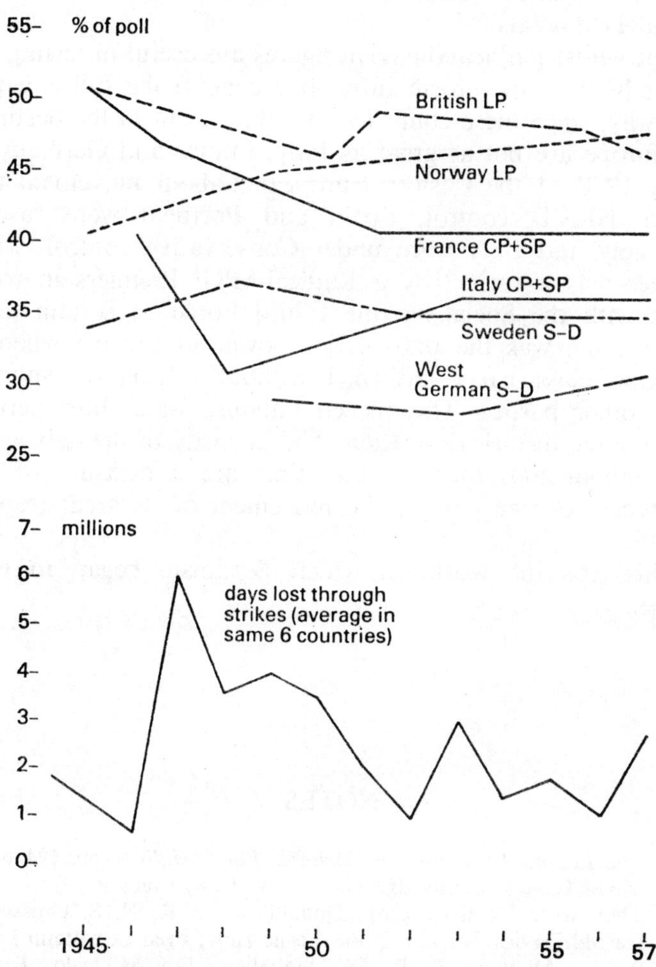

Source: as figure 1 above.

of Kremlin tactics through the domestic Communist parties could cause the most damage. In Norway, Sweden and Britain the very early fifties see a continuing *increase* in the popularity of working class parties represented by the dominant Social Democrats.

But whilst the Scandinavian figures are useful in testing the effect of the Cominform turn, they conceal the full effect in one way, since these countries' specific weight in the destinies of Europe are not as great as Italy, France and Germany.

By 1950–51 the Eastern European Labour movement was under NKVD control, Spain and Portugal were fascist, Germany and Italy were under Conservative control, while France was governed by a Radical-MRP Premiers in coalitions with the Socialists (the 'Third Force').[74] Britain then, for a time, was the only major power in Europe where a working class party governed without relying on support from other parties. This placed Labour, for a short period, in a unique historical position. The intensity of the debates in the Labour movement at that time are a measure of the awareness on the part of the movement of its great responsibilities.

This was the world in which Bevanism began to take shape.

NOTES

1. *The Labour Party and the Struggle For Socialism* (pp. 194–6) by David Coates, Cambridge University Press, London 1975.
2. They were Geoffrey Bing, Donald Bruce, R. H. S. Crossman, Harold Davies, Michael Foot, Leslie Hale, Fred Lee, Benn Levy, R.S.G. Mackay, J. P. W. Mallalieu, Ian Mikardo, Ernest Millington, Stephen Swingler, George Wigg and Woodrow Wyatt. Their names appear on the pamphlet *Keep Left* written by 'A Group of Members of Parliament' published by the 'New Statesman and Nation' in May, 1947.
3. *Parliamentary Socialism* (p. 306) by Ralph Miliband, Merlin Press, London 1973.
4. See *The Labour Party and The Struggle for Socialism* (p. 190 and

p. 193) by David Coates, Cambridge University Press, London, 1975.

On page 190 Coates argues that left wing activity in the post war Labour party 'was restricted almost exclusively to Parliamentary manoeuvring'. On page 193 he says 'Organisationally, the Bevanites were even weaker and more parliamentarily based than earlier Labour Lefts'. With both these views the author takes issue. See below chapter 6 'Bevanite Organisation' which deals extensively with the extra-parliamentary organisation of the Bevanite movement. This chapter also examines the considerable tightness of Bevanite organisation.

5. It is to Zhdanov that the theory of the 'two camps' is attributed. See *Stalin* (pp. 570–572) by Isaac Deutscher, Penguin, London 1966. See also *An Empire Loses Hope* (pp. 117–18) by Anatole Shub, Jonathan Cape, London 1971. See also *The Anatomy of Communist Takeovers* (p. 446) edited by Thomas T. Hammond, Yale University Press, London 1975. The 'two camps' theory eliminated any possibility of a 'third way' or a 'third force' in politics. There was the 'camp' of 'peace and socialism' (the Soviet camp), and the 'Camp' of 'imperialism'. Those like Tito who argued that they were neither for Washington nor Moscow were placed by Stalin in the 'camp' of imperialism.

   The author uses inverted commas around the word 'camp' throughout this study because he does not accept this as a valid approach to the study of world politics. He uses inverted commas around 'east' and 'west' because he does not regard that part of Europe currently under Soviet domination as 'eastern' but as part of Europe and the European tradition, as indeed is Russia itself. Neither does he regard countries such as Japan, Malaya etc. as 'west' or 'western' merely because they are associated with non-Soviet alliances.
6. *America and the British Left* (p. 151) by Henry Pelling, Adam & Charles Black, London 1956.
7. In *The Cold War—A Re-appraisal* (p. 7) edited by David Luard, Thames & Hudson, London 1964, the editor complains that the phrase 'Cold War' is 'remarkable for its lack of accurate definition. It could perhaps be described as a state of intensive competition, political, economic and ideological which yet falls below the threshold of armed conflict between states.'
8. *Keep Left Manifesto. op. cit.*
9. The Guardian, 10.8.78, quoting from *Nachfrost* by Zdenek Mlynar, Europaeische Verlangsanstalt, Cologne, September 1978, gives confirmation of the degree of collaboration between the White House and the Kremlin in more recent times. Said the Guardian report . . .

   'Mr Brezhnev told captive leaders of the Prague Spring in Moscow in 1968 that President Johnson personally assured him that the United States would not move to stop the Russian-led invasion of Czechoslovakia one of the Czech leaders reports . . .' President Johnson's assurances were announced by Brezhnev to the Czech leaders two days before the invasion of 20th August. Mlynar, a former Czech Communist Party secretary is a reliable authority.

'Mr Brezhnev, according to Mr Mlynar, told the Czechs that the Soviet Union was ready to risk a new conflagration if the results of the second world war—Moscow's hegemony over Eastern Europe—were jeopardised . . .'

'Mr Brezhnev said he asked the President whether the US continued to recognise the Yalta and Potsdam Big Three agreements which defined spheres of influence after the allied victory. The response was an "unreserved recognition as far as Czechoslovakia and Rumania are concerned" but that the status of Yugoslavia must be subject to negotiation'.

10. Foot has some interesting comments on 1956 when Britain and Russia simultaneously invaded Suez and Hungary, respectively, within their spheres of influence. On p 534—

> 'Bevan was still captivated by the question which no-one would answer; whether in fact the British decision to go into Suez had spurred the Russians to re-enter Budapest, and sometimes the attempt of Ministers to escape from the implications of that charge impaled them on one even worse. They knew Soviet tanks were moving westwards, across the borders from Russia, from Rumania, back into Hungary; British intelligence supplied the evidence. And yet they had struck at Suez and released the Russians from their moral isolation . . .'

Aneurin Bevan. Volume 2. 1945–60 (p. 534) by Michael Foot, Davis-Poynter, London 1973.

11. *Fascism in Germany* (p. 78) by Robert Black, Steyne Publications, London 1975.
12. *Conversations with Stalin* (pp. 164–5) by Milovan Djilas, Rupert Hart Davis, London 1962.
13. Speech to Congress, 12th March, 1947.
14. *Tito Speaks* (p. 331) by Vladimir Dedijer, Weidenfeld and Nicolson, London 1953. Quoted in *Mao Tse-Tung* (p. 238) by Stuart Schram, Penguin Books, Harmondsworth, UK 1966.
15. David Luard *The Cold War—A Re-appraisal, op. cit.* The excerpt is taken from the chapter entitled 'The Partition of Europe' by Wilfrid Knapp (p. 46).
16. *Shattered Peace—The Origins of the Cold War and the National Security State* (p. 35) by Daniel Yergin, André Deutsch, London, May 1978.
17. See above note on Zdenek Mlynar's book.
18. Daily Mirror, 10.11.47.
19. Tribune, 2.1.48.
20. *The Communist Party of the Soviet Union* (p. 540) by Leonard Schapiro, Methuen & Co, London 1963. In a threat to the

Dubcek leaders in 1968, Brezhnev is quoted by Zdenek Mylnar (*op. cit.*) as saying 'You are relying on the support of the Communist movement in Western Europe. But that lost its importance 50 years ago'.

21. As above (3), p. 541.
22. An extensive article on Bulgaria and Rumania in Tribune, 15.8.47, shows evidence of a far greater interest in the internal affairs of Eastern Europe than is the case with the contemporary Tribune. Nor is this the only example. There were systematic regular reports on the East European States in the period of Michael Foot's editorship.
23. Maniu, the leader of the Rumanian Peasants' Party was arrested in the summer of 1947. Petkoff, the leader of the Bulgarian Peasants' Party was tried and executed in the same year. The Rumanian Socialist Party was forcibly fused.
24. Blajet Vilim. He fled to England in March and wrote regular articles for Tribune for a time.
25. An article by Blajet Vilim in Tribune, 18.6.48.
26. In Poland the Socialist Party was divided into a right wing and a left wing. The left wing was further divided between a minority which supported co-operation with the Communists and a majority which did not. In the Autumn of 1947 the Polish Socialists were forced to allow Communist Party members to attend their meetings and by this means the pro Communist minority within the left was able to secure control of the party. They were then ordered to purge dangerous elements.
    See Hammond, *op. cit.* (p. 355).
    See also Tribune 19.9.47. This report announced that 24 leading Socialist party members, members of the Polish Premier's own party, had been arrested.
27. *Struggle for Germany* (pp. 148–176) by Russell Hill, Victor Gollancz, London 1947. This book contains the most detailed account of the merger.
28. For a full and detailed account of the destruction of the Social Democratic Party in Eastern Germany see the author's doctoral thesis at Transport House library or the Library of the Polytechnic of Central London.
29. *The Major International Treaties 1914–1973, a History and Guide with Texts* (p. 224–5) by J. A. S. Grenville, Methuen & Co, London 1974.
30. See appendix 1 of the author's doctoral thesis on voting in East German elections and in Berlin prior to, and just after, the formation of the SED.
31. See Wilfrid Knapp in David Luard, *op. cit.*
32. A current can exist within a party, and a tendency within a current. There are important differences between the three.
    A party has a constitution, rules and organisational structure which make possible unity for the purposes of elections and

political activity generally. But within a party there may develop *currents* from time to time.

Left currents are a recurring feature of Labour party history. Currents do not initially, and may not ever, develop the paraphernalia of a party. To the extent that they do they may lead in the direction of another party. There was disagreement between left and right in the fifties as to whether the Bevanites constituted 'a party within a party'. The Bevanites themselves disagreed as to the degree of organisation they required for the development of their current of opinion within the party. Bevan, in particular, was wary of tight group organisation.

Tendencies existed within the Bevanite movement. Some wrote for Communist Party journals from time to time and held views approximating towards the Communist Party on certain issues. Others were closely associated with the Trotskyist 'Socialist Outlook'. (See the grid on Bevanite MP's associations in Appendix 9 of the author's doctoral thesis.) Others were associated with the pacifist 'Union for Democratic Control'.

33. David Coates, *op. cit.* (p. 190).
34. See *The Gaitskellites* (pps. 44–60) by Stephen Haseler, Macmillan, London 1969.
35. See below 'The Prehistory of Bevanism' on the Keep Left movement.
36. Tribune 1.8.47. This conclusion was based on a review of the five year plan figures which the Kremlin had just released.
37. Tribune 31.1.47.
38. Tribune 3.1.47.
39. Tribune 3.1.47. A similar idea is expressed in Wilfrid Knapp, David Luard, *op. cit.* (p. 46). 'Between the United States and the USSR lay Germany. Germany united on either side would destroy the balance'.
40. See below section on Zilliacus (p. 52).
41. Tribune 3.10.47.
42. Tribune 11.4.47. 'Half a Europe'.
43. *Economic Policy and Performance—The Fontana Economic History of Europe* (p. 35) by Angus Maddison, Fontana, London 1973 gives the following figures:

Loss of Capital Assets in Europe Through War 1939–45

	Percentage of immediate pre-war stock lost (excluding land)		
	Domestic	Foreign	Total
Austria	16	0	16
France	8	2	10
Germany (F.R.)	13	–1	12
Italy	7	0	7
Norway	6	–3	3
UK	3	15	18
USSR	25	0	25

44. *The Growth of the International Economy* (p. 244) by A. G. Kenwood and A. L. Lougheed, George Allen & Unwin, London 1971.
'For several years after the end of the war, then, the international economy experienced abnormal conditions. The only major country to enter into world trade and commerce without undue stresses on its balance of payments was the United States, which emerged from the war in a highly favourable economic position.'
45. *International Monetary Co-operation* (p. 233) by Brian Tew, Hutchinson University Library, London 1970. Tew quotes M. Gutt's statement on behalf of the IMF.
46. New Statesman 7.6.47, Richard Crossman 'Margate Diary'. An article in Tribune 28.3.47 estimated that the import needs of Europe for 1947 would be roughly $10,000 million and that only $7,000 million of this was covered by loans already granted.
47. Tew, *op. cit.* (p. 177). See also Tribune 15.7.47 for an article on the likelihood of this.
48. See Maddison, *op. cit.* (p. 35), which shows that 25 per cent of the USSR's capital assets had been lost through the second world war. She was thus in no position to sustain the eastern bloc with the kind of economic aid the US proffered to the 'west'. Indeed it was more likely that the USSR would use the eastern bloc economies to supplement the deficiencies of their own. This was certainly the case in Eastern Germany. See below.
49. I. Deutscher, *op. cit.* (pp. 567–8).
'In the meantime Stalin was imposing a state of siege upon the countries of Eastern Europe. Through special agencies such as Soviet-Hungarian, Soviet-Rumanian, and Soviet-Bulgarian Joint Stock companies, he obtained control of their economies. Poland, East Germany, Hungary, Czechoslovakia and Rumania delivered to Russia their coal, machines, bauxite, oil and wheat either as reparations or at extremely low prices, while their own peoples suffered want and poverty . . . Soviet administrators and engineers were supervising the industries of eastern Europe, Soviet generals commanded its armies, and Soviet policemen managed its security forces'.
50. I. Deutscher, *op. cit.* (pp. 567–8).
51. Tribune 30.5.47 and 1.10.48. Tribune led an excellent campaign against the shortsighted and spiteful policy of dismantling.
52. Kenwood and Lougheed, *op. cit.*, p. 303.
53. Kenwood and Lougheed, *op. cit.* (p. 307).
54. *A History of British Trade Unionism* (pp. 227–8) by Henry Pelling, *op. cit.*
55. Tribune, 19.12.47. The Italian Communist Party also favoured the Marshall plan initially, as Tribune reported 10.10.47.
56. Tribune, 10.10.47.
57. At the very start of this wild left lurch, a group of Communist Party members were expelled in Welwyn Garden City and Hert-

ford for 'infantile leftism'. What this could be we can only guess. But it was a remarkable achievement on the part of the expelled members.

58. Tribune, 19.12.47.
59. *The British Communist Party—An Historical Profile* (p. 158) by Henry Pelling, *op. cit.* He says:
'With their activities . . . circumscribed, it was difficult for the Communists in the British unions to make much headway in the direction of the principal Cominform objective of the time—the crippling of the European Recovery Programme and the sabotaging of western rearmament. Nothing to compare to the French political strikes could be arranged, although the French communist union leaders visited Britain to stir the British leaders to similar action. What did occur however was a series of strikes at the London docks and at provincial ports, and there is no doubt that this trouble was fomented and in several cases directly instigated by the party or by Communists from overseas. The Transport section of the Communist dominated World Federation of Trades Unions had now assumed the role in Soviet global strategy that in the twenties and early thirties had been played by the International Seamen and Harbour Workers and during one of the British strikes some of its agents attempted to visit strikers in Britain but without success'. As evidence he cites Parliamentary Papers 1948–9 xxix, p 471.
60. Tribune, 10.10.47.
61. World News, weekly paper published for Communist Party members and supporters 13.8.48. Venom has caused its author to overlook the formalities of grammar.
62. Tribune 26.12.47. Tribune, 5.12.47, reported that the Lorraine miners had been called out *after a secret ballot had rejected strike action* by 75 per cent–25 per cent. French CP union officials removed lamps from miners' helmets. The miners were called out on strike and went back *twice.* A Paris transport strike called by the CGT was ignored and the CGT was forced to rescind it. The strike movement was then called off, the PCF having lost a great deal of support.
63. For details of the Popular Front see *The History of Modern France Vol. 3* (pp. 146 et. seq.) by Alfred Cobban, Pelican, London 1965.
64. *European Unity and the Trade Union Movement* (pp. 23–27) by Colin Beever, Sythoff and Leyden, Netherlands 1960. An excellent account of the post war developments in the European trade union movement is contained in this section.
65. Beever, *op. cit.* (p. 27).
The WFTU headquarters were moved first to Vienna and then to Prague. In 1978 the Italian unions disaffiliated from it, and even the French CGT refused to supply it with a General Secretary, which it had done for most of the intervening period.

66. Comisco was the name originally given to the reborn Socialist International after the war (Committee for International Socialist Co-operation). The Labour Party was largely instrumental in re-establishing the Socialist International (dubbed the 'police international', by those experts in police activity, the Cominform). Denis Healey did a great deal of work in founding the international on a sound basis.
67. Thomas T. Hammond, *op. cit.* (p. 404).
68. Labour Party Annual Conference Reports (LPACR) for 1948 (p. 25), International Department Report.
69. LPACR, 1948 (p. 25).
70. The Italian Socialist party (PSI) finally split in May, 1948. In March the PCI and PCF publicly announced that in the event of war, they would 'back Soviet troops' (Tribune, 4.3.49).
71. There were two waves of Socialist emigrées from Eastern Europe. The first group set up a bureau late in 1947. The second group who sincerely tried to collaborate with their domestic Communist Parties arrived early in 1948 after Moscow's decision to liquidate Socialist parties. There was friction between the 'old' (1947) and 'new' (1948) emigrées. The Socialist Union of Central and Eastern Europe (SUCEE) to which both sets of emigrées were affiliated was still not at this time a member of Comisco, the Socialist International, because western socialists were wary of the Ukrainian, Estonian and Latvian Socialist parties and 'would prefer not to be associated with them' (Tribune 15.7.49). In the seventies Transport House took to inviting East European Communist parties as guests to conference. Since these parties forbid the existence of Social Democratic parties in the states which they rule, and since the SUCEE is now affiliated to the socialist international, this has led to a difficult situation. The question of inviting the oppressors of Social Democracy as observers to conference was not discussed with SUCEE. Things have certainly changed since the forties when the Socialist International defended the rights of their fellow socialists in Eastern Europe.
72. Tribune, 31.10.47.
73. As an example of the kind of tactic that assisted this process we may cite the following—In December 1947, Communist Party deputies were evicted from the French Assembly by troops. The deputies had been hurling abuse at the Radical and Socialist deputies—'Bosches'! 'American Agents'! and 'Traitors'!, behaviour which was doubtless designed to produce the desired result.
74. Cobban, *op. cit.* (Vol. 3. p. 214).
    He says 'When the elections were held, in June 1951, the parties of the Third Force obtained 62.5 per cent of the votes, while the Gaullists had 19.6 per cent with 21.7 per cent, and the Communists with 900,000 votes more than the RPF (Gaullists MJ) had 17.8 per cent to represent an electoral vote of 25.9 per cent.

'In spite of this electoral victory it was apparent that the Fourth Republic could rely on the support of barely half the nation, and that those who did support it were too hopelessly divided amongst themselves ever to be able to form a strong or stable government. The Third Force was still split over the question of state aid to Catholic schools and a proposal to allow their pupils to be eligible for scholarships. The shift to the right continued. In March, 1952 the new Assembly produced, in the person of Antoine Pinay, the first premier from the right since the war.'

Chapter Two

The Prehistory of Bevanism

'Bevan did not create Bevanism; as a refusal on the part of a substantial minority of Labour's rank and file to endorse the leadership's drift of policy and as an affirmation of the need for different policies, it had existed in the Labour Party and in the trade unions long before Bevan gave it his name and his gifts; and it endured and grew in strength after he ceased to give expression to it.'[1]

The years prior to the emergence of Bevan as undisputed leader of the Labour left deserve closer attention. The Cabinet resignations of April 1951 marked, not the beginning, but the culmination of the revolt in Labour's ranks, after which the struggle in the party ascended to a new and higher plane. But the forward thrust of the vanguard took place in a contradictory way and in contradictory world conditions. It followed a period of grace granted by the movement to its leaders between 1948–50. And it coincided with the rallying of sections of the wayward middle class back to its Tory allegiance, which, in turn was part of the general drift in Europe and America to moderation or to the right.

The rightward trend of Europe, though muted, was evident in Britain as early as the autumn of 1947 when the Conservatives made significant gains in the municipal elections. And well to the right of the Conservatives, fascist anti-Semitic activity in Liverpool and London's East End prompted an NEC delegation to Home Secretary, Chuter Ede, in July 1948.[2] But contrary to the experience of the Socialist parties in France and Italy the Labour Party vote stood up extremely well. In the period 1947–January 1950 only one parliamentary seat actually went from Labour to the Conservatives and that was in Glasgow in January 1948. *Labour's vote in-*

creased in 1945, 1950 and 1951, but so did the Conservatives' at all three elections. But whereas the Labour vote increased in 1950 and 1951 by 10.5 per cent and 5 per cent[3] respectively the Conservative increases were 25 per cent and 10 per cent. The surge of Conservative support, was in the main the rallying of the middle class, South of England, voter back to his traditional allegiance.[4] Nonetheless the British Labour establishment rode out the Cominform's offensive far more easily than their Social Democratic cousins on the continent. Indeed Labour's influence in the working class (as distinct from the electorate at large) strengthened very considerably in this period. In all categories, membership of Labour organisations swelled until 1947 and thereafter continued to grow up to 1952.[5] (See Fig. 3)

The quantitative developments of 1945–51, which strengthened the basic organisations of the class, led to a qualitative transformation after 1951 when the rift at the level of government and the Labour apparatus facilitated the public airing throughout the Party of issues and discussions which had, up till then, been agitating small groups of left parliamentarians. The discussions which had opened up inside the Labour left were sharply jolted and derailed by the Cominform turn, and by the 'western' reaction to it. The mass movement's revulsion at Stalin's eastern 'consolidation' had the temporary effect of strengthening the consolidators of the Labour establishment at home. Attlee undoubtedly struck a chord amongst the broadest sections of the Labour electorate when he said,

> 'While overthrowing an economic tyranny of landlordism and capitalism (the Communist Parties of Eastern Europe) have renounced the doctrines of individual freedom and political democracy, and rejected the whole spiritual heritage of Western Europe.'[6]

It was by appealing to such deeply held convictions that Attlee and the Labour leaders were able to steer the movement along a path that led to NATO, the Korean war, and colonial wars in Malaya and elsewhere. All of this had as little to do with the spiritual heritage of western Europe as the terror trials in Eastern Europe.

There is a very real reciprocal relationship revealed here.

Figure 3
Membership of Labour Organisations by Category, 1944–52.

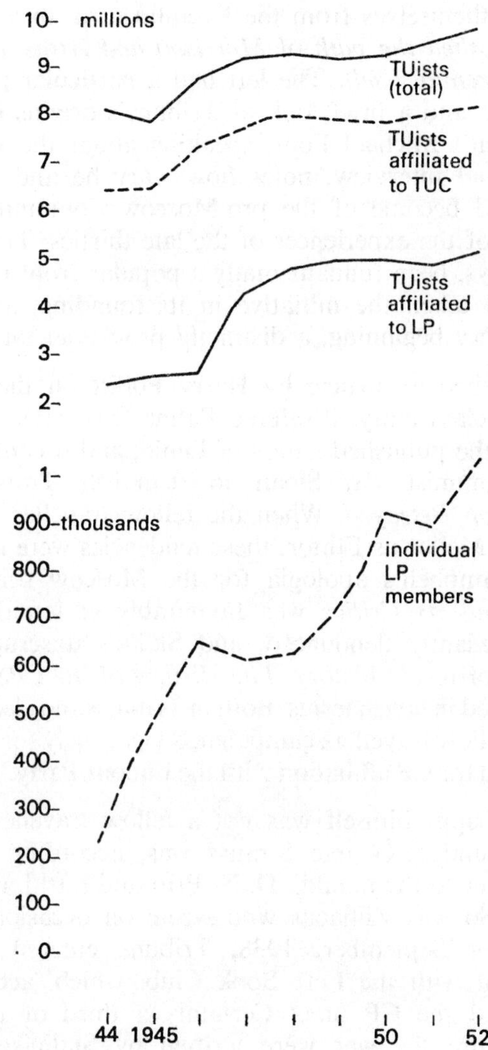

See figure on p. 119.

The leaders of Social Democracy and the Communist Parties used each other's sins as a justification for their own. The Tribune left, despite their best intentions, found that, in separating themselves from the Kremlin turn, they had, ironically, *smoothed the path of Morrison and Attlee hardly less than the Kremlin itself.* The left had a particular problem in this respect, and a brief look at Tribune's origins is in order at this point.[7] Michael Foot, speaking about the late forties in a personal interview, notes how wary he and other left-wingers had become of the pro-Moscow Communist parties as a result of the experiences of the late thirties. Tribune had, in those days, been fundamentally a popular front newspaper. Cripps had taken the initiative in its founding, and it had, from the very beginning, a distinctly pro-Soviet tone.

> 'It published an article by Harry Pollitt on the need for working class unity, it offered Palme Dutt review space to eulogise the published letters of Lenin, and it commissioned the communist Pat Sloan to demolish Trotsky's *The Revolution Betrayed.* When the fellow traveller Hartshorn replaced Mellor as Editor, these tendencies were reinforced. J. R. Campbell's apologia for the Moscow trials, *Soviet Policy and its Critics* was favourably reviewed, Trotsky was incessantly denounced, and Stalin's unscrupulous re-drafting of recent history, *The History of the CPSU (1939)*, was praised in lavish terms. Both in Tribune and elsewhere the British fellow travellers campaigned vigorously for a Popular Front and for CP affiliation with the Labour Party.'[8]

Whilst Cripps himself was not a fellow traveller, another Tribune founder, George Strauss was, according to David Caute, 'closer to the mould'. D. N. Pritt and Laski *were* fellow travellers. So was Zilliacus who wrote on occasions for the paper. After September, 1938, Tribune entered a formal arrangement with the Left Book Club, which, according to Dalton, toed the CP line.[9] Certainly a third of the Club's choices before the war were written by Stalinists such as Thorez and Dutt[10] whilst Orwell's *Homage to Catalonia* had been spurned. All of these concessions of principle to the apologists for Stalin's Russia led the Labour left into a trap which was sprung in 1939 with the Nazi-Soviet Pact. *The bitter memories of this betrayal of the Left has to be borne in mind when tracing the path of Tribune under Michael Foot's editorship in the late forties.* Neither befriending nor cold-shouldering Stalinism was a substitute for understanding it.

The presence of former German Social Democrat Evelyn Anderson on the board of Tribune strengthened the hand of Tribune against the theorists of 'social fascism'. For she had witnessed the damage it could cause in Germany. The Cominform period was to see a partial reversion to the very Kremlin ultra-leftism that had preceded the triumph of Hitler.

Paul Sering was perhaps the most perspicacious of Tribune correspondents. He had a sound grasp of the Stalinist record of tactical zig-zags.[11] Every stage in the Kremlin's forcible fusion of the Social Democratic parties was carefully monitored and Tribune often invoked Marx and Trotsky in defence of the political rights of Socialists in Stalin's domain. The Czech coup was roundly condemned as nothing to do with Marxist or socialist theory. There was, said Tribune, no point in debating Marxism with Vyshinsky, who had been instrumental in the murder of Trotsky and the Russian revolutionary leadership. Marxist theory was not his strong point. The Cominform turn was not Marxism at all, said Tribune, but a total retreat from scientific method.[12] Such criticism was an attack on the Kremlin *from the left*. Tribune writers were intrigued by the continuing allegations of Trotskyism and Social Democracy levelled by the Kremlin at disgraced former Stalinists during the show trials of the late forties,[13] and the equally regular accusations of Titoism after the Yugoslav leader had broken from the Cominform. During the Prague trials Tribune made a withering attack on the outrageous amalgam of Social Democracy, Titoism and Trotskyism, concocted by the prosecutors against their former comrades prior to executions.[14] Just how seriously the Labour movement viewed these events can be gauged from a special NEC statement of 26th July, 1950.[15]

> 'During the last few weeks the communist offensive against the workers of Eastern Europe had reached a new pitch of fury. Savage labour legislation and the destruction of trade union rights have caused unrest and resistance in the fac-

> tories. The communist dictators claim that socialists are leading the workers in the struggle against their oppressors. In Czechoslovakia a new wave of arrests has begun.'

The statement gave details of the arrests of five hundred Social Democrats and concluded:

> 'The NEC of the Labour Party declares that these arrests are a crime against the international Labour movement. It warns those responsible that the workers of the West are watching them. The spirit of freedom cannot be crushed in Eastern Europe. When liberty is restored the oppressors will be punished for their crimes.'

The Wage Freeze

It was against the background of such world events, in which British social democracy alone appeared to offer some hope of an independent course that was neither Washington's nor Moscow's, that Stafford Cripps approached the trades unions for endorsement of a voluntary wage standstill. Appointed Chancellor in late 1947 after Dalton's resignation, Cripps' credentials as a former leader of the Socialist League in the thirties made him the man most likely to succeed in the bid for trade union restraint in the period of Marshall Aid austerity. Just how difficult this task was may be seen by the fact that at the Margate conference of the party in 1947 none other than right wing stalwart Arthur Deakin had denounced proposals for a national wages policy and direction of labour.[16] But although Tribune noted the Southport conference of the TUC in September was to the left of Westminster and Margate, the critical minorities on the floor of conference were unco-ordinated.[17] By October the General Council was considering a government request for a wage stop deal in return for promised retention of food subsidies.[18] By January however, the TUC, in its interim statement on the economic situation, whilst noting the impracticality of 'any external body' determining wage rates and opposing a national wages policy, appeared to have conceded the necessity for voluntary restraint with the exception of the low paid. On 4th February wages and dividend restraint began. The TUC was asked to desist from wage demands except to attract additional labour, or as part of productivity improvements. Tribune followed every move in the wage freeze policy debate but its position was hardly likely to endear the paper either to the pro's or the anti's.

By a vote of five to two a TUC special conference at Westminster endorsed the General Council report on wages and prices, and a review of the resolutions for the Scarborough conference later in the year revealed no serious opposition to the wage freeze.[19] Perhaps this was, in part, because the rate of increase in hourly wage rates had been clearly outstripping that of retail prices in the previous three years. Some on the left, like Ian Mikardo wanted a tougher 'socialist' wages policy. By strange irony they found themselves in a precarious minority. Those who wanted a 'half-baked' policy on wages, Mikardo argued, could comfortably vote aye, 'but those who wanted a real wages policy found themselves, if they voted nay, in the same lobby as the wages anarchists'. Amongst these 'wages anarchists' were Communist Party members for whom the strike weapon was soon to become a valid tool for generating opposition to the Marshall plan. It is instructive that at the special conference the right wing of the General Council were able to use this communist bogey as a means of rallying support for the wage freeze.[20]

Thus when the Margate conference of the TUC came around in September 1948, there was a 70 per cent vote for the white paper accompanied by calls from the leadership for increasing productivity, and denunciations of unofficial strikes.[21] The CPGB was defeated 'all along the line'.[22] Speakers from the Iron and Steel workers union even opposed nationalisation as a communist tactic.[23] The American AFL delegate who had been howled down the previous year received applause on this occasion.[24] Tribune summed it up as 'A Black Week in the Red Calendar'.[25] The following year's conference was of a similar pattern with 'bigger more meaningless majorities than before',[26] but Tribune detected that below the surface there was 'deep dissatisfaction' with wage restrain, even though a six to one vote for wage stabilisation until the end of 1950 would appear to contradict such a judgement.[27]

Early in January 1949, the second Westminster conference

of trade union executives gave the General Council only a narrow majority[28] and the 'anti-General Council faction was bigger than ever before'.[29] However, Mikardo was still of the opinion that 'it is really idle to talk about a planned economy with an unplanned wages sector' and felt it was time for the unions to give up some of their powers to the General Council, or socialism would not be possible.[30] By Spring there was evidence of, what is for contemporary observers, the familiar sign of restiveness that always comes with the second year of any incomes policy. The Easter conference of USDAW flouted TUC policy and the AEU was talking about a strike ballot on its wage claim by the end of June.[31]

Across the water in France a new strike wave, very different from the CP-contrived affairs of 1947–48, gathered pace within the next few months with the support of all trade union centres including the Force Ouvrière.[32]

Tribune was, to say the least, equivocal about the impending doom of the wage freeze, seeing it as a defeat for the prospect of a planned economy and a cause for jubilation by 'Conservatives and communists'.[33]

For trades unionists it had certainly involved real sacrifice. Wages were not exactly frozen but they were kept to within the annual percentage rise in productivity and prices.[34] The goodwill of 1948 became the strained loyalty of 1949. By 1950 the international context of Cripps' national economic strategy intruded ever more obtrusively into the everyday lives of working people. A rapid rise in raw material prices followed the outbreak of the Korean war in the summer. This combined with the effect of the 1949 devaluation to make it impossible for the government and the TUC leaders to hold the line against a movement in the ranks for bigger wage settlements. But the 'revolt' was conducted in the nicest possible way, and was wrapped in *political* loyalty. Electoral support and party membership actually increased. Labour leaders have always found this kind of loyalty uncomfortable and rather difficult to cope with. Clearly had wages policy been the only consideration of workers, this deadly combination of loyalty and revolt would not have been possible.

On the political front those same workers who had declined to voluntarily submit to another year of wage control, could still see evidence of the government pressing forward with aspects of its programme despite Morrison's 'consolidation' speech. There was the battle over the House of Lords and the reduction of its powers. The struggle for steel nationalisation went ahead in the teeth of bitter Conservative and press opposition, when Parliament was recalled early in the Autumn of 1948.[35] The Times was of the opinion that the Steel Bill was primarily a sop to the left wing and the 'demagogy of Mr Bevan'.[36] In July of the same year the National Health Service came into operation. These political initiatives pursued in the backwash of a serious fuel crisis and international pressures from the Kremlin provided the government with an enormous fund of goodwill on which to draw.

But the freeze did not succeed by goodwill alone. Some of the Left's ground was cut from beneath its feet by Cripps' accession to the Chancellorship and by his adoption, either by accident or design, of certain aspects of the Keep Left programme.

The Ministry of Economic Affairs

The Ministry of Economic Affairs experiment was even more short-lived than George Brown's Department of Economic Affairs of the mid-sixties. The MEA came into being on September 29th, 1947 only to be combined with the Exchequer when Cripps became Chancellor shortly afterwards. Cripps had taken responsibility for the MEA after a two year spell at the Board of Trade. Commenting on the creation of the new Ministry, Tribune noted that production, distribution and overseas trade would henceforth be treated as a whole, but that finance was still excluded from its territory. 'The Treasury is still immune' the paper complained. There could not be two masters over these areas.[37] But the proposed structure of the new department was still sufficient to set the adrenalin flowing in the bloodstream of the left.

There was to be a central economic planning staff under Plowden and an economic information unit linked to the economic section of the Cabinet secretariat.[38] Mikardo boasted that the whole idea was a Keep Left one,[39] and indeed the very first point in Keep Left's summarised programme, in Chapter Five, read:

'The job at home: Overall Economic Planning: Turn the central planning authority into a full scale Ministry of Economic Affairs, with a high level Minister who is free from other duties. Abandon the doctrine that departmental ministers must have full autonomy.'[40]

But Mikardo remained somewhat sceptical about implementation. He feared that the new department might simply be one from which pious exhortations would be made to the private sector, and was sure that the necessary developments would not be forthcoming from the private sector itself.[41] Nonetheless, Tribune continued to monitor progress with optimistic enthusiasm. In November it reported that the export promotion department had calculated precise figures for the volume of exports required by mid-1948 and that these were being translated into targets for each individual firm. The department might even seek export returns from each company on a six-monthly basis. It was suggested that order books might be inspected and exports directed to countries with payments surplus in the UK; that sanctions might be applied for non-compliance with targets, but all this was 'assuming Cripps means business.'[42] *By December the following year Mikardo could argue that on the home front Keep Left's main proposals had been accepted by the government.*[43]

Whether or not Mikardo was correct in his assertion, we cannot dismiss the fact that, as one of the three authors of the Keep Left manifesto, he, at least was convinced that some of the Left's advice had been taken to heart. And, if the Left thought that, it goes some way to explaining *why the really serious revolt was delayed until almost four years later.* Attlee's appointment of Cripps was shrewd. It came at a point where Cripps himself was supposed to have been mooting a 'palace revolution' to remove the Labour leader.[44] Even Bevan had threatened resignation if the Steel Bill were to be dropped.[45] MEA appeared to be a bold step in the direction of overall economic planning, the need for which had been starkly revealed in the fuel crisis of that Spring. Cripps had lifted some of the planks of the Keep Left programme and built them into his style of approach, thereby appeasing left critics of 'consolidation'. *No left current can develop against the stream of broad support for the leadership underwritten by a firm deal with the TUC and its membership. Organisational cohesion, determination and leadership ability are important but secondary factors.* The tempo of the struggles of the mass movement, and a clear conception of the international content of national struggles count for far more. The Keep Lefters faced this novel alignment of international and domestic factors which constituted an organic element in the partial and temporary equilibrium at home.[46]

A study of Keep Left's draft programme reveals twenty demands neatly packaged—ten relating to home policy, and ten to foreign policy questions. This hardly bears out the charge of 'almost total preoccupation with foreign policy'.[47] But even if the charge were true, and even if Keep Left had tried to campaign more strongly on home policy questions, the tide of domestic class struggle was not running in their favour, and the partial satisfaction of some of Keep Left's home policy demands *was* a factor in the right wing's ability to buy time. The working class movement does not live by struggle alone. It also thinks. There was a great deal to think about in the years 1947–51. One of the great radical left myths of our time is that a determined 'leadership' can, at any time they choose, dictate the tempo and course of the struggle for socialism by their own volition.

Tribune noted in the Spring of 1947 that the party backed its leaders.[48] The party leadership perhaps construed the surge of membership in 1949 into the party and hugely successful rallies like the one at Filey,[49] as an endorsement of its course. What was happening in this period was in fact more complex. For this was not only a period of 'consolidation' and truce between government and unions. It was also a period of preparation for a new thrust forward which Bevanism was later to give expression to. The ranks of Labour had given its leaders a little time but not a *carte blanche.* The further we move from 1947 and the closer to 1951, the more truce gives way to impatience and revolt amongst the active party workers. There is evidence to show that Keep Left and Tribune embraced and prolonged the truce far beyond the limits of the rank and file's tolerance, putting the loyalty of the left's ranks under something of a strain, and producing tensions and splits even between the signatories of the Keep Left manifesto. Indeed, some of Keep Left's personnel found themselves irresistibly and imperceptibly sucked into one or other of the 'two camps' whilst still paying lip service to 'the third way'. It is to these splits and tensions within the Keep Left as it developed that we now turn our attention.

Keep Left

The curtain raiser to the Keep Left manifesto was a revolt of 72 Labour MPs who voted against the National Service Bill in March 1947, and forced the government to reduce the period of conscription from eighteen to twelve months. Previous revolts had not been pressed to a vote.[50]

A Tribune commentary detected three strands within the revolt—those like Victor Yates and Rhys Davies who opposed conscription on grounds of principle; those like Ian Mikardo who argued the manpower shortage necessitated a cut in national service and, thirdly, those led by Crossman, who were opposed to some aspects of the government's foreign policy and believed that if this were changed an immediate reduction in national service could be secured. Tribune dismissed a fourth contingent as a few 'near communists, who are of no great importance'. The conscription revolt was in effect the first initiative of Keep Left, for the preamble to the manifesto admits that discussions among the signatories had been going on since January.[51]

The vote took place within days of the Truman declaration, and struck at the heart of the 'two camps', in particular the camp in which Labour Britain found itself. Later Montgomery and the Army Council threatened to resign as a body if the period of national service were not increased to assist in the Berlin blockade crisis.[52]

But Tribune's treatment of the conscription revolt brought strong criticism from Victor Yates, Fenner Brockway and other MPs. The journal was accused of minimising the extent of the revolt by its assertion that there was 90 per cent support for the government's conscription bill in the Labour Party.[53] This initial skirmish between the conscription rebels and Keep Lefters on the one hand and Tribune on the other throws into relief the amorphous nature of left opposition at the time.

Whilst there was a great deal of overlapping of personnel and contributors between Tribune and the Keep Lefters, most notably in the cases of Mikardo and Foot, Tribune did not underwrite every action or criticism of the rebels. *At this stage there was not the close relationship between the journal and the parliamentary group that was established in the early fifties.*

It was, after all, the New Statesman and not Tribune which published the Keep Left manifesto. A lead article in late March warned of 'the chasm between the government's socialist aims at home and Mr Bevin's declared belief that our security depends on America.'[54] Such reliance on America made nonsense of any hope of socialism in Britain and perpetuated the division of the world into two ideological alliances. There could not be 'socialism without controversy'. The New Statesman called on the Labour movement to rally and divide the country at least as sharply as the Liberal programme of 1906. Written in April and advertised in the New Statesman in early May, the Keep Left manifesto was a slender 47-page pamphlet, dearly priced at one shilling but eagerly bought up wherever it was on sale.[55]

Miliband sums up the Keep Left approach as one, which, whilst paying tribute to the government's achievement, 'urged greater boldness at home and denounced the fallacy of collective security against communism . . .'[56] A key clause in the manifesto concerned the division of Europe.

> 'The way to make certain that democratic socialism can never be achieved in Eastern Europe is to superimpose on the class struggle the struggle of the Great Powers—the Anglo-Americans supporting the Right, and Russia the Left.'[57]

Fifteen Labour MPs signed it. The three authors Foot, Mikardo and Crossman were to become leading Bevanites. But who of importance on the left of the day did *not* sign the manifesto? There are some non-signatories worthy of note.

Clearly the topmost leadership of the future Bevanite movement were still tied up in government and destined to remain so for a further four years. The Platts Mills group, whom Pelling refers to as the 'crypto-communists' of the PLP, likewise did not sign.[58] Nor did Konni Zilliacus who was expelled along with Hutchinson and Platts Mills in 1948–49. For these people the third way was heresy and the American way was out of the question. Zilliacus was involved with another group, 'Victory for Socialism' of obscure origins and interesting connections, although most commentators are far more familiar with its role as a reactivated force after 1958.[59]

Sidney Silverman, another leading member of VFS, always kept his distance from the Keep Left-Bevanite left, and Bevan himself is said to have regarded him as '51 per cent pro-Soviet'.[60] Another group who did not sign the Keep Left manifesto was the Tom Braddock-Ron Chamberlain group of MPs who later played a leading role in the 'Socialist Fellowship' (1949–51),[61] founded by Ellis Smith and Fenner Brockway. Many of these MPs wrote for Socialist Outlook (1948–54) and some of them for Labour Monthly, a CP-run review.[62] The sole exception here was Harold Davies, who was a signatory of Keep Left and wrote regularly for Socialist Outlook. Thus the architects of Keep Left appear to have been MPs in the mainstream of left-wing Labour politics, genuinely seeking a way out of the movement's difficulties and spurned by the various tendencies apologising for the Kremlin from whatever standpoint and to whatever degree. Jennie Lee, wife of Aneurin Bevan, editorial board member of Tribune, reviewed the manifesto as an expression of doubts and questionings through which the movement was preparing once more 'to lead its leaders'. These questionings would not be a 'synthetic product artificially created by communists or crypto communists'. The aim of Keep Left was to strengthen not weaken the movement, to develop intelligent debate, not slander. Broadly speaking her initial judgement of Keep Left represents a balanced assessment of its motives. Her main disagreements among the twenty points concerned the Keep Left idea of an Anglo-French alliance as the cornerstone of a third force, since it excluded eastern European countries whom she wished to see part of a regional security system under UNO. She also believed the dismantling of German Steel proposal to be 'questionable'.[63]

The discussion around Keep Left had hardly begun when Bevin's 'stab in the back' speech appeared to put an end to the revolt at the Margate conference at the end of May. There was no card vote and the big battalions backed the Foreign Secretary after which, according to Pelling 'only pacifists and crypto-communists kept up their attacks'.[64]

Michael Foot attacked Bevin's oratorical victory and vehemently denied that the battle was one between 'loyal trades unionists and the rebellious intellectuals' as Bevin had implied. He argued that votes at the TUC Congress did not substantiate Bevin's view. Nor was Bevin correct, he added, in choosing to believe that the dividing line for his critics was the issue of relations with Russia. Communist Party sympathisers were largely responsible for Bevin being able to present the issues in such a way, and to avoid the real issues of policy.[65] Crossman in the New Statesman explained that Keep Left MPs had decided that they would not participate in the foreign policy discussion that took place around Zilliacus' resolution since they stood 'somewhere between the Foreign Secretary and Zilliacus'. They had wished to concentrate on manpower and the size of the armed forces but had been outmanoeuvred. However, Crossman warned, Bevin's victory was a hollow one, because Britain could only go on behaving as if she were one of the big three 'until the dollars run out.'[66]

Nonetheless, the threatened revolt had been sufficient to draw a hasty programmatic reply from the right wing. Crossman outlined 'the extraordinary procedure' whereby every delegate to party conference got a copy of 'Cards on the Table' which most people assumed was the official reply to Keep Left. It appears the document was written by Denis Healey, at that time Secretary of the International Section at Transport House, and not an MP. It had been read and authorised by Hugh Dalton although 'no other member of the government or of the Executive had seen it before publication.' According to Crossman this caused something of a 'minor sensation' at conference. It certainly reveals the seriousness with which the party hierarchy viewed the possible response to the Keep Left rebels in the party ranks.[67]

During the TUC-government wage freeze, the left did what it could to stimulate debate on programme. Mikardo published a pamphlet *The Second Five Years—Labour's Pro-*

gramme for 1950–55.[68] This put forward the case for nationalisation of banks, insurance and sectors of industry. G. D. H. Cole argued a similar case for boldness as against compromise in 'Why Nationalise Steel'. As in 1945, he said, the party must lead the nation, and the rank and file must lead the party.[69] But Tribune's tame criticisms of the Cripps' 1948 budget symbolised the problems of the left. The Chancellor was doing 'a very considerable service to the Labour movement',[70] and all that the paper regretted was the lack of a 'bold approach towards a wages policy'. The budget did not sufficiently create the 'right social atmosphere in which restraint on wages is accepted.'[71] Such a viewpoint was hardly likely to bring the trades union ranks into association with the left in the parliamentary party. It is scarcely surprising, then, to find Tribune waxing cynical about the possibility of Hugh Dalton being about to emerge 'as the leader of a new Keep Left group'.[72] All Ian Mikardo could foresee at the next party conference in Scarborough was a closing of the ranks prior to the election, and a battle between Morrison and the 'Nenni telegraph boys'.[73]

There was rancour at the Keep Left inquest, which took place in the columns of Tribune in November-December, 1948, midway between the expulsions of Platts Mills and those of Zilliacus-Solley-Hutchinson. Some Tribune correspondents closer to the Kremlin 'camp' wrote in attacking the Keep Lefters for reneging on the issue of non-alignment, for 'always attacking Russia but never the US'.[74] Michael Foot and Benn Levy were singled out for special criticism. Hugh Jenkins in a surprising piece of fellow-travelling invective, accused Keep Lefters of having 'dropped their pens, buttoned their lips and disintegrated quietly away' after Bevin's speech.

> 'Mr Crossman retired hurt into the literary columns of the New Statesman . . . a safe centre man. Mr Mikardo transferred his attention to smaller and less tender targets. Mr Foot sought to establish his claim to common ground of anti-communism with Hitler and Churchill.'

There was nothing left, he alleged, except Mr Silverman, for whom he thanked heaven. Jenkins called for a new grouping which would not be purely parliamentary, and in which the head would be connected to the tail.[75] Zilliacus joined the fray with a classical piece of Palme-Dutt style polemic. Keep Left's policy was, he argued, 'Bevin's policy of half-war, with its third force vegetarian variant of Morgan-Phillipsising-and-Michael-Footing world communism into extinction by waging a cold war with hot air.'[76] Another contributor called on the 'good' MPs, Zilliacus, Hutchinson, Warbey, Silverman and Leah Manning to form a new group.[77]

Tribune replied by putting the case for a third way, and Crossman spelled out the cause of Keep Left's problems. It was, he maintained, the Marshall plan and the Truman doctrine, which had 'completely outdated our proposal for an independent third force between Russia and America'. With disarming frankness he admitted that since he favoured both the Marshall plan and Western European Union there was therefore no fundamental difference between himself and the Foreign Secretary and 'an organised group is not necessary.' Keep Left had arisen out of purely informal discussions during the fuel crisis and 'its activities went on until the convertibility crisis' which had made the resolutions at Margate 'look silly'. Most of Keep Left's proposals on the home front were now government policy Crossman claimed.[78] This latter claim was made by Mikardo also, when he listed ten points of the programme now adopted by the government: planning, the MEA, greater publicity for policies, withholding labour from inessential trades, more heavy taxation of distributed profits, exposing inefficiency in industry, rationalisation in motor models, reduction of waste of manpower in the services, Western Union and withdrawal of British troops from Palestine.[79]

Mikardo's resignation from Tribune

This post mortem discussion reveals the extent to which Keep Left had given ground to the Attlee-Bevin leadership, and sheds light on the road of good left intentions showing clearly where they led. Crossman by his frankness did as much as the cryptos to assist the process of clarification. The burden of Zilliacus' criticism weighed heavily on Mikardo, but it was not until five months later that Mikardo's disagreement with Foot led to his resigning from the editorial board of Tribune.

Explaining his position in May, 1949 Mikardo said the cause of his resignation was,

> 'Tribune's leading article of a fortnight ago—the one that made me cross the Rubicon from being a director of the paper to becoming no more than a columnist. That article said quite simply, that whatever the Russians say or do we mustn't believe them and we mustn't trust them.'

Coming as it did on top of a series of leading editorials that had given *open and unequivocal support to the formation of NATO*,[80] this article had clearly been too much for Mikardo. But he pledged his continued backing for the idea of the third force whilst refusing to go along with Zilliacus' blanket support for the Russians. Mikardo held that to demand 'unconditional surrender' from the Russians as a price of unifying Germany through free elections would only increase their bellicosity. Russian withdrawal from Eastern Germany could not be demanded whilst the western presence was maintained in the other half of the country.[81] Stephen Swingler MP backed Mikardo and alleged 'to some of Tribune's editors yesterday's meat is today's poison'. He suggested that Marshall Aid and Tito's expulsion from the Cominform may have induced Michael Foot to make a somersault.[82]

Foot's defence of his position makes thoughtful reading. He linked Mikardo's resignation to the ratification of the Atlantic Pact in early May. Despite her follies, the US had made recovery possible, whereas Stalin had lumped democratic socialism, US capitalism and the Commonwealth together, reserving 'a special venom' for the socialists. There was, he went on, no possibility of independence in Eastern Europe.

It was the Yalta conference (in which Stalin and the Western leaders had collaborated) which had led to the destruction of democracy in Poland. It was Potsdam that had ensured the division of Germany and led to the Berlin blockade. The agreements on 'free elections' had led to the total destruction of the Socialist parties. What had to be avoided was a repeat of the Potsdam-Yalta follies. The true third force was one which recognised the complete incompatibility of Soviet ideology with democratic socialism and sought to restrain the forces of anarchic capitalism while forging stronger links with the growing power of labour and liberal ideas in that country. Whilst rooted in the western camp, Foot's spirited defence showed a more profound understanding of the forces behind the division of Europe than the carping of his adversaries. Zilliacus however, irrepressible, attacked both Foot *and* Mikardo. He was not satisfied with the degree of Mikardo's support in the latter's review of his short pamphlet *Dragon's Teeth* in which Zilliacus had argued the incompatibility of NATO, established in April 1949, with the United Nations charter.[83]

Foot rejected the allegation that he had gone back on the position he had held at the end of the war, when he had written the introduction to Zilliacus' book 'Mirror of the Past'. He had not 'swallowed the alibi of the Right', nor embraced power politics. He reminded Zilliacus that the introduction had been an attack on *secret diplomacy* and that nowhere were the common people more excluded from the control of their affairs than in the USSR for which Zilliacus was an apologist.[84] Foot remained impervious to the attacks of Zilliacus but Mikardo continued to be troubled by uncertainty. Mikardo believed there were two sets of forces at work in the USA —one which viewed Britain as 'an airstrip in the coming war against Russia' and Europe as 'expendable'; the other, the New Dealers who were more acceptable to him. But he felt there was a danger of the government becoming identified with the former group.[85] Mikardo was therefore to be found at times at odds with, and at times fortuitously in step with the Kremlin's spokesmen in Labour's ranks. During the Spring of 1950 he was barracked at a meeting of the 'Progressive Businessmen's forum' to which he had been invited, and surmised that it might have been because he disagreed with King Street.[86] But a couple of months later the fact that he had signed a 'Peace Petition' organised by the Stalinist 'British Peace Committee' was reported on the front page of the Cominform journal 'For A Lasting Peace . . .'[87] This drew critical letters in Tribune and an attack on the Committee by Morgan Phillips, who reminded everyone of its proscription. By 1951 Mikardo was opposing Britain's support for the United States UNO resolution which branded China as the aggressor in Korea.[88] But on this occasion he was expressing a growing feeling both in the ranks and the higher echelons of the party.

The Case of Konni Zilliacus MP[89]

The divisions of opinion within the ranks of the future Bevanites is an indication of the havoc caused by the theory of the 'two camps'. But if dispute and recrimination dogged those who found themselves, irrespective of their intentions, drawn into the western 'camp', they could take comfort in the fact that life was even more difficult for those who had opted for the eastern 'camp'. The case of Konni Zilliacus illustrates this most clearly. His fortunes varied wildly under the impact of the foundation of the Cominform, the Nenni telegram affair and the split between Tito and the Cominform. Always at odds with the Keep Lefters, he was expelled from the Labour Party in 1949 only to be re-admitted in the early fifties. Zilliacus was often at the centre of the dispute surrounding the 'crypto communists' in the Labour Party, of whom Platts Mills was the least disguised example. To understand Zilliacus' dilemma we need to look first at the general debate that was raging in 1948–9 concerning the nature of the two 'camps'—a remarkable debate which involved Bernard Shaw, Arthur Koestler, Emrys Hughes MP, and Michael Foot, one of Tribune's joint editors. This debate reached boiling point in the Spring of 1948 after the Kremlin's Czech coup and immediately prior to the Berlin Blockade.

Zilliacus made known his approval of the Czech coup using all the arguments that one might have expected from a card-carrying Communist party member.[90] He even justified the Kremlin's brutal treatment of the Social Democrats by reference to the latter's role in Germany, 1918. By contrast Tribune was enraged at the sequence of events in Eastern Europe and branded the Soviets as the main threat to peace in Europe. The Left would be as well to recognise the unpalatable fact rather than 'indulge in the jesuitical illusions which still seem to comfort the communist fellow travellers'.[91]

Tom Braddock MP, like Zilliacus a signatory to the Nenni telegram waded into Tribune, describing it as a 'distinguished journal that reserved its blessings only for Tory hacks'.[92]

The Nenni Telegram

The Nenni telegram affair became a test case for fellow travellers in the Labour Party. Transport House took a very dim view of the solidarity action of thirty seven Labour MPs who sent a good wishes telegram to the pro-Moscow Nenni Socialist Party who were in a popular front electoral pact with the Communists, against the Social Democrats during the April 1948 general election in Italy. The Nennists set back Italian Social Democracy for a generation and gave electoral leadership of the left to the Communist Party in the post war period.[93]

Sixteen Nenni telegram rebels either recanted or claimed they had not endorsed the telegram. The remaining twenty one submitted to an NEC directive to put in writing, individually, that they would cease 'acting as a group in organised opposition to party policy'.[94] Thus was a similar split in Britain avoided, but the warning shot was 'sufficient to discourage the expression of dissent on the fundamentals, as distinct from the specific applications of the Government's foreign policy'.[95] Though directed at fellow travellers the Transport House stricture was not lost on the Keep Lefters. This may have been a contributing factor in the left's imperceptible slide into the western 'camp'.

By now Tribune was openly inviting Zilliacus to join the Communist Party.[96] The treatment meted out to Benes and Masaryk by the Stalinists in Czechoslovakia was to have a great impact on Labour Party thinking. The Czech situation sparked off renewed conflict between Zilliacus and Tribune. The Gateshead MP accused the Labour government and the NEC of 'acting as agents and accomplices of American Tory intervention against the European revolution', such intervention, if pursued, could only end in fascism, he argued. Tribune countered with the charge that Zilliacus refused to defend the rights of those Social Democrats who would not toe the Soviet dictatorship's line in Eastern Europe.[97] At about this time George Bernard Shaw entered the fray. A long feature article in the Daily Herald drew a front page reply from Michael Foot. Shaw had engaged in 'fulsome flattery for Sovietism'. Foot reminded his readers of Shaw's previous praises for

Mussolini and for Hitler's record in ending unemployment and suggested that the dramatist had 'stopped thinking about fifteen years ago.'

Shaw's article had provided excuses for the means whereby 'Czechoslovakia was robbed of its rights and socialist parties suppressed over a large part of Europe . . .'[98] In June, Foot returned to the attack. He asked why Shaw never ventured the smallest criticism of the methods employed by the Soviet regime. Why was Stalin always right and the British Labour Party always wrong? Why did Shaw pat Stalin on the back for his treatment of Trotsky and laud the dictator as an 'arch fabian'. Were not the Moscow trials 'one of the monstrous frauds of history?'[99] Sidney Silverman and Emrys Hughes came to Shaw's defence in varying degrees, whilst Benn Levy accused Foot of trying to teach his grandfather to suck eggs. In a second reply Shaw pleaded old age, but by now Arthur Koestler had joined the fray attacking the 'Babbits of the Left' whose simple philosophy he ridiculed in the phrase 'East is East and Left is Left'. They had, he said, confused 'left' with the geographical direction 'east'. The decline of Social Democracy in Europe was due to its failure to denounce Stalinism resolutely.[100] The struggle between the Keep Lefters and Zilliacus had already received some international attention[101] but it was not until the expulsion of Yugoslavia from the Cominform that Zilliacus' most serious problems began.

Zilliacus and Yugoslavia

This occurred in June 1948, less than a year after the formation of the Cominform. Disagreements between Russia and Yugoslavia over domestic policy towards the peasantry and the uprising in Greece were at the heart of the dispute. The new capital of the Cominform was moved from Belgrade to Bucharest, and a surrealistic campaign of vilification was initiated under Kremlin orchestration. An ensuing economic crisis forced Tito to seek financial credits from the west. The Kremlin withdrew its ambassador. Russian mechanised divisions were deployed near the Yugoslav frontier.[102] The Treaty of Friendship was abrogated. In November 1949 the Cominform called for insurrection against Tito, who by now was being branded as a 'fascist' and friend of social democracy. In Britain the Anglo-Yugoslav friendship society split into pro- and anti-Kremlin wings. Labour, after initial scepticism about the genuineness of the Tito rift, began to display increasing interest, indicated by a visit of Labour MPs to Yugoslavia in the Spring of 1950.

Zilliacus' interest in Tito's Yugoslavia began some months after this general curiosity in Labour's ranks.[103] He visted Tito just as the Kremlin was denouncing the Yugoslav leader as a fascist. Tribune, whilst commending the member for Gateshead for his 'real courage' in giving a favourable account of the Tito regime, headlined its comments with the ironic 'Zilly Turns Fascist?' In his report Zilliacus had said that if socialism did not mean humanism and respect for freedom and justice, it would not be worth working for. Tribune heartily concurred with the expelled MP.[104] But Zilliacus was not satisfied with this. Worse things had happened in the West than in Eastern Europe he alleged. Tribune suggested he submit an article to Pravda and the Daily Worker entitled 'Why it is a Lie to Call Tito a Fascist' and await the response. And although Zilliacus continued to appear on British Peace Committee platforms[105] Pravda showed how little it thought of his contribution to Moscow's orchestrated 'peace' campaign by branding him as Tito's advocate in Europe. 'On the one hand Zilliacus speaks of peace and on the other he conspires with fascist adventurers and the hirelings of warmongers' said the Soviet paper.[106]

It seemed that Tribune's irony had become today's reality. Like another once-favoured Kremlin Star, Henry Wallace in the US, Zilliacus now fell out of grace with the Kremlin, having already lost his official candidacy in Gateshead in an attempt to advance their cause—worse luck could no fellow traveller have than this!

In November he wrote 'Confessions of a Titoist' for Tribune which marked a distinct change in his position. Fear of intervention and Bevin's pro-American policies had, he said, driven the European communist parties into the arms of Moscow. 'If we ease off the outside pressure, the big CPs of Europe will rapidly become "semi-Titoist" and the Soviet government will cease to be violently anti-Titoist.'

Zilliacus largely anticipated the development of polycentrism and Eurocommunism which was not to become fashionable until a quarter of a century later. He argued that Titoism was really 'self-determinationist' as opposed to 'cominformist'. This principle ought to prevail, and the job of non-communist 'progressives' was to try to understand the issues 'not to take sides in the conflict between them'.[107] Perhaps holding his breath, the Editor of Tribune concurred in this judgement. In 1950 Tribune defended Zilliacus when he was publicly attacked in a Daily Worker editorial and denied the right of reply. Tribune published his answer to King Street in full. In it Zilliacus made clear that he believed Yugoslavia was building socialism along Marxist lines; that he opposed Anglo-American policy but believed the CPSU was assisting Washington to win allies by demanding obedience to all Soviet judgements; that the call to overthrow Tito divided and demoralised the left. Despite the bitter disputes he had endured with Tribune he was beginning to win back some respect for the manner in which he had withstood the cold blooded treatment of the Kremlin propaganda machine in the Tito split.

NOTES

1. R. Miliband (p. 325), *op. cit.*
2. Labour Party Annual Conference Report 1949.
3. These figures have been worked out from *British Political Facts* (p. 184) by David Butler & Anne Sloman, Macmillan, London, 1975.

	Increase in 1950	Increase in 1951
Labour	+1,271,440 (+10.5%)	+682,013 (+5.14%)
Conservative	+2,514,261 (+25%)	+1,214,971 (+9.7%)

4. See Butler & Sloman, *op. cit.* (p. 188) which gives parliamentary seats by region. In Wales Labour seats increased from 25 to 27 between 1945 and 1950 and held steady thereafter, increasing again in 1966 to 32. In Scotland Labour seats increased also in 1950 *and* 1951 (and again in 1955).

	1945	1950	1951
Wales	25	27	27
Scotland	29	32	35
Midlands	64	59	59
Northern England	128	107	99
Rest of Southern England	91	54	46
London (County of)	48	31	29

5. The figures for these diagrams are taken from the following books:

   A Short History of the Labour Party (p. 128) by Henry Pelling Macmillan, London 1973, supplied figures for Labour Party individual membership and TU affiliate membership to the Labour Party.

   A History of British Trade Unionism (p. 282–3) by Henry Pelling, Penguin, London 1973, supplied figures for TU membership and TUC affiliate membership.

	TU membership	TUC affiliates	LP/TU affiliates	Individual LP
1944	8,087,000	6,575,654	2,375,381	265,763
1945	7,857,000	6,671,120	2,510,369	487,047
1946	8,803,000	7,540,397	2,635,346	645,345
1947	9,145,000	7,791,470	4,386,074	608,487
1948	9,319,000	7,937,091	4,751,030	629,025
1949	9,274,000	7,883,355	4,946,207	720,624
1950	9,289,000	7,827,945	4,971,911	908,161
1951	9,535,000	8,020,079	4,937,427	876,275
1952	9,583,000	8,088,450	5,071,935	1,014,524

   The big jump in affiliate membership to the Labour Party in 1947 was a result of a change in the law which replaced 'opting in' to the political levy with 'opting out'.

   Whilst recent press comment has cast doubt on the usefulness of Transport House's Individual Membership figures for determining real Labour Party membership, there is no reason to doubt their validity for comparing one year with another.

6. Attlee, New Year's day broadcast on BBC, 1948.
7. See Michael Foot, personal interview, appendix 3 of the author's doctoral thesis.
8. *The Fellow Travellers* (p. 158–9) by David Caute, Quartet, London 1977.
9. Caute, *op. cit.* (p. 163).
10. Caute, *op. cit.* (p. 163).
11. See Tribune, 10.10.47, an article by Sering on the Kremlin's new turn, in which he reviews past turns and the 'third period'.
12. Tribune, 5.3.48.
13. For good examples see Tribune, 9.4.48, 18.11.49, 16.6.50.
14. Tribune, 16.6.50. Not all of Tribune's articles were as sharp. On 29.8.47 an extremely complacent article predicted that the forth-

coming Hungarian elections would be fair. Some weeks later Tribune reported that Communist Party flying squads had wrecked the elections (See Tribune 5.9.47).

15. Labour Party Annual Conference Report 1950.
16. Tribune, 18.7.47.
17. Tribune, 12.9.47.
18. Tribune, 31.10.47.
19. Tribune, 12.3.48.
20. Tribune, 2.4.48.
21. Tribune, 3.9.48.
22. Tribune, 17.9.48.
23. Tribune, 17.9.48.
24. Tribune, 3.9.48.
25. Tribune, 17.9.48.
26. Tribune, 16.9.49.
27. Tribune, 23.9.49 and 30.12.49.
28. Tribune, 6.1.50.
29. Tribune, 20.1.50.
30. Tribune, 6.1.50.
31. Tribune, 14.4.50.
32. Tribune, 3.3.50.
33. Tribune, 14.4.50.
34. *The Management of the British Economy* (p. 35 & p. 93) by J. C. R. Dow, Cambridge University Press, London 1964.

% Change in	1947	1948	1949	1950	1951
Industrial Production	6	8	6.5	6.5	3.5
Retail Prices	2.4	5.9	3.3	3.0	11.8
Wages Rates	4.1	4.2	1.9	3.4	10.7

See also The Economist, 19.3.75, (p. 92).

35. Tribune, 17.9.48.
36. Foot, *op. cit. Vol II* (p. 227).
37. Tribune, 3.10.47.
38. Tribune, 3.10.47.
39. Tribune, 10.10.47.
40. *Keep Left* (p. 16 and p. 45).
41. Tribune, 10.10.47.
42. Tribune, 7.11.47.
43. See below discussion of Keep Left's fortune, 1947–50.
44. Foot, *op. cit. Vol II* (p. 93–94).
45. Foot, *op. cit. Vol II* (p. 224).
46. One sign of this was that even the British Trotskyists, for whom organisational fetishism was a matter of principle, were forced to wind up the Revolutionary Communist Party. Even they realised that the 1945 vote for Labour was no passing fancy. In 1948, significantly, they entered the Labour Party and were themselves derailed by the international questions that plagued Keep Left. The world Trotskyist movement split early in the fifties. For the Trotskyists, also, the basic problem was whether

there really were two camps, or whether Trotskyism was outside of both. See the section on Socialist Outlook below.

47. Coates, *op. cit.* (p. 190) 'Left opposition within the Labour Party to the policies of Attlee was slow to start, was sporadic and was almost totally preoccupied with questions of foreign policy.'
48. Tribune, 30.5.47.
49. Tribune, 20.5.47. (The Labour Party page). The Filey Rally was a political education camp attended by between 4,000–5,000 people at a Butlin's site.
50. Miliband, *op. cit.* (p. 295–7). Another 'revolt' by Montgomery and the CIGS a year later resulted in an increase in national service from 12 to 24 months. Soviet foreign policy was the argument used by the military to secure this increase. (See p. 48.) In November 1946, 53 Labour MPs signed an amendment to the address warning of the danger of conflict between American capitalism and Soviet communism and calling for a constructive socialist alternative.
51. Preamble to *Keep Left.*
52. Miliband, *op. cit.* (p. 297) footnote quoting from Montgomery's memoirs. The Field Marshal paid tribute to Labour's introduction of peace time National Service after the war. In the face of great opposition 'Attlee and Bevin pushed it through for us.'
53. Tribune, 9.5.47.
54. New Statesman, 22.3.47.
55. Tribune, 9.5.47. Jennie Lee's review of Keep Left.
56. Miliband, *op. cit.* (p. 296) summarising and quoting from the Keep Left manifesto.
57. Keep Left manifesto.
58. Pelling, *A Short History of the Labour Party*, op. cit. (p. 100).
59. Pelling, for a more detailed review of the history of VFS see Appendix 4 of the author's doctoral thesis. See also Coates *op. cit.* (p. 197) on VFS re-emergence in the late fifties.
60. *Sidney Silverman—Rebel in Parliament* (p. 128) by Emrys Hughes, Charles Shilton Ltd. London & Edinburgh, 1969.
61. See Appendix 5 of the author's doctoral thesis for contributors to Labour Monthly.
62. See Appendix 5 above.
63. Tribune, 9.5.47. Jennie Lee's review of Keep Left. Ashley Bramell endorsed her criticisms in Tribune, 16.5.47.
64. Pelling *A Short History of the Labour Party* op. cit. (p. 100). See Labour Party Annual Conference Report for 1947 for the full speech. At one point (p. 179) in a veiled reference to the Keep Left revolt, Bevin complained,

    '. . . when I was in the United States there was a rebellion so-called against me in the House of Commons. What was I doing? Not discussing foreign policy at all. I had telegrams from the Cabinet that the Minister of Food wanted 120,000 tons of grains and 700,000 tons of another cereal and I would do my best with the American government to get the allocation. I did it. . .'

'. . . on the very day I was trying to get the agreement with the Americans to prevent the bread ration from going down, on that very day I was stabbed in the back.'

But in this reply to the discussion, Bevin, interestingly, concentrated his political fire on Zilliacus' Gateshead resolution which was couched in terms equating East with good and West with bad. He clearly found Zilliacus' commitment to the Eastern camp easier to deal with than the Keep Left criticisms.

The Foreign Secretary's speech was wide-ranging—dealing with Greece, Palestine, Germany and relations between the great powers. It is interesting that at no time does he concede that the partition of Germany was either government policy or a permanent situation.

'If anyone in this world has struggled to prevent Europe being divided, the British government has done it, and done it at great cost. The facts are that at Potsdam we agreed on economic unity. At Potsdam we agreed to throw into the pool all the products of Germany before we took reparations of any kind . . .

'But on the pooling of resources for the whole of Germany, we never got one pound of food for the Western zone from Eastern Germany. In addition there was a large area which was transferred to Polish administration which went out of the economy altogether. We have been trying all the time to create economic unity but it has broken down on an entirely separate issue . . .'

Bevin complains in this speech about the reference to 'capitalist America' in one of the critical resolutions and insisted that Labour was not being subservient to the US, that his Washington visit was for the purpose of borrowing, and that the terms of the agreement had been open and fully reported to Parliament. He insisted that he was not discussing foreign policy in Washington.

A final point, worthy of note, on this speech is how basic material shortages, in such things as grain, affected politics, east and west. Bevin refers to the terrible drought of 1946 in Russia 'which was a disaster for the world'. Shortages forced Britain and Europe to beg from America and spurred on Russia to pillage the bread bins of Eastern Europe. All of this contributed to the material foundations of Cold War.

65. Tribune, 6.6.47.
66. New Statesman, 7.6.47, Crossman's 'Margate Diary'.
67. Ibid. See also LPACR 1947 (p. 106) for Zilliacus' attack on the document 'Cards on the Table' and p. 159 for Hugh Dalton's denial that it was a policy statement, but a contribution to discussion.

68. *The Second Five Years—a Labour Programme for 1950* published by Fabian Publications & Gollancz, April, 1948.
69. *Why Nationalise Steel*? pamphlet by G. D. H. Cole, published by the New Statesman.
70. Tribune, 23.4.48.
71. Tribune, 9.4.48.
72. Tribune, 23,4.48.
73. Tribune, 15.4.48.
74. Tribune, letter page, 5.11.48.
75. Hugh Jenkins, later Minister for the Arts in the Wilson government. Tribune, 19.11.48.
76. Tribune, 26.11.48.
77. Tribune, 3.12 48. In the 1950 election the expelled MPs stood as a group of 'Labour Independents' against Labour. The Communist Party called on its members to vote 'Labour Independent' in those seats. They polled well but lost all their seats. It is not clear whether this was the 'new group' that Tribune's critics had in mind.
78. Tribune, 26.11.48.
79. Tribune, 17.12.48. Tribune was very much pro-Europe at this time.
80. Tribune, 18.3.49 and Tribune 25.3.49. See below discussion on NATO.
81. Tribune, 20.5.49.
82. Tribune, 27.5.49. Mikardo made the phrase 'Another Man's Poison' the title of his regular weekly Tribune column after resigning from the editorial board!
83. Tribune, 27.5.49.
84. Tribune, 27.5.49.
85. This predilection for the Democrats and false identification of them with the ideals of British labour was a recurring theme in Tribune during the late forties. See Pelling, op. cit. *America and the British Left*.
86. Tribune, 28.4.50 and 12.5.50.
87. Tribune, 30.6.50.
88. Labour Party NEC minutes for January, 1949. In particular the minutes of the sub committee which were attached, contain 29 pages of documentation and quotations from Zilliacus. He was expelled that year. The NEC minutes for June 1955 contain four pages of documentation relating to his re-admission to the party.
89. Tribune, 9.2.51.
90. Tribune, 30.4.48.
91. Tribune, 2.4.48.
92. Tribune, 30.4.48. Tom Braddock MP worked extremely closely with the Trotskyists on Socialist Outlook, although on the main questions his views were almost indistinguishable from those of the typical fellow traveller.

93. For the rest of the election data see *European Political Facts* by Cook & Paxton, Macmillan, London, 1975.

	Votes	1946 %	Seats
Christian Democrats	8,101,004	(35.2)	207
Communists	4,356,686	(18.9)	104
PSIUP (United Socialists)	4,758,129	(20.7)	115
		1947	
Christian Democrats	12,741,299	(48.5)	305
Communists } Democratic			138
PSI (Nennist) } Popular	8,137,047	(31.0)	38
and others } Front			
PSLI (Saragat)			33

The United Socialists (PSIUP) did better than the Communist Party in the 1946 elections. But the pressure of the cold war brought about conflicts within the PSIUP and the pro-Moscow Nennists within appeared to have a majority. Technically the Saragat Socialists, who favoured Marshall Aid when it was later proposed, 'broke away' early in 1947. Saragat formed the PSLI socialist party and Nenni renamed the PSIUP, the PSI. Nenni entered the popular front arrangement with the Communists as a result of which the PCI improved its representation from 104 to 138 seats, whereas the Socialist representation was reduced from 115 to 71 (38 Nennists plus 33 Saragatists). The Communist Party thus gained from the Popular Front arrangement at the expense of Social Democracy. Indeed it was the most peculiar popular front of all time since it took place after the 'turn' in the Cominform, when the Social Democrats were beginning to be seen, once again, as 'social fascists'. Whilst this reveals to us nothing new about the Italian Communist Party it does shed light on the politics of the Nennists. Only very thick-skinned Social Democrats indeed, fellow travellers, or the politically naïve could have managed a popular front with the Communists in the hysterical atmosphere of 1947–48, and then, probably only in Italy. Even Nenni was forced to take his distance from the PCI later. But by then Italian Social Democracy had suffered a severe setback from which it has not yet fully recovered. The Saragat Socialists later entered a coalition with the Christian Democrats, as indeed Nenni had until January, 1947.

See also *A Short History of Italy* (p. 237–8) by H. Hearder and D. Waley (Editors), Cambridge University Press, Cambridge 1963.

See also Tribune 30.4.48 for an analysis of the Italian Election results.

See also Miliband, *op. cit.* (p. 306).

94. The 21 were:

H. L. Austin W. Dobbie J. Silverman

P. Barstow	Emrys Hughes	S. Silverman
G. Bing	Lester Hutchinson	S. Swingler
Tom Braddock	H. Lever	L. J. Solley
W. G. Cove	J. D. Mack	W. Vernon
Harold Davies	M. Orbach	W. Warbey
S. O. Davies	C. Royle	K. Zilliacus

See NEC report in the LP Annual Conference report 1948.

95. Miliband, *op. cit.* (p. 300).
96. Tribune, 30.4.48.
97. Tribune, 2.4.48.
98. Tribune, 21.5.48 and 28.5.48.
99. Tribune, 4.6.48.
100. Tribune, 18.6.48.
101. See Tribune, 29.8.47. As early as the summer of 1947 both 'Keep Left' and 'Cards on the Table' had been translated into German by the Austrian Socialist party. The introduction to this pamphlet praised Keep Left for attempting to find the right path for socialists and condemned 'the adherents of the little group of supporters of the pro-Communist Labour member Zilliacus' for playing no constructive part in the debate.
102. See Tribune, 2.9.49.
103. See Tribune article, 13.8.48 by Anton Ciliga, founder of the Yugoslav CP. Advertisements for holidays in Yugoslavia began to appear in Tribune and non-communist journals shortly after the rift.
104. Tribune, 9.9.49.
105. i.e. with J. D. Bernal at Hyde Park in September, 1949, (See Tribune 23.9.49).
106. Tribune, 23.9.49.
107. Tribune, 4.11.49.

Chapter Three

The Evolution of Tribune, (1947-51)

A great deal of the polemics relating to the dawn of the Cold War in the nuclear age was chronicled in the pages of Tribune in this preparatory period of Bevanism. But Tribune did not merely record events. It was profoundly influenced and changed by them. At times it hardly appeared possible that it could have become, within a couple of years, a thriving newspaper of a volatile left current challenging for the leadership of the movement.

Up to 1950 Tribune was reflecting a mood of cautious moderation in the Labour movement, and its abhorrence of the new barbarism that had descended over Eastern Europe, led it into the arms of the consolidators and advocates of the 'western' alliance. Whilst running from Zhdanov's terror Tribune embraced his theory of the two camps, by manifestly identifying with one of them. This led Tribune, almost as a matter of course, to accept the Anglo-American drift to war in Korea. Tribune's opposition to the war was extremely belated, and only really developed when the *consequences* became clear in the ranks of the movement, through the effect on living standards and the National Health Service. Tribune halted sharply in its tracks in the late Autumn of 1950, terminated its agreement with Transport House, challenged Deakin's method of dealing with communists in the unions, and began to reflect the more combative mood in the ranks of the unions and the party. The stages of this evolution must now be examined more closely.

The first important change was the resignation of John Kimche as managing editor in the new year of 1948. This resignation was, according to Michael Foot, of no political significance but was a management decision.[1] Foot himself was at that time MP for Devonport and shared the editorship with former German Social Democrat Evelyn Anderson. Foot was also on the editorial board along with Ian Mikardo and Bevan's wife, Jennie Lee. Mikardo was in addition a director, as was former editorial board member Patricia Strauss.

In May 1948 Tribune was appealing for financial help but it received a political fillip when Foot was elected to the NEC at conference that year. Future leading Bevanites, Crossman, Driberg and Mikardo were runners up in the constituency section of the voting.

In January 1949, Tribune began an arrangement with Transport House's Press and Publicity department which was to last until October, 1950. Transport House rented a 'Labour Party page' (in fact it was two pages) on a regular basis. Despite declarations of continuing independence of line, there can be little doubt from the evidence that follows, that the arrangement took on political overtones.

The key role in securing the arrangement was evidently Michael Foot's. It was explained that 'the Labour Party page will offer the means whereby central office and the National Executive may keep in the closest touch with local parties everywhere every week.'[2] The first article to appear in the rented pages was by NEC chairman James Griffiths. The following week secretary Morgan Phillips told readers 'Michael Foot MP, Tribune's joint editor, is taking a keen personal interest in this new venture.'[3] The arrangement temporarily assuaged Tribune's financial problems[4] and circulation increased encouragingly. But the question was—could the journal remain a forthright critic of the government and party within such limits? Foot promised that Tribune would still be critical but subsequent events indicate that criticism was muted. The second LP page began a counterattack on the policies and disruptive tactics of the Communist Party.[5]

The annual Tribune rally was instituted at the 1949 conference where Driberg was elected to join Foot on the NEC.[6] But the clear sign that all was not well was the resignation of Mikardo from the editorial board that same Spring. Mikardo's criticisms of the paper's stance on the western alliance anticipated by a full year the growth of left wing dissatisfaction on this crucial issue.

Tribune and the USA

Allusion has already been made to the recurring theme of pro-Democratic sentiment in Tribune's columns between 1947 and 1950. So marked was it that even Richard Crossman was forced to admit,

> 'I had quite forgotten how unashamedly pro-American the New Statesman, Tribune, Miss Jennie Lee, Mr Foot and I were in those far off days.'[7]

The pro-Democratic sentiment was not surprising. The communists had made much of the Stalin-Roosevelt collaboration in the Grand Alliance. In the New Deal of the thirties Roosevelt's administration had leaned on the American Labour movement and collaborated with it to an unprecedented degree.

Whilst Roosevelt at no time in the thirties embraced Keynesian budgetary policies,[8] it may have appeared to some that there was a parallel between what the Democrats had done in the New Deal period with the backing of the unions, and what the Attlee government was doing in the post war reconstruction period. But there was an important difference. The Democratic Party was an openly capitalist party relying on the external support and collaboration of American Labour. The British Labour Party was, by contrast, a party founded by labour, the political expression of the trade union movement which was structurally integrated with the party at every level. The British Labour leaders saw eye to eye with the Americans on fundamental issues of policy. But the British labour movement on which the government rested had other ideas, and the organisational means of expressing them. Conflict between the government and the movement was inevitable. Hence the Keep Left and Bevanite revolts, for which there is no counterpart in the American Democratic party.

Tribune's pro-American position in 1947 was entirely pragmatic. Britain was in debt to the USA, drew half her imports from that source, relied on her for defence and could 'ill afford to do without the Americans'.[9] When Truman was elected at the end of 1948 Tribune was ecstatic, describing it as a 'great victory for American Labour' and 'the common people all over the world'.[10] There was to be a 'New Deal' style welfare plan and the British Conservatives were alleged to be worried by the Democrats' victory.[11] From this point on Tribune's illusions abounded. The paper quoted American businessmen admiring the Steel nationalisation plan.[12] In the autumn of 1949 a headline ran 'President Truman Reads Tribune' over an article which betrayed serious confusion between the New Deal and a planned socialist economy.[13] This was only marginally less naïve than the Russophiles' belief that the USSR was socialist. It was but a short step from this misconstruction of the nature of the Democrats' domestic policy to endorsement of its strategy in foreign affairs. Tribune made that step with ease. In March 1949 the journal expressed support for NATO as a 'strictly defensive' alliance, 'misunderstood' by the Russians. Any increase in world tension resulting from its formation was a necessary risk.[14] Tribune feared that social democracy would be the chief casualty of 'Soviet imperialism'.[15] NATO was 'made in Moscow'. Had not Hitler sought to destroy democracy prior to launching war? it asked.[16] Assertions that NATO was purely a security pact could not disguise the fact that Tribune was abandoning the third way.

Communist Party members scanning the advertisement columns to see regular half-page displays for the New Leader,[17] New Republic and Socialist Call,[18] might have been forgiven for believing that Washington's influence on 222 The Strand was total. They might also have been suspicious of the close sympathies of Ian Mikardo and Richard Crossman for Poale Zion.[19] At least one correspondent considered that some very fine Jewish socialists who were good on all questions except Palestine 'exercise a weighty influence on Tribune's policy'.[20]

It was the Korean war however which provided the occasion for the full flowering of the pro-American line. Tribune backed it from the start, likening the North Korean tactics to fascism, repeating the accepted view that it was a 'pre-meditated attack' and expressing approval that the 'West had shown it will fight'.[21] And although the paper did not believe the Russians would allow themselves to become embroiled, it was appalled at the rout of the South Koreans in the opening weeks. It 'did not doubt the fighting qualities' of the Americans but felt a 'far greater mobilisation of forces' might be needed or all South East Asia might be lost. The only sceptical note was an expression of pity that the Southern government was not 'more worthy of the support it is receiving from the west.'[22] By July Woodrow Wyatt (a Keep Lefter in those days) used the paper's columns to toy with the idea of threatening the use of atomic weapons. He argued there were worse horrors and that more Jews had been killed by Hitler than died by the use of the atomic bomb in Japan. 'It is worth pondering these figures in considering whether there is any short cut to peace.'[23] Whatever the views of the editors, these lines escaped their censure. The following week protests began. Silverman put his views, and letters from people who had stopped buying Tribune were published. Michael Foot's identification of US and Labour philosophy was immortalised in the sentiment that US soldiers were dying to 'uphold a Labour Party principle.'[24] Tribune was scathing of those who argued that US action was illegal, branding them as 'legalistic appeasers.'[25] It was contemptuous of 'the new pacifism' arising out of the development of atomic weapons. Such people, it explained, preferred Russian occupation to atomic war. Did it really matter whether we were killed by atomic explosions or a firing squad? Thus far had Tribune travelled. It was anticipating the famous American catchphrase of the fifties 'better dead than red'.[26]

But when China entered the war there was a perceptible halt in Tribune's drastic slide into the hawks' camp. It began to dawn on Tribune that big rearmament programmes might be on the way, for after all 'no early success in a war with China could be expected.' Tribune feared that what it had considered action taken to prevent a third world war, might now lead to its breaking out.[27]

The paper supported conscription and even the proposal to extend it to two and a half years.[28] It mooted a plan for a 'rearmament levy'.[29] The moment of truth was near, but it took McArthur's escalation of events in the Far East to cause Tribune to think again.

Tribune and the Government

Enthusiasm for the Democratic party and sublime self-deception about its role within the United States made Tribune all the more able to reconcile itself with the course of the Attlee government during 1947–50. Anglo-American co-operation was fundamental to the strategy of maintaining the status quo in Europe and the world. And there was another dimension to this co-operation. It was in a very real sense 'the form in which Britain's increasing capitulation to America' was taking place.[30] In Greece, Palestine and Persia the United States was relieving Britain of the gendarme's mantle. But Britain possessed one valuable asset which the United States lacked—a viable strong social democratic movement with great standing in the eyes of the European working class. This reputation was augmented as a result of Stalin's consolidation. In Europe where the working class movement was, despite the ravages of fascism, well developed and sophisticated, the status quo could not live by bourgeois parties alone. Parties able to command the allegiance and loyalty of the proletariat were at a premium. In the period 1945–47 the Kremlin had ensured that this valuable service was forthcoming by ordering the parties under its control to disarm partisan movements and enter coalition governments thereby stemming the offensive of the European labour movement. But now that the Kremlin had abandoned this method of preserving its own sphere of influence for the policy of open terror against all parties independent of its control, the role of social democracy in general, and British social democracy in particular, became of crucial importance for Western Europe. It was the British Labour Party and Denis Healey's Comisco that revived the socialist international.

But the tactics of the Kremlin played a greater part than any American funds for journals such as the New Leader and Socialist Commentary, in ensuring the domination of the parties of this new international by representatives of moderate Social Democratic opinion.[31]

Tribune's support for the course of moderation of the Attlee government was not confined to approval of the pro-American stance. On the issues of empire the paper displayed remarkable enthusiasm for the civilising mission. Tribune declared 'unhesitatingly' that the British should stay in Africa to save it from 'catastrophe'!

> 'We do not need to apologise for our mission in Africa. Whatever the reasons which took our forebears there we must stay.'[32]

The sentiments which made the French socialists advocates of French presence in Vietnam and Algeria were obviously as resilient in the heart of Tribune. When British rule in Hong Kong appeared threatened by Mao's victory in China, Tribune proffered advice that might have been expected from a Victorian colonialist. 'To remain calm and behave as though friendly relations were expected as a matter of course is the surest way of continuing the status quo without trouble.' The status quo was, of course, a colonial status, but nonetheless 'considerable investment' meant that 'military expenditure would have to be very high indeed before it outweighed the commercial advantages' of defending Hong Kong from the Chinese communists. What is more, loss of the island could lead to the loss of Malaya to 'communist bandits'.[33] With equal zeal Tribune defended action in Greece against the communists. It argued that the policy of UK–US intervention 'can be defended however evil have been many of the methods employed by the Greek government'.[34] And when the Irish dared declare a Republic, Tribune was most put out.[35] In fact one of the charges Tribune laid at the door of the Conservatives at this time was that they 'neglected the Empire'.[36]

Tribune's drift away from the left was profound. The eulogising of the Anglo-American role in world politics made an easy target for the followers of the Kremlin. The above quoted sentiments were truly a sophisticated apology for empire, dressed in the garb of a socialist commonwealth. But this was hardly surprising. Many of the regular contributors never professed left credentials, and did not even have a radical past like Denis Healey.[37] Editorial policy at Tribune had always been liberal in the accepted sense of the term, denying no person access to its columns. On the other hand Roy Jenkins was a very frequent contributor. As late as March 1951 Tribune published one of his works as a pamphlet, entitled, perhaps significantly, *Fair Shares for the Rich*![38]

Anthony Crosland contributed lengthy economic articles with almost equal frequency. By no stretch of the imagination could either of these men be said to have had very much in common with the Keep Left manifesto, outside of their membership of the same party. Denis Healey and Hugh Gaitskell also contributed, but more often this was under the auspices of the rented LP page of Tribune.

Much of Tribune's defence of government economic policy was undertaken by Crosland and Jenkins in the period of the wage freeze. In the Spring of 1949 Jenkins hoped the LP would not get 'bad nerves about deflation'. He wanted to see a 'substantial reduction in the budget surplus.'[39] Only days before Bevan's resignation he was consoling Tribune readers with the 'view of Treasury experts', that 'the impact of the rearmament programme is likely to be less drastic than many people at first believed'.[40] This was not Tribune's view, but Jenkins did leave it surprisingly late parting company as a regular correspondent.

Anthony Crosland's feature columns finally brought him into conflict with another contributor, Keep Lefter Donald Bruce. In the Spring of 1950 the latter challenged Crosland about the wisdom of a standstill budget. Bruce expressed some of the frustration of the Keep Left group at being lectured by the new economists on the need for restraint and deflation. He wanted the benefits of increased productivity shared fairly amongst the people. Something 'very much better than a standstill budget' was called for.[41] The debate spread over many weeks, foreshadowing the eventual rupture between right and left in 1951.

But these disputes were long arriving. For two years the arrangement with Transport House, the wages truce and the influence of Crosland and Jenkins, combined with other factors to blunt the critical edge which Foot had pledged. The government's economic record was celebrated in Tribune's review of the 'Economic Survey for 1949'. Labour ought to 'be proud' of this 'stupendous achievement' realised whilst the terms of trade were against it.[42] Tribune rejected the charge that it was a 'Tory' budget, but regretted the lefts' advice had been ignored. Had it been a Tory budget Labour might have expected to do well in the counties. But Labour had lost seats there so it was not a Tory budget, the paper argued. One reader complained that Tribune looked like a 'good right wing journal'. He suggested defence of the budget be left to the Herald whilst Tribune revert to socialist criticism. This remark was representative of the concern felt by many Labour activists bemused by Tribune's steady drift to orthodoxy.[43]

But despite the considerable achievement of the Attlee government in riding out the earlier crises, more trouble was to come. The dollar crisis of the summer of 1949 brought regrets that 'slight unemployment may be inevitable'.[44] Devaluation when it followed in September was euphemistically interpreted by Mikardo as an opportunity to intensify the struggle for Labour's policy 'even though it carries with it some increase in the cost of living'.[45] Tribune caused a minor sensation in the national press by demanding a general election, because devaluation marked 'a new stage in Labour's struggle towards economic independence.'[46] Tribune supported devaluation. It called on Labour to demonstrate strength and unity. It called for discipline as an answer to the 'delight' of conservatives and communists. It called for 'sacrifice' and 'self discipline in the cause of British socialism.' Soviet workers had made sacrifices, why, asked Tribune, should we be called 'traitor' for demanding the same?[47] When spending cuts were announced in October Tribune claimed that they were not Labour's fault but criticised the government 'for not presenting the cuts in a more understandable and stimulating way'![48] When Labour won the North Kensington by-election in November this proved to Tribune 'that the people understand why devaluation, and the cost of living increase which is bound to follow it, is necessary.'[49] Tribune had in fact misinterpreted the nature of the support given to Labour. It was the kind of support that the rope is traditionally understood to lend to a hanging man. Support for Labour heralded a new struggle on policy within the party. In the Spring of 1950 a meeting of Labour leaders at Dorking prepared guidelines for permanent consolidation and further retreat from radical policies.[50]

Tribune and the Unions

Underwriting the government's basic economic strategy

caused Tribune to view most unsympathetically strikes which might endanger it. The movement for wages did not get seriously under way until mid 1949 but there was a strike of dockers in the summer of 1948 against the punishment clauses in the Dock Labour scheme. For refusing to load zinc oxide eleven dockers were suspended without pay and lost their entitlement to attendance money. Since they could not get unemployment pay either, this was a serious matter. Tribune thought the dockers were wrong to strike over the issue and described the whole business as an 'unmitigated disaster'. Its reporter however had discovered that communist agitators were not in evidence and that the dockers were 'mostly Labour supporters'.[51] Further trouble on the docks the following year found Tribune hardly more agreeable, though the advice was proffered that dockers needed to make the democratic machinery of their union work more efficiently to ensure the selection of union officials more representative and sensitive to the men's needs.[52]

The 1950 dock strike was more serious still since it involved the hated order 1305, a war time regulation forbidding strikes and lock-outs. The Minister of Labour had persuaded the General Council of the TUC to agree to its peace-time retention.[53] In the course of the dispute the government tried unsuccessfully to prosecute unofficial strikers on the docks and eventually used troops in an attempt to break it. It was left to Sidney Silverman, one of Tribune's critics, to spell out unequivocal support for the dockers' case.[54]

In 1949, the year in which Home Secretary, Chuter Ede, banned May Day processions, Tribune was also to be found remarkably cool on the railwaymen's dispute and decidedly hostile to the NUR secretary Jim Figgins.[55] It suggested that he visit those areas affected by the 'lodging out' strike to persuade the men to accept the union's views about 'the unwisdom' of their industrial action, and it put a number of sharp questions to the NUR leader.[56] Later in the dispute it suggested 'Mr Figgins . . . may be a disciple of some other organisation as his TUC colleagues frequently assert.'[57] This was a scarcely veiled reference to Figgins' pro-CP leanings, but coming at a time of hostile press criticism it was hardly calculated to endear Tribune either to Figgins or the strikers. When the railwaymen's go-slow began in July it was described as 'madness'.[58] Tribune appealed to the railwaymen arguing that they should have 'as their over-riding interest the maintenance of the nation's economy as a whole and the general wage restraint policy which is vital for serving this end.'[59] The railwaymen's pay claim in the autumn received little sympathy. The Railway Executive was 'broke'. The money was not available.[60] Only if the railwaymen accepted necessary redundancies to increase productivity could higher wages be awarded.[61] Those workers who were sacked were sure to find work elsewhere at just as good pay.[62] The explanation of Tribune's hostility is to be found in the fact that it considered the wage freeze *too loose.* It wanted a binding incomes policy. The government White Paper was on the fence between free collective bargaining and a proper wages policy.[63]

Those who sought the removal of the wage freeze at party conference in Blackpool 1949 received stern rebukes from Tribune. The mover, Jack Stanley, secretary of the Constructional Engineering Union, was 'at least as pro-communist as the two MPs whose expulsion the party had endorsed the day before.' The seconder, Ron Chamberlain MP, was 'a frequent contributor to the Daily Worker.'[64] Tribune's venom was prompted by a belief that the industrial action of that summer was purely and simply part of the Cominform's anti-Marshall offensive. In June Tribune attacked the Communist Party and after referring directly to the trouble on the docks and the railways commented . . .

> 'In 1945 the communists committed themselves to the plea for a new Churchill coalition. They never believed in the possibility of a Labour government until it happened. Their present activities both on the electoral and industrial front are directed to assist the return of a Churchill government in 1950'.[65]

By the time of the Labour Party conference the following year Sidney Silverman's resolution which called for an improvement in real wages and the control of prices and profits was accepted by the NEC and adopted unanimously by conference. But it was opposed by Tribune on the grounds that it did not constitute a wages policy![66] Even the TUC at its

1950 Brighton conference, voted to end the wage freeze, as the momentum of a strike movement accelerated.

Tribune and the Witch Hunt

The McCarthy era had not yet arrived but it was dawning. Tribune was treading a very dangerous path. It had difficulty in distinguishing genuine strikes from political intrigue. From justifiable criticism of the CP's adventurism and its leadership's zealous endorsement of terror in Eastern Europe, Tribune was slipping over near to the point of joining the witch hunt now gathering pace in Britain and America, and which was to culminate in the loathsome public trials of the Un-American Activities Committee.

Attlee's decision to remove fascists and communists from certain civil service posts in the Spring of 1948 was endorsed by Tribune. Whilst it was 'dangerous' and 'abhorrent' there were certain exceptions. Did not communists deprive whole nations of their liberty, the paper asked?[67] Thus Mr Attlee's plea could not be rejected on 'the grounds of absolute principle'.

In like manner Tribune supported the ban on communists holding office in the TGWU. 'It is nonsense to denounce the TGWU's ban on communist office-holders as "undemocratic". The decision which, incidentally, also applies to members of the British Union of Fascists, was taken by more than two thirds of the conference delegates.' The CP had only itself to blame. It was not a witch hunt and the only danger of the ban was that it might force the CP to go underground in that union, and make it harder to detect communist influence.[68] But then a change began in the course of 1950. A full page article in May on the issue of anti-communism described it as 'an evil almost as great as communism itself.'[69]

By this time it may have been dawning on leading Tribunites where the paper's indiscriminate fervour for American policy was leading it. McCarthy's allegation of 57 un-named state department officials as card-carrying CP members occurred that Spring. To appease criticism Truman appointed the Republican Foster Dulles and Dean Acheson to government posts. These moves on the other side of the Atlantic coincided with a bizarre press story in Britain involving John

Strachey, who had been appointed to a non-Cabinet, ministerial post at the War Office in February. The story ran that British and US defence chiefs had agreed to withhold military secrets from the Labour minister.[70] The witch hunt to which Tribune had been partially accommodating was now being directed at a Minister in the very government the paper was anxious to defend. Anti-communism was coming home to social democrats. Tribune established the connection between the McCarthyite witch hunt in the US and the press campaign in Britain. 'Lord Witch Hunt goes to war' it declared in a reference to Lord Vansittart's allegations about communists in the Civil Service and the BBC.[71] Leading members of the film industry wrote in to launch a protest campaign against the jailing of left wingers in the American film world.[72] Tribune began to treat the matter of victimisation of communists with more caution, but the adventurist Cominform line made communists difficult people to defend. It presented Tribune with a serious dilemma. Mikardo wrote in November . . .

> 'Just as Soviet imperialism seeks to overthrow Social Democracy by diverting us into military expenditure and away from our positive task of world rehabilitation, so British communism achieves its only victory in diverting the Labour Party into negative anti-communism and away from our positive social and economic programme.'[73]

There lay in this statement the germ of the problem confronting the Labour left—the subtle and contradictory interdependence between right wing social democracy and British Stalinism as representatives of the two camps. How to combat *both*? That was the question. But Tribune had no fully-worked out conception of just what the Soviet Union *was*; just what the Kremlin really did represent in world politics; what the new world role of the USA entailed in the period of Britain's decline. There were in Tribune's pages one or two attempts at an historical accounting with Stalinism's role,[74] but they remained sporadic commentaries on history, unable to assist party activists in the day-to-day task of dealing with CP members in factory and locality. Nor could Tribune assist CP members themselves to break with the destructive leadership of their own party, since the paper was for too long prone to combining historical jibing with an equivocal attitude to the witch hunt. Tribune was no nearer resolving any of the fundamental problems presented by 'two camps' as the movement towards the Bevanite resignations gained momentum in 1950–51.

Keeping Left

Keeping Left was published in January 1950. It proved to those who may have thought otherwise that the Keep Left movement was not dead. The new pamphlet arose out of discussions between the signatories during the summer of 1949.[75] It was an enormous success, selling out prior to publication. New signatories included Barbara Castle, Tom Horabin and Richard Acland, whilst some of those whose names had vanished from the front cover were preoccupied elsewhere.[76] The most noticeable change in the political line was *the tacit abandonment of the third way for acceptance of the western alliance.* It held that Labour Britain should work within this alliance for collaboration between East and West . . . Tribune proclaimed that the pamphlet deserved the widest support.

Keeping Left was a wide ranging policy statement. It was not markedly radical and bore an *unmistakable pre-Korean War* stamp. The battle between left and right, when it eventually commenced was to be less about the modest socialist principles contained in the pamphlet than the practical consequences, in terms of living standards, arising out of the Korean War which broke out five months later.

Whilst Tribune had embraced the war effort, it shrank from confronting the hostility its effects were inducing in the unions and the party later in 1951. Silverman moved a Commons' motion in July 1950 mildly requesting the government to limit the area of conflict and to cease hostilities under UNO supervision. He had the backing of twenty Labour MPs, including Zilliacus. Tribune thought the resolution 'unnecessary'.[77] Even though, as Silverman pointed out, the House of Commons *had never had the opportunity to take a vote* on the UNO war decision.

When Tribune published its October pamphlet *Full Speed Ahead* Silverman criticised it in an article. He argued that it was impossible to fight for socialism from within one of the two 'camps', and that the entire Fulton policy rested on the need for UK-US agreement which patently prevented British Labour from giving the lead for democratic socialism in Europe which Tribune desired.[78]

However from the autumn onwards the split in the Cabinet was clearly developing and news of it leaked out in November. The Daily Telegraph named three Ministers allegedly involved in disagreements—Bevan, Strachey and Strauss.[79] Attlee's public denial in the last week of November did not stem speculation. Equally unconvincing was Tribune's allegation that the entire affair was a 'press stunt'. It advised the government to review the three-year rearmament programme and limit the total spending to that which could be sustained. This was 'surely the only course open to the government.'[80]

On reflection it is ironic that what sparked the left revolt which troubled Labour throughout the fifties was the *hardly radical demand that it should not spend on arms more than it could sustain!* Logically that was the 'only course'. A mass campaign would surely not be required to bring home this simple truth. Not so! In Britain mass movements arise on the basis of such modest elementary logic. False teeth and spectacles become invested with historic significance. Nor is this an expression of the simplicity of British politics, but, on the contrary, of its extreme sophistication—a sophistication not rooted in theoretical reasoning, but in the appreciation by the broad movement of the profound inner class importance of outwardly small things. The drama of over-estimation and over-reaction was about to reach a climax over a figure for arms expenditure which was unrealisable, quite irrespective of its desirability, and the necessary condition for the achievement of which was the partial forfeiture of gains so recently won. Beside this, programmes, theories and polemics took on entirely secondary importance for the movement, which rallied irresistibly to Bevan as the architect of the NHS when the split materialised.

Tribune was still suffering from circulation problems. This may have been due to the drift of its politics but it may have owed something to its literary magazine 'New Statesman' style of layout. It was still a long way from the easy-to-read photo-picture tabloid it was to become in its Bevanite heyday.

But whatever did cause problems for circulation, it could not have been assisted by the sudden termination of the Transport House arrangement in the autumn of 1950. In September Tribune put a brave face on it with the announcement of 'A new venture in publishing'. Closer reading of the venture disclosed that it involved going fortnightly instead of weekly. But there was to be a monthly Tribune pamphlet of between 20,000–30,000 words which could treat subjects in greater depth and obtain a much wider circulation for socialist ideas. The new venture was supposed to be undertaken in the spirit of the tradition of Robert Blatchford, Brailsford, Tawney and the Left Book Club but Tribune admitted it would have preferred to remain a weekly.[81]

What did cause Transport House to end this effective subsidy to Tribune? Certainly, in the broadest sense, it was evidence of the drift of the government's course, which meant it was becoming ever more sensitive even to modest left wing criticism. But there was a more immediate and identifiable cause. The 'new venture' was announced on September 15th. The first fortnightly appeared on September 22nd, and the last LP page on October 6th. The issue which flared up at this time and which the present editor of the paper confirms was the issue which contributed to the ending of the arrangement was a dispute with TGWU chief, Arthur Deakin.

Deakin had begun a concerted campaign against communist influence in his TGWU. A ban had been imposed in 1949, forbidding Communist Party members to hold paid positions. Tribune had frequently been critical of the bureaucratic structure of the Transport union and the remoteness of its leaders from the ranks,[82] particularly on the docks. Now it reminded Deakin that not all strikes were caused by communists. The occasion of this reminder was an infamous Deakin press conference during the weekend of September 16–17,[83] in the course of which the union chief had demanded the outlawing of the CP and the suppression of the Daily Worker. Deakin's outburst was prompted by a strike of London busmen and wages disputes gathering pace on the docks among road haulage men. He had clearly been impressed by the Minister of Labour's reference to the fact that three leading London dockers had just returned from a visit to Poland, where they were alleged to have been briefed concerning the 'dislocation of the British economy'.[84]

However, these wages disputes had a simpler explanation. The wage freeze had all but broken down. The patience of trades unionists was running out and there was a revival on the industrial front from the relative lull of 1948–49. This merged with the dissatisfaction of the TGWU members with their union's structure. These disputes anticipated to some degree the revolt of the dockers against the union bureaucracy in 1954. Had not Tribune made a stand on this issue it is doubtful whether it could ever have come to lead the left in the fifties, because the dissatisfaction in the TGWU was an expression of a new forward thrust of the working class directed against Deakin and the right wing in the government. It really is not an accident that this was the issue which sundered apart the cosy relationship between Tribune and Transport House. Deakin's union leased the Transport House premises to the Labour Party whilst Tribune only leased two pages of its paper. Apparently the landlord's lease proved a more powerful influence on the NEC than Michael Foot's. In its attack on Deakin, Tribune conceded that the Communist Party was 'most likely plotting to disrupt industry', but said it believed the broad mass of opinion in the Labour movement regarded the CP with 'healthy contempt'. The paper opposed a sterile and mainly negative anti-communist campaign, and further accused Deakin himself of borrowing totalitarian methods by his suggestion of a ban. The article was entitled pugnaciously 'Chuck it, Deakin!'[85] The special relationship between Tribune and Transport House was at an end.

The new venture was remarkably successful. There was sufficient buoyancy in the left current to enable Tribune to survive without the Transport House supplement. One of the first of the monthly pamphlets *John Bull's Other Island* by Keep Lefter Geoffrey Bing, an indictment of the Ulster government, sold over 150,000 copies.[86] Ian Mikardo was elected to the NEC in October. The Keep Left Brains Trusts, which were to become an immensely successful feature of the Bevanite movement, began that same month at the Labour Party conference. Mikardo was in the chair and amongst the thirteen speakers were many leading Bevanites-to-be, and seven signatories of 'Keep Left'. But the financial problems did not disappear.

Duff relates how 'in late March or April' Michael Foot had taken her to the west room of the Tribune offices and told her 'in confidence, that he expected that as a result of the budget some Ministers would resign. That would give Tribune new opportunities, a new lease of life'.[87]

This may have been speculation, yet the fear it was designed to placate was very real. It was the 'one and only time' he had openly spoken about the possibility of the paper closing down. At this time, three weeks before the resignations, Foot appears certain of the outcome and its implications for the paper.

Ministry of Labour

In his definitive work on Aneurin Bevan, Michael Foot devotes less than one page and an extensive footnote to Bevan's three-month stay at the Ministry of Labour. The events on the Labour front that occurred between January and his resignation in April are presented very much as off-stage noises to the debate on the arms programme. This may well betray Foot's own parliamentary debating perspective of historical events. Is there a case for attributing greater significance to Bevan's experiences as Minister of Labour as a contributory factor to his resignation than the biography allows for? If the intention of moving Bevan from the Health Ministry to the Ministry of Labour was to remove him from a contentious area of administration before health charges were imposed, it was not a wise move. The Ministry of Labour's bed of nails is a poor resting place for those with troubled political consciences. Why was Bevan moved *there*, and did it have any influence on his subsequent decision to resign?

The wage freeze was at an end. Railwaymen, bank employees, gasmen and dockers began to press wage claims. A Times leader in January feared yet another round of wage claims issuing from the Easter conferences and prophetically warned that it was quite likely that the unions would attempt to ditch compulsory arbitration. This was the conclusion the editor drew from the effect on rank and file union opinion of prison sentences imposed on ten gas maintenance workers for unofficial strike activity.[88]

Referring to the wage demands The Times considered them not only reasonable but even modest were it not for 'the consequences of the international situation'.[89]

When George Isaacs resigned his post, he stressed the onerous nature of the job he had held for five years and his need to relax after it. The Times now saw the Ministry of Labour as a 'key post'. Mr Bevan's appointment was,

> 'A measure of the growing importance of this department at a time when circumstances compel the government to embark on a big rearmament programme and to make the inevitable adjustments in the country's industrial economy.'[90]

Bevan, in other words, had been put in charge of a Ministry where he was most likely to meet the full force of the wages offensive, the movement to end compulsory arbitration and the system of war-time regulations for the prevention of strikes associated with it, the infamous order 1305.[91] Foot says of Bevan's sojourn at the Ministry of Labour that 'He had time to prepare the abolition of the long detested war-time regulation, Order 1305 . . .'[92] The actual unfolding of events leading up to its abolition is, however, very much more complex.

Early in February Merseyside dockers struck in opposition to a dockers' delegate conference decision to accept an offer of 21 shillings a day. Merseyside wanted 25 shillings, one of the five points of the popular 'Dockers Charter'. The London docks gave only partial support to the strike. Arthur Deakin accused 'communist saboteurs' of being responsible and when Bevan was questioned on the content of Deakin's revelations he said he found it an 'interesting' document which deserved 'wider circulation' and which shed considerable light on the 1949 docks dispute. Such remarks must have given comfort to those who sought to explain the dispute as a communist manoeuvre.[93]

By February 8th the Liverpool men had abandoned the attempt to fully involve the London docks and the strike was weakening. At this point, four London and three Liverpool dockers were arrested in a raid on an East End pub and charged with conspiracy to organise an illegal strike. Two noteworthy dockers' leaders, Bill Johnson and Harry Constable, were among them. Nothing could have been better designed to rally the dockers. Sympathy strikes began immediately. From a wages dispute it became a struggle for the abolition of 1305, after a vote on a Merseyside resolution. And since 1305 was the main sanction of compulsory arbitration it meant an end of that as well.

When the seven appeared at the Old Bailey in April, daily sympathy strikes and marches to the court room took place on each of the nine days of the hearing. Many thousands of dockers participated. There were mounted police charges and the dockers sang 'Britons never shall be slaves'.[94] On April 19th, four days before Bevan's resignation, the dockers were discharged and a great victory had been won which led to the ending of 1305 in August. The dockers had done it. In the course of these events Bevan had a personal encounter with the dockers at a rowdy Bermondsey meeting prior to the trial. The heckling turned to cheers when he said,

> 'I will never be a member of a government which makes charges on the National Health Service for a patient.'[95]

For Harold Wilson, as for others, the Bermondsey speech ended speculation about whether Bevan would resign or not.[96] But if that is the case, ought not Bevan's experiences at the Ministry of Labour be given their rightful place in the formative influences on his decision to resign. And ought not the dockers be credited with the main responsibility of ending 1305!

The wages offensive, the struggle against 1305, the arms budget and the imposition of NHS charges were many sided aspects of an international crisis penetrating the Labour movement. The dockers were the spearhead of the union ranks pressing forward to end war-time restrictions on free collective bargaining, removing the obstacles to a wages movement necessary to compensate for the inflation resulting from the Korean war.

Bevan's Cabinet revolt was a manifestation of this same forward thrust expressed within the Labour party and the government. It was an attempt to protect the gains of the 1945–50 period, now threatened by international crisis. But the Ministry of Labour interlude is a vital clue to the relationship between the political revolt in the Cabinet and the industrial offensive of the workers. In this three months the chief political representative of the left found himself on the wrong side of the fence to those whose champion he was to become in the months ahead. Bevan's revolt cannot therefore be *equated* with the forward movement from below. It was a distorted reflection of it. His resignation had been in the air on three occasions—1947, 1949, and 1950. It took the mass movement for him to make up his mind. The period from Keep Left to Keeping Left had been an important preparatory period of the Bevanite revolt. The Keep Left leaders were to become the general staff of the Bevanites. Two of them, Foot and Mikardo, had, with Tom Driberg, been elected to the NEC since 1947. The debates they had conducted were to become the debates of the Bevanites. But none of the basic theoretical or programmatic problems had been solved. They preferred pamphlets to theoretical works. Between *Keeping Left* in January 1950 and Bevan's resignation in April 1951 came the Korean war, the real father of the Bevanite current. With the Korean war the age of innocence ended for the left. The grim consequence of uncritical alignment with Washington was clear. The effects were all pervasive—inflation, charges on the social services, war service for the youth, the extension of anti-communist hysteria on a frightening scale. Yet the other camp offered continuing terror trials and repression.

Towards the end of February 1951, Bevan's speech in the defence debate was published in Tribune in full in a particularly aggressive and business-like issue of the paper, (despite its marginally reduced format). Alongside it was a major editorial on 'War Aims in Korea' and a leading article by Mikardo on the arms programme. It was in this defence speech that Bevan made known his view that events in South East Asia did 'not have their seat in the Kremlin at all' but 'under the influence of historical forces.' Whilst recognising the need for defence he warned of imitating 'other places' where the rearmament clamour and witch hunting went together.[97] The speech was billed in Tribune as 'Britain's Policy for Peace'.

When a mass movement is generated it does not seek perfect programmes, impeccable leaders, fully rounded-out theories and stream-lined organisation. It seizes upon what is at hand. In the Labour party the discontented activists fearing the loss of what had been gained from the post-war Labour government, sensing the danger of the return of a Conservative government, turned to the left they had spurned in 1947 and the prodigal son who had returned. Despite all its weaknesses, divisions and past sins, it was all they had.

NOTES

1. Michael Foot, in a personal interview with the Author at the House of Commons, 8th August, 1978. See Appendix 3 of the author's doctoral thesis.
2. Tribune, 7.1.49.
3. Tribune, 14.1.49.
4. *Left, Left, Left,* by Peggy Duff, Allison and Busby, London 1971. 'One of the life saving plans which began shortly after I arrived was an "arrangement" with the Labour Party. They paid us (I can't remember how much) for the regular use of two pages of Tribune. In addition they sent out to their mailing list a leaflet advertising the paper and appealing for sales through local parties. As a result we built up fairly rapidly the sale of several thousand copies a week. Apart from its effect on bulk sales, the "arrangement" with the Labour Party did us not much good.' Its two pages were abysmally dull and Tribune withdrew from the bargain in 1950.
5. Ironically it was over the issue of Arthur Deakin's witch hunt of the Communists that Tribune's arrangement with Transport House was terminated. For details see the end of this chapter.
6. Duff, *op. cit.* (p. 27).
7. *America and the British Left* (p. 152) by Henry Pelling, *op. cit.* Pelling in turn takes the quotation from Crossman in the New Statesman 9.4.55.
   In the passage from which the quotation is drawn Pelling says, 'Just as in the period of the Marshall Plan the Labour Left had found ideological reasons for its friendship with America by emphasising the significance of the Fair Deal and Truman's fourth point and exaggerating the significance of the American Labour movement, so now the Bevanites justified their alienation by stressing the instability of American capitalism, the like-

lihood of an early economic depression in the US, the influence of "big business" in the counsels of the Republican party (which returned to power in 1952) and finally the irrepressible character of the anti-Communist witch-hunt which reached its climax under Senator McCarthy's leadership in 1953–54.'

8. It is commonly thought that Roosevelt was an early convert to Keynesianism. This is not so. See *Franklin D. Roosevelt and the New Deal* (p. 264) by William Leuchtenburg, Harper and Row, New York 1963.
   On p. 337 Leuchtenburg quotes Keynes' open letter to the President in which the economist expresses his optimism at Roosevelt's election. But Roosevelt on 16th May 1933 called for stabilisation of currencies at international level, a distinctly monetarist move. He began to revise his views on this when monetarism conflicted with his New Deal policies. On page 256, Leuchtenburg, writing of the 1937–38 recession says the President was still unconvinced by his Keynesian advisers.
   > 'Harry Hopkins and Aubrey Williams armed with a memorandum from Leon Henderson sped to Georgia to try once more to win the President over to multi-billion dollar spending. This time they succeeded.'

   So Roosevelt's reversal of his anti-Keynesian position was not until Spring 1938 but 'he still had not embarked on the kind of massive spending which the Keynesians called for. He seems to have been even less impressed with Keynes than the British economist was with the President's grasp of economics.' Only part of the 1938 spending programme was based on an increase in government debt.
9. Tribune, 3.1.47.
10. Tribune, 14.1.49.
11. Tribune, 12.5.48.
12. Tribune, 25.2.49.
13. Tribune, 9.9.49.
14. Tribune, 18.3.49.
15. Tribune, 25.3.49.
16. Tribune, 18.3.49.
17. Tribune 6.8.48 and 8.7.49 for example.
    New Leader—a publication for British and Foreign Labour parties. In 1973 Radical Research Services, London, alleged CIA money was partially responsible for the revival of this newspaper as an organ of right wing social democracy. The conspiratorial tones of this publication however, demand critical reading. *New Leader* contributors were James Burnham, John Dewey, Louis Fischer, Arthur Koestler, Bertrand Russell, Herbert Johnson, George Orwell.
18. *Socialist Call* was the organ of the USA Socialist Party.
19. Tribune, 28.4.50 and 4.3.49. However the Soviet Union was one of the UNO members who voted for the establishment of Israel

in 1948, so that Communist opinion would not have been as hostile to Zionism as is the case today.

20. Tribune, 7.12.48.
21. *The Hidden History of the Korean War* (pp. 1–23) by Irving Stone, Turnstile Press Ltd., London 1952. Stone produces evidence to show that the North Korean invasion of Sunday, 25th June, 1950 was not the surprise 'Pearl Harbour' affair that officialdom in the USA at first suggested. He is also convinced that Russia did not want war, and that her absence from the Security Council when the crucial vote was taken is evidence that Russia was taken by surprise by the North Korean invasion. On p. 44 however, Stone argues 'Has the real truth been hidden in the murk of dispute between pro-Communists and anti-Communists, the former unwilling to admit that the North may well have prepared and planned an invasion, the latter unwilling to look at facts which cast any shadow on South Korea's role as the poor little Serbia or Belgium of what might become World War Three?'

    In *Korea—The Limited War* by David Rees, Macmillan, London 1964, there is a more thorough treatment of the subject. This book starts not with the invasion, but the Potsdam agreement between the Russians and the Americans as it affected Korea. This agreement made the 38th parallel the approximate dividing line of the two nations' sphere of influence. Despite 'fanatical resentment' (p. 11) of the American presence in the South, the Moscow Foreign Ministers Conference agreed to 'work out trusteeship proposals for a period of up to five years.' Russia dealt with the indigenous Northern partisans, the Korean Volunteer Corps, by merging all groups into a 'front' as had been engineered in East Germany and Kim Il Sung, a major in the Soviet occupation forces was elevated to a position of national leadership. By this means the peoples' committees which had arisen spontaneously all over Korea and which had been suppressed in the South, were contained in the North. However a question mark must surely be placed over Rees' assertion that the Northern invasion was a 'Soviet war plan worked out by General Antonov . . .' (p. 19). Whilst this is entirely possible, insufficient evidence is presented for definite proof. It may well have been that Russia resented the North Korean's upsetting of the Potsdam agreement. Her actions at the Geneva conference in 1954 in underwriting the continued partition of Vietnam even after the routing of the French army by indigenous communist troops, does not suggest Russia was given to adventurous acts of unification except where she stood to gain directly from it.
22. Tribune, 7.7.50.
23. Tribune, 7.7.50.
24. Tribune, 28.7.50.
25. Tribune, 14.7.50.

26. Hugh Jenkins was associated with this new pacifism. See Tribune, 8.9.50 and 15.9.50.
27. Tribune, 12.1.51.
28. See Tribune, 28.10.49. Selective extension to 2½ years should be considered although reduction was still to the long term aim.
29. Tribune, 3.11.50. The idea was to spread the cost of rearmament more evenly.
30. *Where is Britain Going* by L. Trotsky (p. 3) New Park Publications, London 1970.
31. See *The Labour Party and the CIA* (p. 13) by Radical Research Publications, London.
32. Tribune, 20.8.48.
33. Tribune, 21.10.49.
34. Tribune, 21.10.49.
35. Tribune, 29.4.49.
36. Tribune, 1.4.49.
37. See author's interview with Michael Foot, Appendix 3 of the author's doctoral thesis. Foot warns of retrospective labelling of people's political views.
38. Tribune pamphlet, published 30.3.51.
39. Tribune, 1.4.49.
40. Tribune, 9.3.51.
41. Tribune, 31.3.50.
42. Tribune, 18.3.49. Indeed the recovery after 1947 was remarkable.

Balance of Payment on current A/c £m.

1945	–875	94	= Terms of Trade Index (fall = adverse movement)
1946	–230	95	
1947	–381	88	
1948	26	85	Figures from *Butler & Sloman* (pp. 310–11), *op. cit.*
1949	–1	86	

43. Tribune, 15.4.49.
44. Tribune, 1.7.49.
45. Tribune, 7.10.49.
46. Tribune, 30.9.49.
47. Tribune, 23.9.49.
48. Tribune, 28.10.49.
49. Tribune, 11.11.49.
50. Tribune, 16.6.50, quoted the Sunday Times which had referred to 'the Dorking Conference and the new socialist line', which it considered underlay Morrison's policy speech at Perth.
51. Tribune, 25.6.48.
52. Tribune, 29.7.49.
53. *A History of British Trade Unionism* (p. 224–9), Henry Pelling, *op. cit.*
54. Tribune, 28.4.50. 'In Defence of the Dockers' by Sidney Silverman. Tribune's attitude in this dispute is in marked contrast to its passionate involvement in the 1954 dock strikes, emphasising the change that occurred after 1951. The Trotskyists in Social-

ist Outlook were closely involved with this strike. Dockers' leader Harry Constable wrote occasionally for the Outlook.

55. *The Railwaymen* (p. 626–7) by Philip S. Bagwell, George Allen & Unwin, London 1963 contains some interesting material on Figgins' career. Beneath Tribune's sniping was the suspicion that Figgins was a fellow traveller, and of course the Communist Party was, along with the Cominform parties in the middle of an anti-Marshall Plan offensive. Professor Bagwell says this of the 1948 General Secretaryship campaign in the NUR,
'Because Mr. Figgins had been associated with Communists in the Railwaymen's Minority Movement in the 1930's, and more recently had been in sympathy with them in opposition to a "standstill" on wages, the Railway Review, in the course of the campaign for the election of a General Secretary, had asserted that he was a Communist. Mr. Figgins therefore drafted a letter to Harry Pollitt in which he stated that he was not a member of the Communist Party, and he read this letter, and Pollitt's reply, endorsing the truth of his statement to the EC, which decided to make no formal resolution on the matter.'
Of the Minority Movement in question, Professor Bagwell comments (on p. 522) (of the RMM and the re-named Railwaymen's Vigilance movement—MJ) it 'tended to isolate militants from the rank and file.'
The Black Circular issued by the TUC in 1934 prevented Communists from openly holding office in many unions.
56. Tribune, 3.6.49.
57. Tribune, 17.6.49.
58. Tribune, 23.9.49.
59. Tribune, 1.7.49.
60. Tribune, 16.9.49.
61. Tribune, 2.12.49.
62. Tribune, 1.12.50.
63. Tribune, 13.2.48.
64. Jack Stanley was a moving spirit of *Socialist Outlook*. Ron Chamberlain was for a time very closely associated with it.
65. Tribune, 10.6.49.
66. Tribune, 20.10.50.
67. Tribune, 19.3.48.
68. Tribune, 15.7.49.
69. Tribune, 5.5.50.
70. The story appeared in the Sunday Dispatch and was based on 'an unfounded Press Association Report'. Strachey had been a CP member in the thirties.
71. Lord Vansittart's House of Lords speech on communists in the Civil Service occurred simultaneously. See Tribune, 7.4.50.
72. Tribune, 5.5.50.
73. Tribune, 3.11.50.
74. Tribune, 11.8.50.

75. See the introduction to *Keeping Left* published by the New Statesman, London, January 1951.
76. See appendix 3 of the author's doctoral thesis. Michael Foot was not associated with it because he felt there might be conflicting obligations with his NEC work at the time. Mikardo's name does not feature. It is known that he had resigned the Tribune editorial board over disagreements in regard to the western alliance, but this does not necessarily explain his absence from the list of authors.
77. Tribune, 21.7.50.
78. Tribune, 3.11.50.
79. Daily Telegraph, 21.11.50.
80. Tribune, 1.12.50.
81. Tribune, 15.9.50.
82. Tribune, 22.9.50. Also *Trade Union Leadership* (p. 282–4) by V. A. Allen, Longman, Green & Co., London 1957. The TGWU journal had carried an article by Deakin 'Trades Unionism versus Communism—the Gloves are Off' only weeks before the July 11th biennial conference in 1949.
83. At a press conference 18.9.50, quoted in Tribune, 22.9.50.
84. World News, 7.10.50, (p. 474).
85. Tribune, 22.9.50. 'Chuck It Deakin!' Tribune had already allowed a TGWU official space to put the Union's case. This was Tribune's reply.
86. Tribune, 12.1.51.
87. Duff, *op. cit.* (p. 29).
88. The Times, Editorial, 8.1.51.
89. The Times, 8.1.51.
90. The Times, 18.1.51.
91. Conditions of Employment & The Dock Labour Scheme.
92. Foot, *op. cit., Vol II* (p. 317).
93. The Times, 6.2.51 & 30.1.51 Sir Hartley Shawcross gave details of police enquiries into aspects of the dispute.
94. Socialist Outlook, May 1951.
95. The Times, 4.2.51, quoted also in Foot, *Vol II, op. cit.* (p. 320).
96. See Foot, *Vol II, op. cit* (p. 320).
97. Tribune, 23.2.51.

Chapter Four

The Socialist Fellowship, (1949-51)

Tribune's involvement with Transport House in the consolidation period, combined with the Communists' self-imposed sectarian quarantine, meant that the field of critical left-wing politics in the Labour movement was relatively open for two years or more. At this very time the British Trotskyists, studied practitioners of sectarianism, made a remarkable turn towards the Labour Party and began to work in the left current. In December 1948 a modest monthly, Socialist Outlook, was launched from the North London home of the Labour Publishing Society[1] by a group of left wingers which included Trotskyists, fellow travellers and some left Labour MPs and trade union leaders.

Socialist Outlook grew into an impressive little monthly that was able to transform itself into a fortnightly and then a weekly in the course of 1952. A measure of the importance of this historically neglected publication and the organisation associated with it—'Socialist Fellowship'—is to be gauged from a list of those who, with varying degrees of regularity, contributed articles to the paper, or were involved in meetings and joint activities.

Regular writers and columnists were Labour MPs Tom Braddock, Ron Chamberlain, Harold Davies, Ellis Smith and MP-to-be Frank Allaun. Occasional articles were submitted by MPs Stephen Swingler, Konni Zilliacus, H. L. Austin, Santo Jeger, S. O. Davies, Fenner Brockway, Frank Beswick, Bessie Braddock and John Parker. Nor were the trade unions absent. Constructional Engineering Union secretary Jack Stanley was, with Trotskyist leader Thomas Gerard Healy, a co-founder of the newspaper and wrote frequently for it. NUR secretary Jim Figgins was another leading contributor, as were Ernie Roberts and Bernard Dix. Bob Willis, Compositors' secretary, and TUC General Council member, wrote for the Outlook on occasions. So did NASD secretary Dickie Barrett and Frank Moxley, editor of the NUR's Railway Review.[2]

Closely associated with the Outlook was the organisation Socialist Fellowship, founded by MPs Ellis Smith and Fenner Brockway in the summer of 1949. This led a modestly successful existence until its proscription at the time of the Bevan resignation in 1951. The Outlook and the Fellowship differed in one important respect from Keep Left and Tribune. Whereas the latter were at this time almost exclusively parliamentary in orientation, the Outlook and the Fellowship represented the first serious post-war attempt to bring together MPs, trade union leaders and rank and file party members into organised association with each other for the purpose of conducting left wing campaigns and conferences within the Labour Party. Tribune up until 1950 was largely neglectful of this aspect of left wing activity. But once the Brains Trusts became popular and Bevan began to associate with Tribune after 1951, the Outlook quickly receded to the periphery of events and became superfluous to the left's requirements and the development of its struggle. An historical accounting of the experience of the Fellowship is long overdue and helps complete the picture of the prehistory of Bevanism.

Although they numbered less than one hundred people nationally, a short review of the immediate post-war activities of the British Trotskyists is called for. Whilst neither the Outlook nor the Fellowship were explicitly Trotskyist enterprises, Trotskyists played a leading, if not dominating role—certainly on the paper, though not entirely in the organisation. The two tendencies of British Trotskyism had fused in 1944 to form the Revolutionary Communist Party (RCP) which optimistically set itself up in competition to both the Labour Party and the British Communist Party. Within the RCP 'entrist' factions began to push for entry into the British Labour Party. The most important of these factions was led by Gerard Healy.

By December 1948 this entrist faction had begun work as Labour Party members and established the Socialist Outlook as a vehicle for conducting a dialogue with Labour's left wing. But the Trotskyists had no one of the intellectual and political stature to make the exercise worthwhile. The RCP's 'open' journal Socialist Appeal continued to publish until the summer of 1949 when that organisation broke up. At the time in question British Trotskyism did not present the picture of anarchic fragmentation with which we are familiar today, and the Healy entrists, after losing a small faction at the time of the Korean war, quickly established unchallenged leadership over the small forces of the main stream of British Trotskyism. They became known as 'the Club', and worked clandestinely as part of the Labour left.

The Socialist Fellowship 1949–51

At the Labour Party conference in Blackpool in June 1949 a fringe meeting attracted 160 or so delegates.[3] The meeting was addressed by MPs Ellis Smith and Tom Braddock, and the Editor of the Outlook, Trotskyist John Lawrence. Ellis Smith who was also President of the United Pattern-workers union announced the intention of forming a 'Socialist Fellowship'. It was a particularly fortuitous time for such a venture. Aneurin Bevan had aroused a certain resentment on the left by his remarks about industrial unrest being due to the fact that 'our people have achieved a material prosperity in excess of their moral stature'[4] at the Labour rally in Blackpool. Tribune was only five months into the arrangement with Transport House and Jack Stanley was able to jibe,

> 'One can appreciate your paper's attitude now you have, at least for the time being, been taken under the aegis of the National Labour Party, for occasionally economic circumstances force us to act against our better judgement. However there is always a day of repentance and your temporary absence from the critical field leaves the way open for the expansion of the Socialist Outlook.'[5]

The idea for the Socialist Fellowship appears to have come from Ellis Smith, who was not a Trotskyist. The Outlook congratulated him on his proposal in its June issue, and the Trotskyists had clearly decided they were going to work within it.

The first national founding conference of the SF was held in London on November 27th. One hundred delegates from 29 towns where branches had already been set up in the interim period, resolved to attain a membership of 30,000 within eighteen months and to raise a fund of £1,000. The statement to aims was short and to the point.

> 'The Socialist Fellowship is an association of Labour Party members pledged to work for an early attainment of Socialist society. It expects members to give practical proof of their devotion to socialism by sustained activity within their Labour, Trade Union or Co-operative organisations. It advocates socialisation, workers' control, ending the gross inequalities of income, a socialist Europe and freedom for the colonies.'[6]

The very general nature of these demands made it difficult for Transport House to raise any immediate objections, especially in the light of an impending election.

The economic demands that the first SF conference urged on the government never went as far as the programme outlined by Lawrence in the columns of his paper. The conference called for food and clothing subsidies to meet price increases due to devaluation, maintenance of the building programme and social services, the linking of pensions and benefits to a cost of living scale and, finally, the dropping of the wage freeze. All of this could be achieved through 'better technique and organisation of industry, defence cuts, increased taxation of the top bracket, death duties and capital gains tax. Fenner Brockway, former ILP leader, supporting the main resolution said,

> 'We are starting out on an adventure of great hope. The ILP made the great mistake of leaving the Labour Party in 1932. If we are to succeed where the ILP failed we must remember we are first and foremost members of the Labour Party, desirous of serving it. Membership of the SF must mean not less work for the Labour Party, but more'.[7]

Ellis Smith was elected President of the Fellowship and Brockway was on the committee along with Lawrence and six others. Vice-Presidents were MPs Tom Braddock and Ron Chamberlain, and the Secretary was Fred Emett. All of these officials were from the greater London area, to ensure a real working executive, but there was also a national council with regional delegates. Smith appealed for delegates to sell 'Labour's Northern Voice', 'Forward' and 'Socialist Outlook' so that, at this stage at least, the Outlook was not the official organ either of the SF or the 'Club' within it. However the links between the paper and the SF were extremely close. Its leaders wrote extensively for it and Smith congratulated the Outlook on its 'excellent service'.[8] This looseness of association proved to be a positive benefit when, some eighteen months later, Transport House wielded its proscription axe.

The January issue of the Outlook called upon all members to spare no effort in the election campaign and a big rally was called with six MPs, a trade union leader and the editor billed as speakers. But the March issue and a planned February SF conference were dropped to ensure 100 per cent electoral activity. In the close run election victory Tom Braddock lost his Mitcham seat and Chamberlain was ousted in Norwood. Ellis Smith wrote the lead article in which he insisted that Labour should not retreat from its programme, nor compromise with the opposition. He called for a government investigation into raw material and production costs, interlocking directorships and accounting techniques. Salford Labour Party, where the Fellowship was strong (Allaun was the Chairman of the Manchester SF) demanded a national conference of the Labour Party at the earliest possible date. Lawrence concluded that the election result had underlined the need for the SF.[9]

The successes of the movement in this period were a foretaste of what was to come in 1951 when many of the MPs associated with the Fellowship were to rally round Bevan. Indeed Harold Davies and Stephen Swingler were Keep Lefters too, and thus were involved in all three movements. SF called a conference 'Labour and the Future' with Santo Jeger, Brockway and Lawrence as main speakers.[10] Bessie Braddock, no relation to the former Mitcham MP, also spoke on SF platforms and wrote articles for the Outlook while she remained on the left of the party.

By May 1950 the Merseyside Fellowship was reported to have 120 members from eighteen constituencies. In Manchester's Fellowship, where Frank Allaun was Chairman, was one of Aneurin Bevan's closest personal friends, his parliamentary private secretary Will Griffiths MP. Stanley May, regional secretary of the NFBTO (Building workers) was another prominent member. Preston, Birmingham, S.E. London and South Norfolk established Fellowships which attracted not only rank and file militants but Councillors, Trades Council and local LP officials.[11]

It became practice to hold monthly meetings of the Fellowships. All areas called post election conferences and discussed a strategy to keep out the Conservatives at the next election, which could not be long delayed. The prospect of a Tory victory activated all layers of the movement. The first London regional conference of the SF was attended by just under 300 delegates from 85 Labour Party and trades union branches. It was addressed by Santo Jeger and London dockers' leader Harry Constable who played such an important part in the abolition of wartime regulation 1305. Anticipating some of the problems which were to confront the Bevanites, Constable, who with two other strike leaders had been expelled from the TGWU, called for a struggle inside that union for its democratisation and the election of all officials. The conference condemned the use of troops by the Labour government in industrial disputes.[12] Regional conferences were also held in Manchester and Birmingham at this time.

A measure of the SF's breadth of approach is provided by some of the issues on which it campaigned. That summer the SF national committee published a resolution opposing the dismantling of the giant Reichswerke-Salzgitter steel mill-blast furnace complex employing some 50,000 German workers in the British zone, under the terms of the Potsdam agreement.[13] This issue was raised at Labour and trade union meetings wherever SF members were present. It was a brave campaign which ran counter to the prevailing anti-German sentiments unscrupulously exploited by some in anti-German rearmament campaigns. Links were established with German socialists and trades unionists, some of whom wrote for the Outlook on the dismantling question. When the German rearmament debate developed later these same correspondents reported the strikes and demonstrations that swept West Germany. But about

East Germany and the forcible fusion of the Labour Party's sister party, the SDP, nothing appeared in the Outlook or the Fellowship's conferences. It was their blind spot. Fellowships mushroomed in the early summer of 1950 in new areas —amongst them Slough, Windsor, Staines, Chertsey, Thames Valley, North West and Central Nottingham and East London. The ambitious 30,000 membership target seemed in sight. Outlook announced plans for weekly publication.[14]

Split in the Fellowship

In June the Korean war broke out. This war produced a major split in the SF, and in the Club within it. A tiny group later known as the 'International Socialists' emerged as a result. But more important for the Left was that the Korean War had set in motion the train of events which produced the Bevanite movement.

The July issue of the Outlook had already been published when the first shots were fired and a special supplement[15] was rushed off a duplicator. A statement by the Editorial Board declared opposition to the war and demanded the withdrawal of all British armed forces from the Far East, from China, Malaya, Korea and the rest of the colonial world, and for a free and united Korea. The statement denounced UNO as an instrument of American policy and demanded working class action to prevent Korea developing into 'the third world war', and declared that the issue of which side crossed the frontier first was irrelevant.

> 'The very existence of an artificial "frontier" which was imposed on the Korean people by the Allied powers in 1946 is in itself an act of imperialist aggression.'[16]

Now of course one of these allied powers was the Soviet Union itself, yet this point was never made explicitly, since that might imply that the Soviet Union was partly responsible, or even 'imperialist'.

Nor was any mention made of the Soviet Union's boycott of the UNO security council, which facilitated the war decision.[17] The Outlook's editor, far from relating Moscow's past opposition to the revolution in China, and its agreement to partition Korea after the war even gave the impression that Russia's role was somehow beneficial in South East Asia. So much so he felt forced to emphasise,

> 'We are far from suggesting that the Russian Government, *at all times* and *under all conditions*, supports progressive movements.'[18]

A powerful lead article by Nenni-telegram signatory, Merthyr MP, S. O. Davies denounced Synghman Rhee and recounted his recent shattering election defeat and execution of opposition MPs.[19] Lawrence paid tribute to S. O. Davies and Emrys Hughes, the only two Labour MPs who voted against the government's intervention in Korea. These two stood out against the prevailing feeling in the PLP. The Outlook's editor denounced Tribune's support for the war as 'blackleg'.

> 'As for Tribune—erstwhile journal of "left" socialism—it has now become so blatantly imperialist that it sternly rebukes even those few MPs who, *having supported the government's actions in Korea*, now plead pathetically for a "localisation" of the conflict.'[20]

This was a veiled reference to SF leaders Ellis Smith and Fenner Brockway who backed the Silverman resolution, but between Tribune and the SF, Lawrence detected a further tendency, which, while conceding that the USA's role was reactionary and demanded the withdrawal of British troops, considered that Russia too was imperialist and equally bent on world domination. As a result, this tendency refused to support either side in the war. By November these people, led by Tony Cliff, separated themselves off from the Fellowship and the Club, and the first issue of 'Socialist Review' a duplicated news sheet appeared, declaring, 'neither Washington nor Moscow but international socialism'. Stan Newens and Raymond Challinor were among those writing for this paper when it became a printed edition in 1952. Whilst the national council of the SF convened on 25th June, before the outbreak of the war, it nevertheless had passed resolutions opposing conscription and calling for 'no participation in the war plans of imperialism.' It declared that it would not lend its support to the campaigns of the British Peace Committee because this committee divorced the struggle against war from the struggle for socialism.[21]

On July 5th the SF national committee met and accepted the resignation of its President Ellis Smith, and Fenner Brockway after confirming its opposition to the war.[22] But the MPs own reasons for resigning were not published[23] only their opposition to the SF resolution itself. The secretary declared that the main SF branches had supported the anti-war motion. The September Outlook carried the news that the 'Socialist Fellowship Lives and Grows', and that the 'great majority' of the 39 SFs supported the national committee. Of those that did not, none supported the Smith-Brockway endorsement of the war, but rather the view of the 'Socialist Review' tendency.[24]

Problems of Programme

The second national conference of the SF met but no figures were given for attendance in the November issue of the paper. A new committee was elected and only Lawrence remained of the original committee. Tom Braddock became President. The international situation had created very serious problems and the Korean war had provoked a deep crisis in the SF's ranks, in marked contrast to the successes of its first year's activity. A new sharper note was struck at this conference, reflecting frustration and impatience. In place of the modest demands of the first conference, the second conference maintained that only a 'vigorous socialist policy can save the country from economic collapse, subservience to international capitalism and destruction in a third world war'. It called for *all* large scale industry to be taken over by the state and transferred to the control of the workers, so that 'it can be run in accordance with a national plan'. In the meantime, 'pending the adoption of such a programme', the SF called for higher wages to defend living standards.[25] The departure of Brockway, Smith and a number of other MPs appears to have produced an over-reaction in the SF. Whilst courageously standing out against the war, the SF paid little attention to how the campaign against it might be carried into the daily struggles even of those workers who at this stage backed UNO. Agitation around a programme of minimum demands gave way to demands for the maximum programme: as the Outlook put it 'Second Conference adopts *full socialist policy.*[26] This programme was published as a pamphlet which Tom Braddock both wrote and then reviewed in the following vein,

> 'There is no half way house here at all. The mixed economy is nuts. And the Fellowship utterly condemns the idea that we can continue it. *From Labour to Socialism* contains a programme that would make us 100 per cent socialist democracy—and it would have it done NOW.'[27]

The relationship between the minimum programme of the day-to-day struggle (wages, reforms) and the maximum programme (socialist society, planned economy) has always presented Marxists with problems. To spurn the former leads to self-isolation. To postpone the latter leads to 'liquidation' into the reformist mass. Now whilst Braddock was not a member of the Club, he was working very closely with the Club inside the Fellowship. The Club appears to have gone along with this new turn of Braddock's quite uncritically. No attempt was made to find a bridge between minimum demands originating in the broad movement to the maximum programme and the establishment of socialism. *From Labour to Socialism*[28] appeared almost co-incidentally with the Communist Party's new programme 'The British Road to Socialism'.[29] In Braddock's programme the task of assessing the world situation and the difficulties created by Marshall and the Cominform was abandoned in favour of a return to fundamentalist affirmations of the rightness of socialism. Braddock denied that it was an extremist document, denied that it was possible to move towards socialism 'step by step'. He saw socialism simply as an instantaneous possibility dependent only on determination and activity by leadership.

The campaign against the Korean war now became the Outlook's pre-occupation. Yet the adoption of the 'full socialist programme' could only stand in the way of formulating demands on the basic issues facing working people which were objectively and indissolubly linked with the war itself—conscription, serious inflation, health service cuts. These were at the heart of the Bevanite revolt when it began only a few months later.

The budget that cut the health service was a direct consequence of the arms programme necessitated by the war and demanded by the USA. The ranks' criticism of Labour centred not on their failure to achieve 'full socialism' but, more simply, on Labour's retreat from its own programme of reform and even the partial dismantling of some of its achievements. It was Bevan's stand on these questions that won him the leadership of the left, not his advocacy of a maximum programme. Even Bevan's more modest disagreements brought him close to expulsion. How much more easy, then, had the SF made its own proscription by relapsing into demands for the maximum programme. Ironically, less was required to mobilise a mass movement, and far more thought required to assist its direction.

Despite the media's war fever, anti-war feeling did begin to grow on a moderate scale among Labour and trade union supporters. Even leading Fabian G. D. H. Cole spoke out against the war and possible conflict with China.[30] The SF went ahead and called a successful rally. The January and February editions of the Outlook had not given news of the SF's activities, but in March a new, larger, more attractively produced newspaper, with photographs, reported the February 25th anti-war rally. Four hundred delegates and visitors attended, including delegations from seventeen Constituency and Borough Labour Parties and 29 trade union branches. The conference's main speaker was S. O. Davies MP, and the main resolution, opposed by six delegates called for an end to all war alliances 'with capitalist countries', the withdrawal of British forces from Korea and an emergency conference of the Labour Party.[31]

This latter demand was in line with a growing body of opinion in the movement. The Engineers' union had itself demanded such a conference of the NEC.[32] Taken together with the TUC's request that the government re-examine wartime order 1305[33] relating to compulsory arbitration and strikes, this decision of the Engineers indicated the beginnings of a powerful current from below which was gathering strength and was soon to prise Bevan from his Cabinet post. There was a successful ban on piecework by Manchester engineers against the recently concluded wages agreement, big demonstrations and half-day token strikes by building workers in London and Manchester for a sixpence an hour rise, and, overshadowing all this, the dockers' mass mobilisation throughout their High Court battle. The SF and the Outlook were undoubtedly benefiting marginally from this groundswell. Dockers' leader and court defendant, Harry Constable and a number of prominent engineering stewards were in evidence at SF functions by this time, and writing for the Outlook.[34]

The anti-war rally was reconvened on March 18th, and whilst little advance was recorded in terms of delegation, additional anti-war conferences were held in Manchester and Birmingham.[35] An emergency conference campaign committee was established[36] and played some part in promoting resolutions in unions and constituency parties which began to flood into Transport House.[37] This growing demand for an emergency conference was opposed by 'Victory for Socialism'[38] and by the Communist Party in the ETU conference[39] that May. East Salford Labour Party, one of the biggest in the country at that time, with over 4,000 individual members was suspended by Transport House later in the year for its attempt to mediate in the docks dispute in Manchester. The Fellowship was strong in the party and its delegate to party conference the previous year had been mandated to oppose the NEC on the Korean war.[40]

One aspect of the SF's anti-war campaign was the moving case of Corporal Bill Tyler. He was one of the young leaders of the fellowship who had been called up to serve in Korea. Initially he had considered refusing to fight but he decided to go into the army to conduct anti-war propaganda. He sent regular letters home about his discussions with soldiers at the front. Some of these were published in Outlook. They were collected and published as a small pamphlet and circulated around the anti-war layers in the Labour Party after his death. The pamphlet received a warm tribute from Frank Allaun and from MPs.[41]

By now the Outlook's publishers—the Labour Publishing Society—had a small print works. Circulation was claimed to be between 9–10,000 which, if reliable, was a remarkable achievement in just over two years.[42]

Transport House now decided to act. The sudden upturn in

the class struggle, the modest successes of the Fellowship's anti-war rallies, despite the departure of Smith and Brockway, all of this was brought to a head by the April of 1951. The same NEC meeting that gave broad approval to Gaitskell's arms budget also approved an edict placing Socialist Fellowship on the list of proscribed organisations.[43] This was testimony to the effectiveness of the SF over the previous two years. Notwithstanding that they had been a collection of people with widely differing aims and views from the start, it must be conceded that, whether by design or fortune, they had anticipated by many months the resurgence of a powerful current in the Labour Party. They had worked for it from the grass roots right up to the level of the PLP.

Proscription

The fact that the SF had survived its split to present a threat to the NEC is proof of its political weight and the specific weight of the Club within it. It may be they regretted the reversion to the ultimatism of 'full socialism now' and the publication of a separate Fellowship programme in Braddock's pamphlet *From Labour to Socialism.* This had been an ill-considered move, arising out of temporary isolation and reaction to the defection of Smith and Brockway. Certainly it provided Transport House with the justification for proscription before the party membership. It was several weeks before the NEC's decision was conveyed to the Constituency parties in a circular which contained the following sanction,

> 'The NEC has had under review for some time the activities of the Socialist Fellowship and has come to the conclusion that they are advocating a *programme* and policy which fundamentally varies from that laid down by the annual conference of the Labour Party and therefore decides that membership of that organisation is incompatible with membership of the Labour Party'.[44] (*my emphasis—M.J.*)

The NEC's sudden reverence for annual conference decisions as the determinants of party policy must have struck a hollow note with the Fellowship but they did not defy the ruling. They immediately went into liquidation and this decision was warmly welcomed by the editor of the Outlook, who now began to take his distance from the SF, no doubt for tactical reasons. Lawrence, who remember was on the SF's national committee, commented 'They(!) have very wisely decided not to be driven out of the ranks of the Labour Party but to stay inside and fight it out,' because even though the Fellowship was finished the ideas for which it fought 'will, we are sure, become the official policy of the movement in a shorter time than the witch hunters imagine'.[45] The paper scornfully rebuked VFS for its volunteer letter to the NEC proclaiming its lack of connection with the SF.[46] In their final act, a letter to the NEC after the proscription announcement, SF's leaders bowed to the decision in the following manner,

> 'As loyal members of the Labour Party who have never had any interests separate and apart from the Labour Party we are obliged to accept the decision of the NEC.'[47]

The NEC may have recognised this as a paraphrase from the Communist manifesto of Marx and Engels, which contains a passage stating that communists have 'no interests separate and apart from' the interests of the working class, and that they will struggle for the unity of the class. The same passage says 'The communists do not form separate parties opposed to those of the working class.'[48]

Although it accepted the decision, the Outlook now began to organise readers' meetings all over the country wherever it had support.[49] There began a campaign to win readers in the unions and local parties.

The mystery is why the NEC did not proscribe the paper as well as the SF? The Outlook and the SF jointly sponsored meetings, rallies and conferences. The personnel of each were virtually identical. It is possible the NEC felt that proscription might drive the prominent MPs (some of whom were 'Nenni rebels') associated with the paper into the arms of Tribune, which would then have presented a single pole of attraction for the left. Or perhaps at this stage the party leadership simply wanted to remove the SF organisational framework which might have set a dangerous precedent in a period of growing revolt in the party as a whole. Certainly the fact that the Fellowship was proscribed at the same meeting where the Gaitskell budget was broadly approved cannot be regarded as accidental.[50] Within days of the Fellowship ban Bevan, Freeman and Wilson had resigned the Cabinet.

The SF had achieved a great deal in a very short space of time. Its great strength was its breadth of appeal. It was not a barren 'rank and file' type of organisation but embraced all layers of the party. It generated discussion and campaigned on the major issues confronting the movement. It was linked to a newspaper which carried news of its successes, opened its columns to widely differing currents of opinion and rallied its forces for campaigns. The weakness of the SF was its lack of a theoretical journal to pursue the movement's problems back to fundamentals. At the crucial moment of the Korean war apparent agreement on immediate programmatic points fell away to expose fundamental differences in which the Trotskyist leaders of the Fellowship found themselves barely distinguishable from Stalinists and fellow travellers.

The Outlook and the Trotskyists

The Outlook now temporarily put aside the maximum programme, made a tentative bloc with the Bevanites and campaigned on the demand 'No election before an emergency conference of the Labour Party'.[51] In the light of subsequent developments this slogan conformed closely to the requirements of the left, if not the party as a whole. Attlee's decision to call an election which was announced on September 18th caused the conference to be shortened. Normal business was dropped in favour of exclusive concern with election preparations, finance and the manifesto. The necessary discussion on the budget, the health service and the arms programme was therefore shelved for electoral considerations and criticism muted. The Fellowship's proscription was easily endorsed and the Trotskyists' role in it revealed to conference.[52]

In terms of the consequences for the Labour Party, Attlee's decision to call an election was second only in importance to MacDonald's step in entering the coalition National government, but MacDonald at least had the excuse that he was leading a minority government in conditions of world slump. MacDonald's decision split the Labour Party and put it out of power for fourteen years whilst Attlee's resulted in Labour being out for thirteen, under conditions of left-right war within the party. But whereas MacDonald's actions occurred in a situation of defeat and falling standards for the working class, Attlee's move took place in conditions of steady advance in organisation and living standards. It may well be that Attlee felt certain of a mandate.[53] Labour did, after all, achieve its highest vote ever. But there was sufficient doubt about this to lend weight to the Outlook's demand that the Tories should not even be given the chance for a few years, and that the left needed time to fight out policy questions within the party.

Like the Korean war, the election defeat temporarily disoriented the Outlook. They had recovered from the early setback resulting from their stand against the war when they were derailed for a second time. The calling of the election and its result were a serious setback for the working class movement. But the Outlook had failed to grasp the profound changes of the post-war period. Whilst the paper maintained that the strength of the class and its desire for a Labour government was undiminished, it continued to allege that the Tories had learned nothing from their six years in opposition, and that they would revert to the policies of the thirties.[54] Quite apart from the fact that such a strategy might only be visited on a dispirited and demoralised populace, which in no way conformed to the current state of morale, the SF leaders gloomy prognosis revealed a failure to grasp the extent of the influence of the 'right progressives'[55] in the Conservative party, which in turn was a result of the profound influence of social democracy on the party of Churchill. If Baldwin had domesticated the Labour Party, Attlee had socialised the Conservatives.

For a time the vagaries of the trade cycle may, to the superficial observer of the SF, have lent credence to fears of a major world recession in the very early fifties. But as time went on this schema was increasingly unrealistic. Whereas 1951 saw a serious payments crisis, the following three years brought surpluses. The wages movement after 1951 ensured that earnings more than kept pace with the cost of living. The advantages of commonwealth preference were still in evidence. Europe and Japan were still far from recovered to present the serious challenge to British trade that they were to become fifteen years later.

British Trotskyists found it very hard to come to terms with reality. They lived on shallow slogans, failed to make any serious analysis of the trends in the world economy and world politics that their teacher would no doubt have insisted on. Such economic understanding as the Trotskyists possessed was borrowed from the Communist Party. It can be summed up as the 'slump-war perspective'. It was as if these twin-catastrophies were the agencies that would solve the intractable problems presented by the two camps. The analysis of the world economy, and all the other vital tasks that those who aspire to revolution need address themselves, could therefore be dispensed with.[56]

The Trotskyists and those like Jack Stanley who worked with them, might have asked themselves whether the SO itself should not have gone into liquidation. There was a good case for winding the paper up in 1951, and it became even more convincing in 1952. The left clientele within the party for which the Outlook catered was the same market that Tribune was trying to reach. After Bevan's resignation Tribune turned towards the left in Labour's ranks. The Outlook and Tribune found themselves in competition. In 1952 both papers achieved weekly publication in what almost appeared to be a race. The main forces of Labour's left were undoubtedly gathered around Tribune. What use, therefore, did the Outlook serve? Those MPs and ex-MPs who remained associated with it tended to be former Nenni-telegraphists or trade union leaders like Figgins and Stanley who either displayed an uncritical attitude to the USSR, or reserved their choicest barbs for the Bevanites themselves. Whilst the Bevanites were in need of constructive criticism and advice, this might best have been achieved from within the Bevanite current. It was, in fact, only when the Socialist Outlook was proscribed in 1954 that the Trotskyists began to work in this way, writing for and selling Tribune as constructive critics of the Bevanite current. This might have been done three years earlier if assistance of the left had been uppermost in the minds of the Socialist Outlook's editors. Nonetheless the 1949–51 episode demonstrates that the Socialist Fellowship grouping had earned a place for itself as a tendency within the Bevanite current had they wished to participate in the process of clarification. They had made a number of mistakes, but then who had not? It would certainly not be fair to compare the Trotskyists of the fifties with the macabre and clownish behaviour of their successors in such groups as the WRP in the seventies.

NOTES

1. The Labour Publishing Society was registered under the Provident Societies Acts (1893–1928). It was a co-operative organisation. The Provisional Management Committee's officers were: Chairman, Jack Stanley, General Secretary of the Construction Engineers Union (who later attended the Moscow Economic Conference and sponsored the Vienna Peace Congress).
Vice-Chairman, Ernie Roberts (Regional Executive of the West Midlands Labour Party).
Secretary, Daphne Barnes, Holborn & St Pancras South Labour Party.
Treasurer, Councillor Jasper Ridley, Holborn & St Pancras Labour Party (who quickly resigned and joined the Communist Party).
2. Bernard Crick, Reg Groves, Dr Stark Murray, Hyman Levy and Jim Allen also contributed varying amounts of material at different times.
3. The meeting was in fact a 'Socialist Outlook meeting' advertised in the June 1949 edition. Ellis Smith, Tom Braddock and John Lawrence were billed as speakers.
4. See Socialist Outlook, July 1949. 'The moral stature of Aneurin Bevan' by John Lawrence.
5. Socialist Outlook, July 1949.
6. Socialist Outlook, January 1950.
7. Socialist Outlook, January 1950.
8. Socialist Outlook, January 1950.
9. Socialist Outlook, April 1950.
10. Socialist Outlook, April 1950. The Conference took place on April 30th at Holborn Hall.
11. Socialist Outlook, May 1950.
12. Socialist Outlook, June 1950. See also Butler & Sloman, *op. cit.* (p. 298). The Labour government twice invoked Emergency Powers—on both occasions against Dock strikes. The first occasion was on 29th June, 1948 against the strike opposing disciplinary clauses. The second was against a solidarity strike for Canadian seamen.

13. Socialist Outlook, June 1950.
14. Socialist Outlook, July 1950.
15. Published 4th July, 1950. But it was also inserted in the August issue.
16. Socialist Outlook—special July supplement on the Korean War (July 1950).
17. *The Major International Treaties* (pp. 449–450) by J. A. S. Grenville, Methuen & Co, London 1974.
'The day after the invasion, 26th June in Korea, 25th June in the United States, the Security Council met, passed its first resolution stating that the North Korean attack constituted a "breach of the peace", and called for an immediate end to hostilities and a withdrawal of North Korean forces to their own side of the border. In the absence of the Soviet representative (owing to Soviet protest at the seating of the Nationalist Chinese Representative), this resolution was adopted by a vote of 9–0 with Yugoslavia abstaining. The United States decision to provide the South Korean forces south of the 38th parallel with all-out air and naval support was taken by Truman on the evening of 26th June, and orders were issued at once. On the afternoon of 27th June the Security Council adopted a second and stronger resolution calling upon members to give all possible help to the Republic of Korea to repel the invasion and to restore peace and security in the area.'
In *The Hidden History of the Korean War* (pp. 65–66) by Irving Stone, Turnstile Press, London 1952, the author deals with US officials anticipating possible Soviet attendance at the Security Council.
'Mr Hickerson: We did not know whether Malik would turn up and veto this resolution.
Senator Ferguson: What were you going to do if he did turn up? You knew he would veto it.
Mr Hickerson: He did not turn up though.
Senator Ferguson: I say, if he had.
Mr Hickerson: We were going to ask the Secretary General to call a special session of the General Assembly. We had one small group of people working on the plans for that and drafting a sort of statement that we would make if he did that'.
18. Socialist Outlook, August 1950.
19. Socialist Outlook, August 1950.
20. Socialist Outlook, August 1950. This was a reference to Sidney Silverman's resolution supported by Ellis Smith and Fenner Brockway, among others.
21. Socialist Outlook, August 1950.
22. See Socialist Outlook, September, 1950 which carried this announcement. For more details of the disputes within 'the Club'

in 1950 see *The Origins of the International Socialists* edited by Richard Cooper, Pluto Press, London 1974. To the author's knowledge this contains the only known reference in print to the Socialist Fellowship (although it is not mentioned by name). On p. 96 we have . . .
'The Korean war also exposed the "allies" of the club leaders. For a long time the SO did not find it necessary to utter a word of criticism and warning about the reformist stand of Ellis Smith, Mrs Braddock and Brockway. Now the three of them have come out openly in support of UNO (Read American and British Imperialism). The other "stars" of the club leaders—Tom Braddock and more recently S. O. Davies—are not less ready to jump on the opposite bandwagon: Braddock is chairing a British Soviet Society meeting and S. O. Davies is speaking under the auspices of this Stalinist propaganda organisation.'
'The Korean war and the visit of Morgan Phillips and Co. to Belgrade must convince even the blind that the declarations of the Club leaders about Tito moving in a Trotskyist direction are pure illusion'.
This book also contains interesting material on the debate about the nature of the Eastern European states after consolidation.

23. 'The Voice of Labour' decided to merge with the SO and its Editor, T. Mercer, announced this in September.
24. In a private interview with the author, Lord Brockway suggested Trotskyist domination of SF was the main reason for his resignation. But in *Towards Tomorrow,* his autobiography he admits he has 'always regretted' not having followed the example of S. O. Davies over Korea.
25. Socialist Outlook, November 1950.
26. Socialist Outlook, November 1950.
27. Socialist Outlook, February 1951. This was not the first time an 'alternative programme' had been mooted. John Lawrence in August 1949, right at the beginning of the SF's existence had outlined an extensive programme of his own, couched in suitably either/or terms, for discussion by the movement. Needless to say the adoption of the new programme is anticipated before any discussion or vote, quite apart from the fact that it did not represent the aspirations of the mass movement.
28. *From Labour to Socialism* by Tom Braddock, John Stafford Thomas, London Dec. 1950. The pamphlet was issued by the Socialist Fellowship for the consideration of the Labour movement.
29. Adopted January 1951. See H. Pelling *The British CP—A Historical Profile*, A. & C. Black, re-issue of 1975 (p. 161). Whilst this programme spoke of conquest of power through parliamentary means, it was published in the context of a 'radical' interpretation of this parliamentary road in a period of extreme sectarian denunciations of Tito, Bevan, the Labour left and social

democracy. See Appendix 7 to author's doctoral thesis: 'Two versions of the "British Road".'

30. Socialist Outlook, March 1951.
31. Socialist Outlook, March 1951.
32. Daily Worker report, 1.3.51, said the NEC had rejected the AEU's demand.
33. Socialist Outlook, March, 1951.
34. For an example see Socialist Outlook, July 1951, 'The Real Causes of Unofficial Work Strikes' by Harry Constable.
35. Socialist Outlook, April 1951.
36. Socialist Outlook, May 1951.
37. For a list of resolutions see Socialist Outlook, June 1951. Over 100 from Trades Unions and Labour Party branches.
38. Socialist Outlook, June 1951. VFS letter to all LPs. It did not even protest against the SF ban.
39. Socialist Outlook, June 1951. ETU conference May 7–12.
40. Socialist Outlook, November 1951. Gives full report on events of April 1951 when the party tried to mediate in the docks dispute over compulsory overtime working. This strike was connected with the notorious order 1305.
41. Socialist Outlook, August 1951 announced the pamphlet 'Letters from Korea'.
42. This figure was claimed by Tom Braddock in Socialist Outlook, March 1951, in a letter to readers. At the same time however the editorial board continued to call for 5,000 *weekly* subscriptions for the planned Weekly Outlook. But even a figure of 5,000 would have been a considerable achievement in so short a time.
43. Socialist Outlook, May 1951.
44. Socialist Outlook, September 1951.
45. Socialist Outlook, May 1951.
46. Socialist Outlook, June 1951.
47. Socialist Outlook, September 1951.
48. *The Communist Manifesto*, Marx and Engels.
49. Socialist Outlook, November 1951.
50. Socialist Outlook, May 1951.
51. Socialist Outlook, August 1951.
52. Labour Party Conference Report, 1951.
53. Foot, *op. cit. Vol II* (p. 349) quotes Attlee's concern for King George VI's health as the main consideration.
54. In fact there had been considerable re-thinking in the Conservative party. Nor did this begin with the years of opposition. Harold Macmillan was an early convert to Keynesianism in the thirties, and this was the leadership that was grooming itself in the shadow of Churchill-Eden. See *The Conservative Nation* by Andrew Gamble (pps. 28–60), Routledge & Kegan Paul, London 1974. On p. 29 Gamble says,

    'It is a mistake, however, to imagine that the Conservative Party at this time was preparing to restore the glad days of the Depression. The Conservatives' acceptance of what became the post-war settlement had already made great strides by 1945. Nowhere was this clearer than in the work of the Coalition Government, which had set up numerous committees to plan social and economic policy after the war . . .'

'Churchill had wanted the Coalition to continue after the war was over, and carry through the whole of its projected social programme. This the Labour Party would not agree to, and so forced an election in July 1945. With the exception of nationalisation, the parties fought the election on virtually the same policies.'

Of course left wing groups like the SF could not be expected to be familiar (or even interested) in internal policy disputes of the Conservatives at the time. And their belief that the Tories had not changed was probably, in any case, shared by many in the working class movement who had lived through the Baldwin-Chamberlain era.

55. Gamble, *op. cit.* (p. 33).
56. Socialist Outlook, November 1951. See James Figgins, NUR secretary, 'The Consequences of the Election' (reprinted from the Railway Review).

'This is 1931 all over again . . .' he begins, in an article prophesying further increases in the arms programme. In fact as we now know, Churchill *reduced* the estimates for the arms programme contained in Gaitskell's 1951 budget, and acknowledged Bevan's correct assessment of the impossibility of its achievement. (See Foot *Vol. II, op. cit.*, p. 355). Churchill said 'We shall not however, succeed in spending the £1,250 million this year (The part of the £4,700 million allocated for the first year) and some of the late government's programme must necessarily roll forward into a future year. The point was, I believe, made by the Right Hon. gentleman for Ebbw Vale after his resignation . . .'

However, the SF never followed Bevan's arguments as closely as they might have done.

Chapter Five

The Dimensions of Bevanism

In his standard work *Parliamentary Socialism,* Ralph Miliband entitles the chapter dealing with the Labour government 1945–51 'The Climax of Labourism'.[1] Since he is recounting the history of the dominant socialist ideology in Britain, and since that is undoubtedly 'Labourism' or parliamentary Social Democracy, it is impossible to take issue with him that the Attlee government represented its climax.

But the mass movement is not identical with the party and governmental superstructure, with what we might call the apparatus. The apparatus is sustained and nourished by the mass movement, and is able, with varying degrees of success, and within tight limits, to modulate the tempo and intensity of the struggles of this movement. To the extent that it can do this the apparatus becomes an *essential part* of the state machine. Mediation in these struggles, reconciliation of the aspirations of the movement, and their accommodation within the social order over which the state presides—herein lies the value of the apparatus to the state. But the struggles of the movement have a motion and tempo of their own which can, on occasions, bring it into conflict with the apparatus. When this occurs *the conflict is not pure.* It does not consist in the lining up of the mass movement on the one side and the apparatus on the other. The first effect is the creation of tensions and fissures *within the movement, but, more especially, within the apparatus itself.* If this did not occur it would mean that the apparatus was purely and simply an alien agency within the movement, and if it were only that it could be clearly comprehended as such and could not, therefore, perform its role of mediation of the movement's struggles. This in turn would render it of little value to the state machine.

The secret strength of the apparatus lies in the mystery that shrouds that boundary where the *necessary self-organisation* of the mass movement for the *propagation* of its struggles becomes transformed into the organisation of *the state* for the *accommodation* of these struggles (to the extent that they are capable of being resolved within the existing social order).

The career of Aneurin Bevan is a graphic illustration of how a working class militant moved through this self-organisation network only to find himself in the heart of the state machine. Yet the conflicts generated within the apparatus were of such intensity that they thrust him back into the arms of the movement. For the rest of his remarkable career Bevan oscillated between the two. At Morecambe he was the representative of the mass movement within the apparatus. At Brighton, finally, the representative of the apparatus within the mass movement. However the struggle between Bevanites and the party establishment went on at branch, regional, national conference, PLP and Cabinet levels. It was pursued within the trades unions at all levels also. This indicates not only that those who gave expression to the struggles and aspirations of the mass movement were present within the Cabinet, which is unquestionably part of the state machine, but that the lower echelons of the apparatus had its following in the mass itself to no small degree.

The Labour movement does not consist of a pure, undefiled mass presided over by a self-evidently alien party bureaucracy. Therefore we shall not attempt here to portray the Bevanites either as an expression of the movement's purity or merely as a dissident faction of the party bureaucracy. The mysterious boundary to which reference has been made is to be found *within every organ of the Labour movement from top to bottom.* It even runs through the careers of Labour politicians as that of Aneurin Bevan himself. But at the top, at the level of the Cabinet the tensions are greatest for here the welded joint is clearly visible.

Here the 'dignified' extra-parliamentary aspirations meet the 'efficient' parliamentary state machine.[2] To the extent that the Bevanites gave partial expression to demands of the mass movement that conflicted with the deepest requirements of the state and its machine, they met the full ferocity of the party apparatus that was closest to that machine. This is what underlay the initial dispute over rearmament and NHS charges. The climax of Labourism was followed by a period of intense inner party strife. This needs to be explained. The conflicts within the apparatus arose out of the intensity of the struggles and aspirations of the mass movement. There is a great deal of evidence to show that from the *point of view of this mass movement, as distinct from the party and governmental apparatus,* the climax of Labourism was not 1945 *but later between 1951–53*. This is not for a moment to underestimate the importance of the achievements of the Attlee government for the working class.

The validity of this thesis can be confirmed only by empirical data. It is not a matter of 'opinion', but of what the statistics reveal. Statistics are the indices of the movement's struggles, and even, to a degree, a pointer to the level of political consciousness and sophistication of the participants.

The period 1951–53 saw the peaking of the party's membership figures, of its women, youth and student sections and of its popularity with the non-party mass. 1951 was the sole occasion in the history of British Labour when a Labour government, visibly 'consolidating'[3] and soft-pedalling on the radical programme which had brought it electoral success *received an increased vote.* In 1931 and 1970, and from all appearances in the present period also, Labour governments who disappoint their followers lose votes. In 1951 they lost the election with an increased vote, having received *the highest vote for any British political party in history before or since.* Indeed we could go further—only as late as 1969 did a Social Democratic (or Communist) Party receive a higher vote at a genuinely free election, and that was in Western Germany where the SPD's 14,065,716 votes capped Labour's 1951 total of 13,948,605.[4] Labour's record 1951 vote was achieved despite austerity, consolidation,[5] rationing, the use of troops against strikes, imposition of charges on the health service, higher national service to prosecute colonial wars, involvement in Korea, the biggest jump in the retail price index for ten years[6] and a serious split at Cabinet level.

The voters weighed all this against the positive aspects of Labour's rule in terms of full employment, social welfare, disengagement in India, Greece and Palestine, and the prospects for a return to the aspirations of *Let us Face the Future.*[7] The party activists and its loyalist supporters hoped to keep the *government* in power whilst pursuing the internal struggle for the party programme simultaneously. Never before had such a prospect been embraced.[8]

Labour's total vote rose in the 1945, 1950 and 1951 general elections. And even though its share of the poll fell from 47.8 per cent in 1950, *it rose again to 48.8 per cent in the year of electoral defeat.* Scottish and Welsh Labour representation held up well.[9] However Labour's electoral thrust forward did not end in 1951. The Labour share of the poll in borough council elections rose to a 55.4 per cent peak for the decade 1947–57 in 1951.[10]

Nor were these high percentage polls achieved on small turnouts by the electorate. In the 1951 general election turnout was only marginally down from the record 84 per cent of 1950, whilst the 1952 County Borough election turnout represented a five per cent increase on 1951.[11]

Figure 4
Labour's Share of the Poll in General and County Borough Elections, 1945–55.

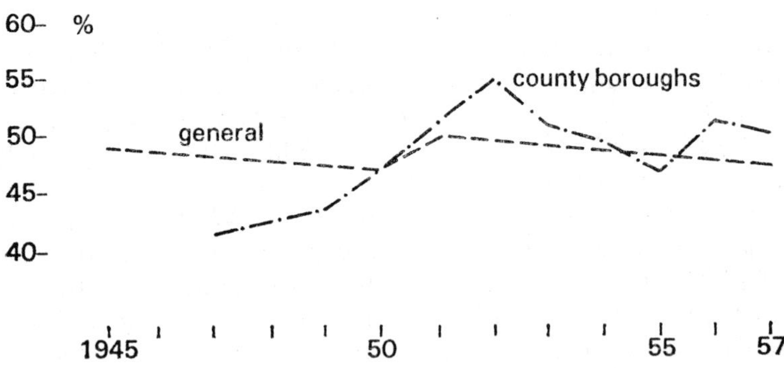

What kind of a class was it—this working class whose most organisationally and politically conscious layers swept in to swell the ranks of the Labour party and the trades unions in the early fifties? What was motivating it and driving it forward to place Labour in office?

The structure of population for the year 1951 reveals that the under-19 age group accounted for a smaller proportion of the total than today, in the seventies. On the other hand the 20–39 and the 40–59 age groups were each a larger percentage of the total than today. Taken together they accounted for over five per cent more at 55.4 per cent of the total. The over-sixties were three per cent less than today's figure, but at 15.7 per cent they were over 4 per cent up on the 1931 census figures.[12]

So in 1951 the very young and the very old accounted for less of the population than today when they represent over half. The figures take on importance when one considers the experience that had moulded the consciousness and political awareness of these working population deciles. A man aged forty in 1951 may have lost a relative in the first world war during his infanthood. In 1921 he would have been ten, and if his father *had* survived, he might well have been among those two million unemployed that made it a peak year for the twenties. By 1931 the young man would have been twenty and by 1932 unemployment was worse again at just under three million, a peak for the thirties. As a man of thirty he might have found himself in uniform in jungle, desert or tundra.

Such a man might well have been typical of the mass of soldiers who cast their vote for *Let Us Face the Future*. In contrast to his pre-war experience, the post-war years had seen a Labour government with an overall majority, full employment for the first time, a National Health Service and the introduction of a large measure of public ownership in the basic industries. For such a man rationing and austerity would not have detracted from Labour's achievements. So his response to the close electoral victory of 1950 would be to turn out again for Labour in 1951 to urge his workmates and neighbours to do the same, or maybe even to join the party. It was not the thirties alone that had framed his consciousness *but the experience of 1945–50 by contrast with the thirties.* It was concern at having all the gains of the Labour government possibly snatched back from him. Hence the vote of nearly fourteen million for Labour in the lost election of 1951. Fear of the Tories was as great an asset to the Labour leaders as their election programme.

But these are purely electoral expressions of the national mood which nourished the Bevanite current. Examination of the statistics of organised Labour itself reveals just how shallow is the view that Bevanism had 'no organised working class roots'. Membership of unions affiliated to the TUC, trade union affiliate membership of the party and individual party membership stood respectively 10 per cent, 27 per cent, and 50 per cent higher in 1957 than they did in 1947 despite intervening fluctuations. By far the biggest increase in all three categories occurred *in the period up to 1953–54* when Bevanism was in the ascendant.[13]

The validity of individual membership figures has recently come under scrutiny, and there can be little doubt that the methods of accounting inflate the true figures somewhat, but, for comparative purposes, we have no reason to consider one year's figures less reliable than another. Certainly of the three indices individual membership is the most reliable guide to the state of political consciousness in the working class. This is especially the case since 1946 when 'contracting in' to the Labour Party by trade unionists was replaced by a 'contracting out' clause, which means that trade union affiliate membership of the party is automatic unless a member signs a form releasing him from the political levy. By contrast the individual member makes a conscious decision to join the party and at the same time recognises that trade union organisation alone is insufficient to protect and advance the interests of himself or his class.

At no time in the thirties or since have such conscious decisions been made on anything like the scale of 1945–53. The biggest increase in the thirties was recorded in the year 1932—75,000. But in 1945 individual party membership rose by 222,284—just short of a quarter of a million! Thereafter the increases were as follows:

Figure 5
Labour Party and Trade Union Membership 1947–57.

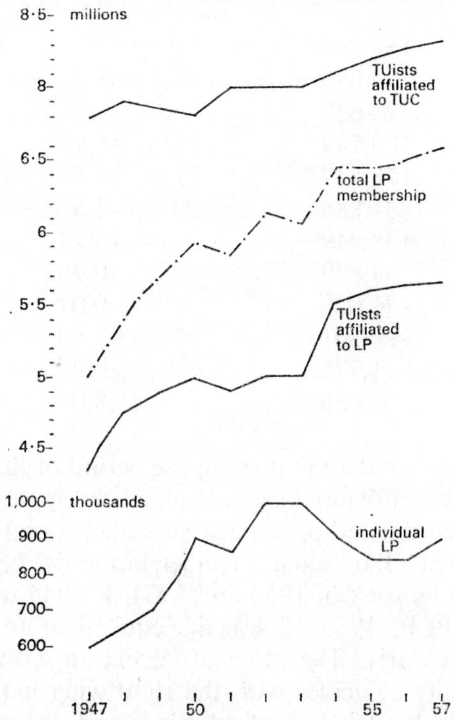

The following figures on which the graph is based are taken from Pelling *A Short History of the Labour Party* op. cit. (p. 172). Trade Union figures are taken from Pelling *A History of British Trade Unionism* (op. cit. (p. 283).

Year	Individual LP Membership	Trade Unions Affiliated to LP	Co-operative Society membership. Excluding the Co-op party	Socialist Society Membership	Total LP Membership	Total TU members affiliated to TUC
1943	235,501	2,237,307	25,200	5,232	2,305,240	6,642,317
1944	265,763	2,375,381	25,100	6,501	2,672,845	6,575,654
1945	487,047	2,510,369	33,600	7,681	3,038,697	6,671,120
1946	645,345	2,635,346	33,600	8,067	3,322,358	7,540,397
1947	608,487	4,386,074	36,960	8,778	5,040,299	7,791,470
1948	629,025	4,751,030	33,600	8,782	5,422,437	7,937,091
1949	729,624	4,946,207	33,600	7,516	5,716,947	7,883,355
1950	908,161	4,971,911	30,800	9,300	5,920,172	7,827,945
1951	876,275	4,937,427	28,000	7,300	5,849,002	8,020,079
1952	1,014,524	5,071,935	14,000	7,200	6,107,659	8,088,450
1953	1,004,685	5,056,912	28,000	7,425	6,096,022	8,093,837
1954	933,657	5,529,760	28,000	7,610	6,498,027	8,106,958
1955	843,356	5,605,988	28,000	7,650	6,483,994	8,263,741
1956	845,129	5,658,249	28,000	6,850	6,537,228	8,304,709
1957	912,989	5,644,012	20,000	5,550	6,582,549	8,337,325

Annual Increases in Individual Labour Party Membership[14]

Year	Increase	Increase as a percentage on previous year's total
1946	158,298	32.5
1947	–36,858	–5.7
1948	20,538	3.4
1949	100,559	15.97
1950	178,537	24.50
1951	–31,886	–3.5
1952	138,249	15.78
1953	–9,839	–0.96
1954	–71,028	–0.07
1955	–90,301	–9.60
1956	1,773	0.2
1957	67,858	8.0

Between 1947 and 1952 then, in the period of the emergence of Bevanism, individual party membership increased by 406,037! Even the end of the war surge between 1942–47 cannot equal that. Individual membership only began to fall slightly from its peak in 1953 and 1954. If 1945 was the flood tide of the PLP, 1952–53 was its equivalent for the extra-parliamentary party. The onset of decline in individual membership broadly coincides with the right wing inquisition, the break up of the Bevanite leadership and the accession of Gaitskell in 1955.

Congress-affiliated trade union membership experienced similar fortunes up to 1951, but growth was steadier and less dramatic. But whereas party membership declined after 1952, trade union membership continued to rise at a fairly steady pace.[15]

This trend of divergent party and trade union membership has been an enduring and more accentuated feature in the sixties and seventies. But the key to the Bevanite period lies in the third index, that of trade union affiliate membership of the Labour Party. The number of trade unionists affiliated to the Labour Party coincides broadly in contour with the curve for trade union membership, as might be expected after the establishment of the 'contracting out' clause. But there is a glaring anomaly in 1954–55 which invites closer investigation. In 1954–55 membership of trades unions increased only marginally, LP affiliations by *almost half a million*, whilst individual party membership goes into a two-year decline. These divergent trends are more clearly seen in Figure 6. In 1954–55 the rate of change in LP, trades union affiliation is moving in the opposite direction both to TUC affiliations and individual party membership.

Three questions arise here. First, why is the 1954–55 trend for LP affiliation far more accentuated than the trend of straightforward trade union membership? Secondly, why is

Figure 6

Annual Percentage Rate of Change on Previous Year for Trade Union Membership Affiliated to TUC, Trades Unionists Affiliated to the LP, and Individual Party Membership.

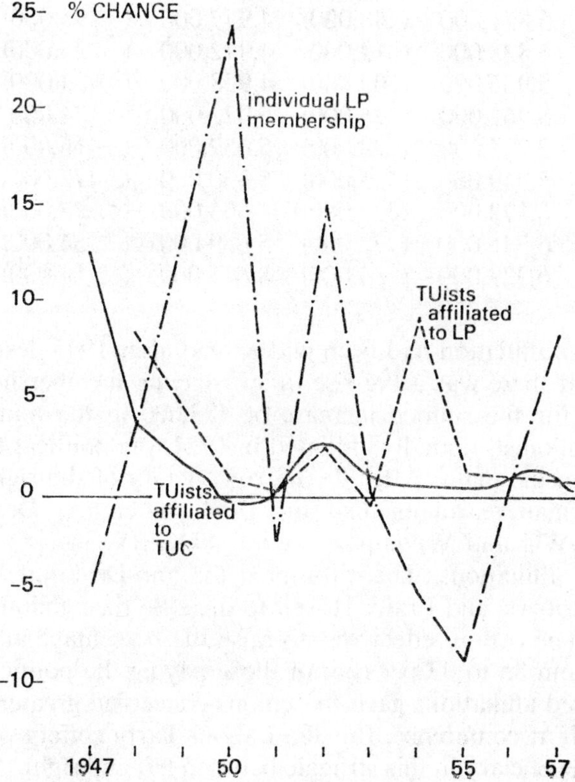

the LP affiliation trend the inverse of the trend in individual membership? And finally, do these trends have any bearing on the fortunes of Bevanism?

The answer to the first question is that the figure for trade unionists paying the political levy to their union does not coincide with the figure of trade unionists actually affiliated to the Labour Party. Unions do not affiliate fully to the party as the table reveals.[16]

Year	Trade Unionists Paying Political Levy	Change on Previous Year	Trade Unionists Actually Affiliated to LP	Change on Previous Year	Percentage Affiliated
1947	5,613,000	(n.a.)	4,387,000	(1,751,000)	78
1948	5,773,000	(160,000)	4,752,000	(365,000)	82
1949	5,821,000	(48,000)	4,947,000	(195,000)	85
1950	5,833,000	(12,000)	4,972,000	(25,000)	85
1951	5,936,000	(103,000)	4,938,000	(–34,000)	83
1952	5,962,000	(26,000)	5,072,000	(134,000)	85
1953	5,924,000	(–38,000)	5,057,000	(–15,000)	85
1954	5,949,000	(25,000)	5,530,000	(473,000)	93
1955	6,173,000	(224,000)	5,605,000	(75,000)	91
1956	6,245,000	(72,000)	5,659,000	(54,000)	91
1957	6,329,000	(84,000)	5,645,000	(–14,000)	90

Under-affiliation had been widespread after 1945 despite the fact that there was a big rise in levy paying membership. The reason for the sudden increase of 473,000 in the number of trade unionists actually affiliated in 1954 was political factionalism, in the main. After the narrow victory of the right wing on German rearmament at the 1954 conference, Deakin of the TGWU and Williamson of the NUGMW increased their unions' affiliations. This prompted the anti-Deakinites led by Bryn Roberts and Frank Haxell to increase their unions' affiliation. The overall effect was to raise the percentage affiliation level from 85 to 93 per cent of those paying the political levy. Increased affiliations gave the unions concerned greater voting strength at conference. But the Labour Party coffers were the chief beneficiary in this struggle between left and right.

Figure 7
Levy Paying and Nationally Affiliated Trade Union Membership 1947–57.[17]

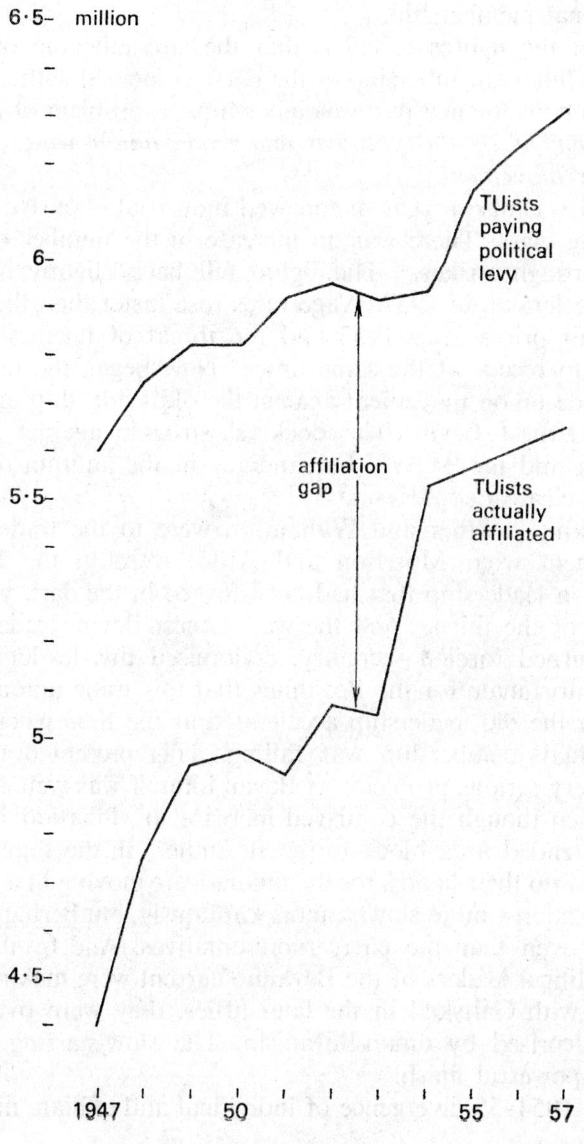

Did this manoeuvring distort or rectify the true picture of the relationship between party membership and individual membership? Figure 7 confirms that the figures are not a distortion. The real trend of trade union affiliation *was sharply upwards after 1954*, coinciding with the downturn in individual membership.

What the figures reveal is that the strengthening of trade union affiliate membership of the party coincided with a downturn in constituency party membership—a problem of *uneven development of the political and trade union wings of the Labour movement.*[18]

1954 was also a year of renewed industrial offensive by the working class. There was an increase in the number of days lost through strikes.[19] The figure fell back slightly in 1956 but accelerated in 1957. Wage rates rose faster than the index of retail prices after 1953 and the threat of unemployment began to recede at the same time.[20] Now began the revolt of the trade union movement against the old leadership moulded under Ernest Bevin. The dockers' struggle against Arthur Deakin and the TGWU bureaucracy in the autumn of 1954 was its clearest expression.

Deakin, Lawther and Williamson were to the trade union movement what Morrison and Attlee were to the Labour Party—a leadership that had been forged in the dark years of defeat of the thirties and the war. Ernest Bevin, trade union boss turned foreign secretary, epitomised this leadership. It was unfortunate for the Bevanites that this trade union revolt against the old leadership accelerated at the time when party individual membership was falling. This presented the left with very serious problems as Bevan himself was well aware.[21] Yet even though the contrived increase in affiliation in 1954 was intended as a block to the Bevanites, in the long run it played into their hands, for the unions were moving in a Bevanite direction—more slowly, more cautiously, but perhaps more surely even than the party representatives. And by the time the political leaders of the Bevanite current were making their peace with Gaitskell in the later fifties, they were overtaken and surprised by union-Bevanism. The slow-starting unions had a powerful finish.

The 1954–55 divergence of individual and affiliate membership synchronises also with the emergence of the Crossman-Wilson 'centre-left' of Bevanism, the beginning of the decomposition of its parliamentary wing.[22]

The surge forward in trade union affiliations in 1954 was the harbinger of important changes impending in the union leaderships. Most of the increases took place in the General unions. Ironically its immediate effect was to swell the vote for Gaitskell in the Treasurership vote in 1955. But it also cannot be accidental that the TGWU, which experienced this rapid growth, also produced, within a few more months, a radical left leader like Frank Cousins, who did so much to upset the balance of forces within the party and to prepare the way for Gaitskell's defeat on unilateralism in 1960. This is not for a moment to suggest that the TGWU underwent a sudden left-wing 'conversion'. The left winger, Cousins, was no more a perfect expression of his union membership's political viewpoint than the right winger, Deakin. Leadership always reflects imperfectly and indirectly developments in the mass movement. Cousins was as well to the left of his membership on many matters as Deakin was to their right. It was rather in its greater consideration, tolerance and thoughtfulness that the Cousins leadership approximated more closely to the mood of the TGWU ranks,[23] and thereby to the Bevanite current in the Labour Party.

The extent of party growth in the early fifties is also evident in the figures for women, student and youth movements of the Labour Party.

The number of women's sections of the Labour Party in existence was increasing throughout the fifties, but the biggest increases appear to have come about between 1947 and 1952. The number of delegates to the National Conference of Labour women rose from 647 in 1947 to a peak of 936 in 1950, declining thereafter.[24] The number of student Labour clubs affiliated to NALSO (the National Association of Labour Student Organisations) increased from 12 in 1948, a year after NALSO was formed to 46 in 1954 but membership proper rose from only 1500 to around 3,000 in the same period.[25]

The LLOY (Labour League of Youth) had only 260 branches in 1948, but this had risen to 806 by 1951 only to decline sharply by the mid-fifties.[26] At the week-long Filey

Figure 8
Circulation of Labour, pro-Labour and Other Journals—1947–57.

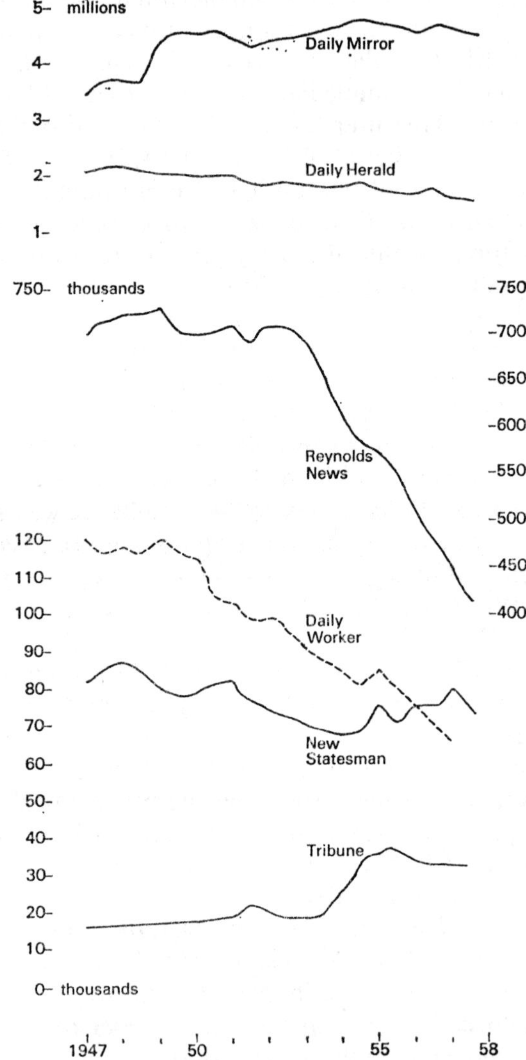

Figures for these diagrams were kindly provided by the Audit Bureau of Circulation, 19 Dunraven St, London W1 to whom the author expresses his thanks. They are also contained in Appendix 6 of the author's doctoral thesis.

rally in 1950 75 per cent of those attending for a week of intensive political training and discussion were of LLOY age.[27]

The ferment in the mass movement enabled Labour to employ more full time professional staff.[28] These were at a peak in 1951 when there were 296, the greatest numbers being in London (121), Lancashire (53) and South Wales (41).[29] It is also expressed in the circulation figures for Labour, pro-Labour and other left wing journals[30] during the Bevanite period. The New Statesman experienced two peaks—in 1948 and 1951. The Daily Mirror's circulation rose very sharply between 1948 and 1951. The Daily Herald's high point came earlier, in 1948, and the Sunday Reynolds News, 1949. Tribune's figures are not reliable after 1946 when it disaffiliated from the Audit Bureau of Circulation. Figures from the different sources do not tally. Michael Foot believes that the average weekly sales were around 18,000, but there were some exceptionally high sales of 'over 40,000' in some weeks according to Richard Clements.[31] In that same period Transport House put the 1951 circulation at 22,000[32] and it certainly rose in the years following. But both Foot and Clements agree however that the peak for circulation in the forties and fifties was 1954–55. The New Statesman experienced a second but lower peak at about the same period, that is, four to five years after the peaks of the wars circulation of Herald and Reynolds News. Whilst the latter two went into slow then rapid circulation decline after 1948–49, the Statesman and Tribune picked up strongly, their 'vanguard' readership being *carried along by the momentum of the political surge of the early fifties* even after it had begun to falter in the mass movement.

The figures for individual party membership, trade union affiliation, membership of Labour's women student and youth movements, readership of pro-Labour and left wing Labour journals appear to prove that the climax of the mass movement in the post war period was not the mid-forties but the early fifties. But might it not be argued that the phenomenon of Bevanism is purely coincidental with this, and that there is no causal relationship between the upsurge in the mass movement evident in 1950–51 and the maturing of the Bevanite current? It still needs to be demonstrated that the two are organically related.

Elections to NEC (Constituency Party Section)—Figures from NEC Minutes and LPACR's

Name	47	48	49	50	51	52	53	54	55	56	57
(B) A. Bevan	646(1)	736(1)	756(1)	849(1)	858(1)	965(1)	1142(1)	—	—	Treas	Treas.
H. Dalton	624(2)	670(2)	575(5)	654(4)	545(7)	—	—	—	—	—	—
H. Morrison	592(3)	580(4)	597(4)	671(3)	595(5)	—	—	—	—	—	—
(L) H. Laski	571(4)	505(6)	—	—	—	—	—	—	—	—	—
J. Griffiths	539(5)	544(5)	605(3)	781(2)	597(4)	700(4)	913(4)	953(4)	853(5)	—	—
E. Shinwell	475(6)	581(3)	528(6)	604(5)	(410(5))	(146(12))	(351(10))	—	—	—	—
P. Noel-Baker	460(7)	(340(8))	—	(363(8))	(249(10))	—	—	—	—	—	—
(B) M. Foot		420(7)	644(2)	—	—	—	—	—	—	—	—
(B) T. Driberg	(251(9))	(279(10))	323(7)	588(6)	646(3)	744(3)	842(5)	869(6)	790(6)	831(4)	753(4)
(B) I. Mikardo	(190(10))	(207(11))	—	367(7)	561(6)	630(6)	637(7)	815(7)	777(7)	717(6)	719(5)
(B) B. Castle				(Women Sct)	676(2)	868(2)	1026(2)	1024(2)	1034(2)	952(1)	855(3)
(B) H. Wilson				1950		632(5)	934(3)	1043(1)	1066(1)	877(3)	886(2)
(B) R. Crossman	(334(8))					620(7)	788(6)	910(5)	897(4)	740(5)	578(6)
(L) Aty Greenwood								962(3)	969(3)	899(2)	911(1)
(L) S. Silverman	(113(12))				(185(11))	(129(14))	81(14)	(169(12))	(252(8))	675(7)	(533(8))
J. Callaghan				(184(12))	(142(14))	(196(11))	315(11)	(495(8))		(358(8))	565(7)

(B = Bevanite, L = Left)

NEC	47	48	49	50	51	52	53	54	55	56	57
Successful Bevanites:	646*	1156*	1723	1804	2741	4458	5368	5623	5533	5691	4702
Successful Other:	3261	2880	2305	2710	1737	700	913	953	853	—	565
Total Votes for Top 7 Seats:	3907	4036	4028	4514	4478	5158	6281	6576	6386	5691	5267
Bevanite % of Vote for top Seven:	14·8%	28·6%	42·8%	40·0%	61·2%	86·4%	85·5%	85·5%	86·6%	100%**	89·3%

(* Excludes Laski. ** Includes Greenwood & Silverman)

Note: Due to insufficient data it has not proved possible to calculate the Bevanite vote as a percentage of the *total votes cast for the NEC*. Some year's figures are missing and some do not show all the unsuccessful candidates' votes. Since these do not amount to a very great total, the picture is not distorted.

At this point examination of the voting for the National Executive Committee is appropriate (page 128). The pattern is instructive. It exhibits the 'momentum effect' alluded to in relation to the Tribune/New Statesman circulation figures.

The alignment between the surge in the mass movement and the representation of Bevanites on the NEC *is not direct but staggered.* This can be seen more clearly in Figure 9. The quantitative influx of the early fifties is transformed after a few short years into a qualitative change in the political complexion of CLP representation. By 1956 this section is 100 per cent Bevanite and left, and Bevan himself Treasurer, even though individual party membership had been *falling since 1953.* This momentum supplemented by new influxes into the party after Hungary and a further rise in party membership in the early sixties could even be said to have contributed to the accession

Figure 9
Bevanite and Left Representation on NEC Constituency Section.

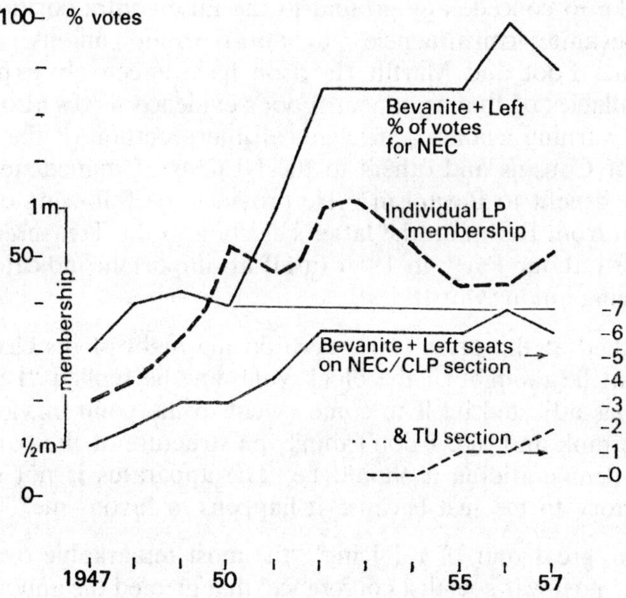

into the leadership of the party of Wilson and Crossman and Castle in the Sixties.

Nor is the momentum effect confined to the Constituency section of the NEC. In 1954 trade union affiliation increased dramatically, bringing it more into line with the underlying rise in levy-paying TU membership. In 1955 Frank Cousins stepped up into the NEC. He was joined by Raymond Casasola in 1956, and the following year, Tom Hollywood of the NUR. This represents quite an important change in the complexion of the union representatives of the NEC in only a couple of years. When Cousins stood down it was to succeed to the General Secretaryship of Britain's largest union, but the election of these three between 1955 and 1957 was a pointer to the complexion of trade union representation on the NEC in the future. Once again the growth of left representation is staggered, but, unlike CLP representation, left wing union representation exhibits a steady consolidation. The union lefts of the sixties were not being carried along by the momentum of a movement on the wane, but one which was penetrating ever-new layers of the working population. Even so it would be a mistake to concede any ground to the false contra-positioning of Bevanite constituencies to anti-Bevanite unions. Both Michael Foot and Martin Harrison have effectively exposed the fallacies of that argument. Foot's evidence serves also as a stern warning against a mechanical interpretation of the election of Cousins and others to the NEC as of immediate and direct benefit to Bevanism.[33] He provides the following observation from Bevan on the latter's election to the Treasurership of the Labour Party in 1956 (itself an important indicator of changing union sympathies).

> 'Asked at the press conference on the night of his election what he thought of the block vote now he replied "I think it has adjusted itself to some extent to the point of view of the rank and file. I don't think the structure of the party is as democratic as it should be. The apparatus is not satisfactory to me just because it happens to favour me".'[34]

The 'great roar of rejoicing', 'the most remarkable ovation of any post-war socialist conference' that greeted the announcement of the vote indicates that the movement appreciated that the voting was, at last, beginning to reflect the movement in the ranks of both unions and CLP's. But once again, it was not proportional. Just as the British electoral system distorts party majorities, the bloc vote distorted and over-emphasised the left-wing complexion of the unions after 1956 as surely as it had the right wing complexion beforehand. It is extremely doubtful, for instance, that the TGWU membership was as unilateralist as TGWU voting at conference later implied.

Another contributory factor to the distortion of representation is the degree of union affiliation at General Management Committee level of the CLPs. In effect unions are doubly represented in the Labour Party. Apart from the bloc vote at conference, their votes on management committees affect the complexion of CLP politics also. If the *locally* affiliated unions contain a greater proportion of unions with a left or right complexion then clearly something less than a true picture is the result. These figures taken from the Bevanite period indicate the problem.[35]

Percentage of affiliations to CLPs in different unions

Union	Number of Branches	Branches Affiliated to CLPs	Year	%
Amalgamated Society of Woodworkers	1,414	547	1954	38.60
Electrical Trades Union	664	135	1955	20.30
London District of NUGMW	292	161	1952	55.10
United Society of Boilermakers etc	281	254	1957	90.37
National Union of Furniture Trade Operatives	280	55	1957	19.60
National Union of Tailors & Garment Workers	244	60	1957	26.70
Power Group of the TGWU	196	48	1957	24.40
National Union of Sheet Metal Workers & Braziers	104	58	1958	55.76
Scots Painters' Society	98	38	1957	38.70

Now union delegates are very often bound to abide by union policy on GMCs. Thus if, for instance, predominantly left wing unions also had a higher percentage of CLP affiliation this could materially affect the balance of forces in the local parties. Hence the danger of interpreting CLP Bevanism as a purely constituency phenomenon and counter posing it to union hostility.

Harrison's study identifies four union groups in the fifties.[36] Summarised they read as follows:

Extreme Left (1)	Moderate Left (2)	Unreliable Right (3)	Right (4)
ETU	ASSET	ASW	TGWU
Vehicle Builders (NUVB)	AEU	UPW	NUGMW
CEU (Construction Engineers)	NUR	Patternmakers	NUM
Boilermakers	USDAW		Bisakta
Metal Mechanics (NSMM)	NUFTO		Textile Workers
Chemical Workers	PTU		Seamen
Tobacco Workers	AESD		NUBSO
FBU (Firemen)	NUTGW		Blastfurnace Men
Foundrymen			

All four categories were split amongst themselves on certain issues. But apart from the TGWU none of the unions in category four was known to have voted against the NEC from 1945 to 1957. Category three hovered between 'orthodoxy and dissent',[37] although 'often carelessly classified as right wing'. The moderate left was less sharply defined, but 'voted fairly consistently against the National Executive'.[38] The extreme left group normally voted and spoke alike, but Harrison notes,

> 'Several normally left wing unions were influenced by the sudden switch of the Communists to supporting the British Hydrogen Bomb in 1957. The 1957 Conference offered the rare spectacle of the ETU and other Communist-led unions defending the NEC against "irresponsible" unilateralists. When the issue became really heated in 1959 Communist influence helped several Executives rally their conferences to the official line.'[39]

Harrison concludes that there always had been a substantial left wing in the trade union movement with two or three of the six largest unions voting against sections of official policy at any one time, whilst the constituencies were on balance to the left of the unions,

> 'the overlap is considerable.This overlap is one reason why the two wings have held together through all the party's internal upheavals.'[40]

These observations are of great importance. They help explain why the expulsion crisis of 1955 never ended in a split,[41] and warn against superficial deductions based on short-term trends, the political opinions of leaderships and single-issue stands made by different unions.

If the ETU and TGWU stood on opposite sides in 1954, they did so again in 1959, but this time the ETU was the bulwark of the right. Apparently we have here a perplexing pattern, a meaningless game of musical chairs. But beneath the surface a singular process is common. The struggle against the bureaucracy was proceeding in the ETU as well—the rebellion against the ETU leaders' support for Russian action in Hungary was already beginning.

Bevan's decision to campaign for the Treasurership of the Labour Party when Arthur Greenwood died in 1954 was based not upon personal ambition but on his own conviction that the struggle against bureaucracy was under way in the unions and would eventually find expression, even if staggered by some years. He understood this better than any of his contemporaries and was unquestionably right. He knew that initial defeat was certain. 'It will take us three years to win this particular fight' he told his sceptical supporters. In fact it was won in two. The Blue Union dispute had begun the revolt but soon there were other indicators that Bevan's campaign on the unions was a realistic one determined by the forms and tempo of the struggle. The Treasurership intervention only accelerated the process.

The Treasurership Campaign Against Bureaucracy

This assessment of the Treasurership campaign, and its importance for the movement conflicts perhaps with the view of some commentators on the period who would argue, along with David Coates that the Bevanites,

> 'had no organised working class roots outside constituency parties, as had the ILP, nor did they manage to mobilise rank and file support in the trade union movement.'[42]

The facts do not bear out Coates' contention that the NASD dispute comprised the Bevanites' 'one excursion into trade union politics.' It is surprising that after eighteen years since Harrison's eloquent and encyclopaedic study[43] of the relations between the party and the unions in the fifties, such superficial judgements still pass for wisdom.[44] That viewpoint appears to blithely overlook the real, existing, *historical, organisational connection* between the party and the unions established by *the working class itself*, in pursuit of some undefined parallel or substitute 'organisational roots' which its author considers necessary 'to link industrial and political struggle.'

Bevan *did* carry the struggle into the trade union organisations at all levels. The success he had is testimony to the superfluity of 'rank and file' organisation. What follows is evidence that the Bevanite campaign for the Treasurership aroused the union membership to the importance of the inner party struggle, and that it set in motion a profound questioning of undemocratic procedure that had been commonplace in union decision making.

Harrison reveals that most unions still left nomination and voting for the Treasurership and other offices in the Labour party to their Executives. And this could have been a crucial factor in explaining the unrepresentative nature of the composition of the trade union section of the NEC. As regards the Treasurership . . .

> 'In all the "Big Six" but the NUM Executive decided nominations and in all but the TGWU and USDAW it also decided how the delegation should vote.'[45]

and Harrison adds,

> '. . . it was only when the dispute broke out that most unions gave their members the least information about how they voted.'[46]

He concludes that,

> 'It is in the deciding of the votes for members of the NEC that trade union "representative democracy" is at its weakest.'[47]

The supporters of the right in the party viewed their membership's new interest in democratic procedure in the unions with dismay. AEU President Openshaw, a solid anti-Bevanite member of the NEC complained about his union's delegation to conference insisting on their right to nominate for the Treasurership.

> 'It is strange . . . that after all these years during which the Executive have nominated for the Treasurership and other posts, suddenly in the last two years there has been all this clamour that someone else should have the right.'[48]

Tiffin of the TGWU invoked 'custom and practice' as justification for the TGWU Executive to nominate. Alan Birch, General Secretary of USDAW resisted attempts to nominate Bevan at his union's own conference in 1956.

Nor was this an organisational matter purely and simply. The antagonists well understood the *policy implications* to the party of the election of Bevan as Treasurer. The same Mr Birch complained about,

> 'the tendency to make the annual election of the Treasurer a cockpit of ideological strife.'[49]

The clamour of which Openshaw complained was evidently considerable and points to the fact that Bevan's supporters in the unions, far from setting up rank and file bodies, were busy asserting their rights and *taking hold of their unions' organisations.*

Bevan's campaign began in 1954, and when he was defeated for the Treasurership at the 1955 LP conference the dispute between the AEU delegation and the union's executive was referred to the AEU Final Appeal Court, which found in favour of the delegation. The Executive promptly challenged this decision by issuing a circular to all branches re-affirming the Executive's right to decide how votes would be cast. The closeness of Communist Party leaders to the right wing in the course of these events was thrown into sharp relief at the AEU National Committee conference in the Spring of 1956, the report of which produced mutual rebukes in the columns of Tribune and the Daily Worker.[50]

It was not until July 1957 that the AEU agreed to accept the decision of its Final Appeal Court. In the meantime the CP must have found it extremely irksome to have been accused of siding with the bureaucracy of the union against the rank and file, especially in view of the fact that the party was—at last—publicly backing Bevan for Treasurer.[51]

In the ETU the revolt of the ranks against the Stalinist-dominated union bureaucracy went much further. But the beginnings of this struggle date from the same time as the struggle in the AEU, revealing it as part of a generalised move from below against bureaucracy in all its forms. In the very same issue of Tribune which covered the AEU dispute we find the editors answering disconsolate CP members in the ETU who did not like the way their conference was reported by the paper.[52] Sam Goldberg of the ETU's Executive described Tribune's report as 'nauseating bilge'. The paper replied that union leaders had better start 'getting used to criticism'. A major feature of the conference had been the protest from the floor against Executive policy in relation to the responsibility for the division of Germany. The union's CP leadership had refused to accept the implication that the USSR may have shared some of the responsibility for that country's division. There was also a wrangle concerning the voting on one of the resolutions. A year later however, after the Hungarian revolution, this mild protest escalated into rejection of the CP-dominated leadership's apologia for the Russian invasion of Hungary. The conflict came to a head over the General Secretary Haxell's personal decision to invalidate certain branches' votes in the election for his office, invalidations which, it appeared to some, were conducted inconsistently. So began the ballot-rigging scandal. From the very beginning of the battle inside the ETU, the Bevanites' paper attacked Haxwell's autocratic methods as consistently as they had those of Deakin and his allies in other unions.

Evidence of this generalised struggle in the unions is to be found in the NUM also. In February 1956 simultaneous with Yorkshire miners' decision to back Bevan, Tribune turned the spotlight on the issue of pit closures in South Wales which resulted in letters from local miners scathingly critical of the CP miners' leader, Will Paynter.[53]

In performing this role as crusader against bureaucracy of every hue, Tribune was continuing the work it had begun in the TGWU in 1954. Its reporting constituted a protracted campaign to carry the Bevanite struggle into the union ranks which found a warm and growing response. Derby, Kent and Lancashire miners began to turn their votes over to Bevan. Nor was the campaign confined to the ranks. In the autumn of 1955, NUPE Secretary, Bryn Roberts, engaged the new TGWU secretary Jock Tiffin in debate in Tribune's columns about the way membership of the General Council was engineered behind the scenes.[54] Although he represented a union that had grown from 13,000 members in 1934 to 200,000 in 1955, he had been turned down for membership of the General Council on each of the twenty times he had been nominated.

This campaign was not 'necessary' if all that was at stake was Bevan's membership of the NEC. He could have had that any time he wanted on the constituency section. Bevan and Tribune pursued the Treasurership campaign and did not neglect agitation in the ranks, at union conferences, nor in the higher bodies of the big unions and the TUC. And who dares say they did not succeed?

> '. . . of the 3,029,000 votes which brought him the Treasurership, at the very minimum 1,980,000 were trade union block votes—and he may have won as many as 2,322,000 union votes. While the overwhelming majority of local Party votes came back to him (his opponents shared 100,000) Mr Bevan's support in the unions *was always considerable and finally decisive.*'[55] (*My emphasis—M.J.*).

And this was managed *before* the ranks' challenge to the Executives in the General Unions and the AEU over the issue of the rights of delegates had finally carried the day. Even on the NEC the monolithic right wing trade union bloc was a myth,

> 'During the Bevanite controversy the NEC did tend increasingly to split into blocks, *but the trade union members were always divided.* They were still divided on the final battle—the proposed expulsion of Mr Bevan.'[56]

Sufficient has been recounted here to indicate that the Bevanites were capable of substantial and lasting victories on the issues of democratic procedure in the unions, in a remarkably short space of time and with the *minimum of organisational apparatus.*

And if the ILP and the Socialist League are the models for left organisations within the Labour Party then we ought to pose the question of why no such organisation materialised in the fifties, sixties, and seventies? And if it is necessary to the success of left currents how did the Bevanites achieve so much with such economy or organisation? In other words is there something to be learned from the Bevanites' experience in the field of organisation and the continuous disputes they had about what kind and what degree of organisation the left required?

NOTES

1. Miliband, *op. cit.* (p. 272 et. seq.).
2. *The English Constitution* by Walter Bagehot, Fontana, London 1975. This classic work distinguishes between the appearance of government, the 'dignified' aspect, and the actuality of decision making, the 'efficient' aspect. The former is public, ornamental and the mythical side of the Constitution by which men's hearts are won. The latter is rather secret, practical and mundane. Yet the Constitution, he argues, requires both its dignified and efficient aspects. Men's hearts must be won before their minds could be governed. Bagehot's method of approach has interesting applications in the sphere of Labour politics. Popular mythology has it that party conference is the highest body and the policy-making body. This is the 'dignified' part of Labour's constitution. The policies of Labour governments, however, have not necessarily very much to do with conference decisions, and are arrived at by quite different procedures far removed from conference debates. Richard Crossman's diaries and George Brown's memoirs contain valuable accounts on these procedures.
3. The phrase used in Chapter 9, Ralph Miliband, *op. cit.* (p. 272) concerning the achievements of Labour 1945–51.
4. British figures taken from Butler & Sloman, *op. cit.* (p. 184)

German figures from Cook & Paxton, *op. cit.* (p. 98). In 1972 the SPD again broke Labour's record, polling 17,175,169 votes! Prior to 1951 the record had always belonged to the SPD. In 1911 they polled 11,509,100. Thereafter the party split and rivalry with the KPD reduced its poll until the discredit of Stalinism in the post-war period eliminated the KPD as a rival.

5. Miliband, *op. cit.* (p. 298) Herbert Morrison's speech to the LP conference in 1948 stressed 'consolidation' as one of the aims of Labour's next programme, '. . . you must expect the new programme to be of a somewhat different character and a somewhat different tempo to the last . . .'.
6. Butler & Sloman, *op. cit.* (p. 307).

Retail Price Index 1963 = 100

1940	38	1945	49	1950	61
1941	42	1946	51	1951	67
1942	45	1947	54	1952	73
1943	47	1948	57		
1944	47	1949	59		

7. *Let us Face the Future*, the title of Labour's election manifesto in 1945.
   The 1950 programme was *Let Us Win Through Together*. In 1951 Labour produced a one-page leaflet headed simply *Labour Party Manifesto* which laid emphasis on past achievements rather than future plans.
8. The closest similar occurrence *since* was in 1966 when a Labour government increased its vote and representation. But the vote was almost one million less than the 1951 total and the circumstances were quite different.

	1964	1966
Labour Vote	12,205,814	13,064,951

9. See Butler & Sloman, *op. cit.* (p. 184). See also figures, above, in footnote 4, p. 56. Labour representation in Wales remained constant in 1951 while Scottish seats fell by only 3. It was in Southern England that their greatest losses were sustained in terms of seats.
10. Figures from Butler & Sloman, *op. cit.* (p. 184—General & p. 338—County Borough).

Labour's % share of poll in General & County Borough Elections

	G	*CB*		*G*	*CB*		*G*	*CB*
1945	47.8		1951	48.8	n.a.	1957		50.00
46			52		55.4	58		
47		41.7	53		52.0	59	43.8	
48			54		49.2			
49		43.2	55	47.6	47.6			
50	46.2	46.2	56		51.1			

Turnout in the elections was as follows:

General Elections			County Borough Elections					
1945	72.7	(NB. Only in	1945		1950	45.5	1955	43.8
1950	84.0	1910 was	1946		1951	44.4	1956	37.6
1951	82.5	there a higher	1947	52.6	1952	49.9	1957	40.0
1955	76.7	turnout—	1948		1953	45.2	1958	40.3
1959	78.8	86.6%)	1949	52.2	1954	42.8	1959	41.0

11. See previous footnote.
12. Population structure figures given in Butler & Sloman *op. cit.* (p. 265).

	1931		1951		1971	
10–19	32.9		28.9		31.2	
20–39	31.6)	55.6	28.7)	55.4	25.9)	50.1
40–59	24.0)		26.7)		24.2)	
Over 60	11.5		15.7		18.7	

13. See Figure 5, p. 119.
14. See Figure 5, page 119.
15. See Figure 5, page 119.
16. *Trade Unions and the Labour Party* (p. 62) by Martin Harrison, George Allen & Unwin, London 1960. Harrison quotes the LP Constitution, Clause X (1), as evidence that 'The Party's Constitution clearly commits organisations to affiliate their entire levy paying membership. Not all do! '
17. Based on figures in Harrison, *op. cit.* (p. 62).
18. The divergence between individual and LP membership has become a permanent trend since 1954 and individual membership of the LP represents a continually decreasing percentage of total membership as trade union affiliation membership continues to rise.
Individual LP membership as a percentage of total party membership. Calculated from figures in Butler & Sloman, *op. cit.* (pp. 135–36).

1955	13%
1960	12.4%
1965	12.6%
1970	10.9%
1973	10.8%

19. B. R. Mitchell, *op. cit.* (p. 391)
Days lost through Strikes, in thousands

1952	1,792
1953	2,184
1954	2,457
1955	3,781

20. See Dow, *op. cit.* (p. 93), Table 3.3 The British Economy 1955–59
Prices and Wages (% change in year)

	1955	1956	1957	1958
Retail Prices	6.0	3.3	4.4	1.5
Wage Rates	7.0	7.6	5.7	3.6

Maximum unemployment figures for year, from Butler & Sloman *op. cit.* (p. 300)

1951	367,000
1952	468,000
1953	452,000
1954	387,000
1955	298,000
1956	297,000
1957	383,000

21. Foot, *op. cit. Vol II,* (p. 492 Footnote 1).
Bevan saw the obstacle in the democratic issue . . . 'the thrust could not find expression in the upper reaches of the party'. He added that 'the key to this failure must be looked for in the way the constitution worked.
'I knew that at least for some years my defeat (for the treasurership of the LP) was practically certain . . . the Party will never regain its health until the stranglehold of the bureaucracy is broken.' Bevan believed that the unions were ready for a new thrust forward. He was right.
22. See below, 'The Organisation of Bevanism'.
23. For example, see Foot, *Vol II, op. cit.* (p. 577).
'That was Brighton 1957. Nothing happened there that counted for very much, not even the huge vote of 5,836,000 to 781,000 recorded against the Norwood resolution nor the novel democratic spectacle of the general secretary of the Transport and General Workers Union asking for time to consult his delegation and finding himself outvoted for 16 votes to 14.'
and on p. 514,
'. . . the speech of Frank Cousins, the newly-elected General Secretary of the Transport and General Workers Union, offered an entirely fresh prospect of the relationship between the party and the unions. Yet the vote of the Transport Union that year had gone to Brown not to Bevan, so difficult was it for even a powerful union leader like Cousins to escape from the entanglements of the past.'
24. Labour Party Annual Conference Reports 1947–57—Labour Women.

Increase in No. of Women's Sections Reported	Total No. of Women's Sections Reported	Delegates at National Conferences of Labour Women	LPACR in which figures appear
+241	n.a.	647	1947
+185	n.a.	806	1948
	Re-Organisation of CLP's		
	1,843	833	1949
+297	2,140	936	1950

+169		716	1951
+225		739	1952
'further development'	2,362	731	1953
'further increase'	n.a.	679	1954
'an increase'	n.a.	549	1955
'an increase'	n.a.	604	1956
'an increase'	n.a.	536	1957

25. Labour Party Annual Conference Reports 1947–57—Labour Students.

Comments in LPACR	No. of NALSO Clubs	Membership	LPACR in which figures appear
	12	'nearly 1,500'	1948
	32	'about 3,500'	1949
	33	'about 3,500'	1950
'Some' in TTCs	36	'nearly 3,000'	1951
'largest' SO Student movement in world	44	'exceeds 3,000'	1952
	46	'about 3,000'	1953
	46	n.a.	1954
		n.a.	1955
	'about 40'	n.a.	1956
'largest attendance ever' at conference.		n.a.	1957

26. Labour Party Annual Conference Reports 1947–57—Labour League of Youth.

Comments in LPACR	Branches	Year	
	260	1947	(This 1947 figure is in 1950 report)
	310	1948	
	561	1949	
	788	1950	
349 delegates + 200 visitors at LLOY Conference	806	1951	
	670	1952	
	538	1953	(Calculated from 1954 Report)
121 delegates + 200 visitors Plan to reorganise LLOY	366	1954	(Calculated from 1955 Report)
'Youth Sections' introduced	237	1955	
	301	1956	
	275	1957	

27. LPACR, 1950.
28. Labour Party Annual Conference Reports 1947–57—Full Time Agents Employed.

Year	F/T Agents	Year	F/T Agents
1947	n.a.	1953	250

1948	n.a.	1954	252
1949	Increase of 79 reported	1955	227
1950	279	1956	204
1951	296	1957	221
1952	274		

These figures are very slightly distorted by the 'boom/slump' effect of general elections on full time agent employment. The National Union of Labour Organisers Executive Committee in a report to its own conference in 1949 complained that 'many more appointments could have been made' if parties with substantial resources had been prepared to turn part-time posts into full-time ones.

29. NULO/EC Report, 1950, delivered to conference of NULO, Sept. 30th to Oct. 1st, 1950, Cliftonville.
30. See Figure 8 and Appendix 6 of the author's doctoral thesis.
31. See Appendix 3 of the author's doctoral thesis (Interviews with Foot and Clements).
32. NEC Minutes, 12.12.51. Enquiry into the press and the election.
33. Foot, *Vol. II* (p. 557). At Brighton 1957 Cousins consulted his delegation on the Norwood resolution and was defeated 16–14!
34. Foot, *Vol II, op. cit.* (p. 514) footnote 2.
35. The percentage figures are calculated from the data in Martin Harrison, *op. cit.* (p. 112). This book is without doubt the most comprehensive work in print on relations between the Labour Party and the trade unions.
36. Harrison, *op. cit.* (pp. 212–13).
37. Harrison, *op. cit.* (p. 213).
38. Harrison, *op. cit.* (p. 213).
39. Harrison, *op. cit.* (p. 237).
40. Harrison, *op. cit.* (p. 239).
41. See Chapter on 'The Organisation of Bevanism'.
42. Coates, *op. cit.* (p. 194).
43. *British Political Parties* by Robert McKenzie, Heinemann, London 1964 (p. 502 & 597). Whilst McKenzie concurs with Harrison's judgement in denying a permanent union–CLP split on voting at conference, he does concede that it has happened notably in the debates on SEATO and German rearmament.
44. Coates, *op. cit.* (p. 194).
'Their one excursion into trade union politics (in which they gave their support to the NASD in its dockland struggle with the Transport and General Workers Union) came late, and was not part of any systematic attempt to link industrial and political struggle.'
It is the view of the author that, to the extent that industrial and political struggles *are linked* (not artificially but in actuality) they are *bound to find expression politically*. The Taff Vale dispute produced a rapid development of political consciousness in the 1900's. The experiences of the 1926 General Strike played a great

part in placing Labour in office in 1929. More recently the problems experienced by the unions with the Conservatives' Industrial Relations Act had a great deal to do with Labour's victories in 1974.

The difference between the Bevanites' attitude to the labour and trade union movement and the one which Coates laments the lack of, is the difference between those who regard the movement as their own and who struggle within the organisational framework *established by that movement*, and those who regard themselves as outsiders who seek to work within the Labour movement.

45. Harrison, *op. cit.* p. 317.
46. Harrison, *op. cit.* p. 319.
47. Harrison, *op. cit.* p. 319.
48. Harrison, *op. cit.* p. 318, quoted from the Manchester Guardian, 2.5.56.
49. Harrison, *op. cit.* p. 318.
50. The CP's veteran columnist Walter Holmes accused Tribune of having 'smeared' Reg. Birch, CP member and one of the AEU's leaders. (Daily Worker, 21.5.54). Tribune asserted that Birch had cut short a debate on the issue of the executive's right to decide how votes should be cast at the LP conference, and that he had earlier backed the anti-Bevanite executive of the AEU against the pro-Bevanite ranks. He was also accused of being anxious not to strip the executive of its powers because he hoped shortly to preside over a 'Communist controlled executive'. Peter Sedgewick retaliated with allegations of anti-Communist bias in Tribune's reporting of the pending election for the Presidency of the Union in which Birch and William Carron were candidates. Former Socialist Outlook correspondent, Norman Dinning as the delegate who was at the centre of this struggle in the AEU, came to Birch's defence in Tribune arguing that 'the real issue . . . is that the (EC's) nominees must reflect union policy.' (Tribune, 18.5.54). But Tribune stuck to its guns and revealed the most embarrassing fact that a CP card holder and delegate to the National Committee was actually on his feet to reply to the President's speech on the AEU vote at the LP conference when Birch terminated the debate by moving the vote. Tribune's editor went on 'to vote for the standing orders committee ruling that the nominations were no business of the National Committee was, in effect, to vote in support of the Executive. If Mr Birch did not realise this most of his Communist Comrades on the National Committee did. They voted the other way'. (Tribune, 25.5.54).
51. World News, 31.7.54. The Communist Party's orientation towards Bevan dates from the German Rearmament campaign which reached its peak in that year. Since the party had some influence in the unions, this support for Bevan did help to swell the vote for him.

52. Tribune, 25.5.54.
53. Tribune, 2.3.56.
54. Tribune, 23.9.57. Bryn Roberts complained of 'back door' offers of General Council seats, through the offices of the NUGMW. However, Roberts' attitude to bureaucratic action and lack of elections in communist China's unions was hardly as rigorous. See Tribune, 20.12.57 for an apologia for the lack of democracy in Chinese unions.
55. Harrison, *op. cit.* p. 317. In a footnote Harrison adds, 'The unions which should have supported Mr Bevan were NUM (678,000); USDAW (324,000); NUR (300,000); ETU (140,000); NUPE (100,000); Boilermakers (61,000); Foundry Workers (50,000); Painters (46,000); Vehicle Builders (39,000); Loco Engineers & Firemen (29,000); Sheet Metal Workers & Braziers (27,000); Draughtsmen (26,000); Constructional Engineers (19,000); Scottish Bakers (16,000); Fire Brigades' Union (16,000); Patternmakers (14,000); Plasterers (15,000); 11 other unions 45,000. The possible supporters were: Tailors & Garment Workers (88,000); Building Trade Workers (70,000); Plumbing Trades Union (37,000); Natsopa (37,000); Printing, Bookbinding Paper Workers (30,000); Furniture Trades Operatives (23,000); Bakers (15,000); and London Typographical Society (12,000).
56. Harrison, *op. cit.* p. 322.

Chapter Six

Bevanite Organisation

The organisational weakness of Bevanism is a popular theme with historians of post-war Labour history.[1] Does empirical research verify this view? Indeed how much empirical research has been done on the subject? Very little, it would appear. This review of Bevanite organisation may serve as a balance to the popularly held prejudice of Bevanism as a poorly organised, 'academic' movement.[2] But it is prefaced with the reminder that tight organisation of itself is neither necessarily desirable from the point of view of programmatic clarification, nor is it a guarantee of political success. The defeats of the Stalinised Communist Parties of China in 1926, Germany in 1933, Spain in 1939 should serve as an antidote to organisational fetishism. Organisation comes a poor third behind political clarity and the conjuncture of objective circumstances. In addition, it is important to avoid the mistake of *abstracting the Bevanite movement from the mass organisations of which it was an integral part*—the British Labour Party and trades unions. The British working class movement has few rivals in the sphere of organisation, and the Bevanites were very much part of that movement, with no interests separate and apart from it. At the time in question Transport House had undertaken the task of reconstructing the Socialist International in Europe, which underlines the point! The Bevanites *were* organised—too well organised some thought. Not for nothing was the 'party within a party'[3] allegation launched by the press in 1952. There were, of course, differences within the Group; comings and goings; overlaps with other groupings, and defections. Bevanism was never a party: It was an organised *current* within a party. This current became a group but contained within it emergent and sometimes ill-defined tendencies. A current is by its very nature amorphous and the degree of organisation of the Bevanites reflects this. It would be true to say the Bevanites had the degree of organisation that their level of theoretical clarity justified. Crossman's lamenting the lack of 'coherent ideology' and Mikardo's dissatisfaction with the degree of tightness in organisation[4] are complementary assessments of the Bevanites' level of political development. The Keep Left group existed as an organised group within the Labour Party from November 1946; became the Bevanite Group when many joined in 1951, and finally furnished the main personnel of the refurbished Victory For Socialism which reappeared publicly in the mid fifties as a rallying centre for the left.

The organisational history of the Keep Left-Bevanite movement falls into the following periods.

1. a. The Old Keep Left Group (November 1946–November 1950).
   b. The expanded Keep Left group (November 1950–April 1951).
2. The public Bevanite group (April 1951–March 1952).
3. The 'open' Bevanite group (March 1952–October 1952) under Standing Orders.
4. The clandestine Bevanite group (October 1952–1954).

Victory for Socialism, whilst it embraced many former Bevanites in an organisation which had rank and file membership and national conferences cannot strictly be called a continuation of Bevanism since more than one of its leading personnel (i.e. Sidney Silverman and the now re-admitted Konni Zilliacus) had always kept their distance from the Bevanites, and VFS didn't begin to attract the interest of the left until after the Brighton conference.

The Old Keep Left Group

After the drubbing they had received at the hands of Ernest Bevin during the conference of 1947 little was heard of the Keep Left group. In January 1950 they published their second manifesto, 'Keeping Left'. In the interval between the two pamphlets however the Group continued to meet, publish papers and concert activity on a regular basis. Minutes were kept,[5] annual financial statements were produced and regular subscriptions were required from members.

It appears, however, from attendance records that by 1950 an average of only about ten MPs were turning up for the weekly meetings chaired by Crossman in a House of Commons Committee room. Of these ten, Crossman, Mikardo, Swingler, Wigg and Hale were authors of the original Keep Left manifesto of 1947 whilst Barbara Castle, Marcus Lipton and Tom Horabin were regular attenders from the ranks of the authors of *Keeping Left.* Non-attenders at this time were the following authors of the original Keep Left manifesto—Bing, Bruce, Foot, Mallalieu, Wyatt and Fred Lee. In the autumn of 1950 Deakin's call for the banning of the Communist Party led to the termination of the Tribune-Transport House arrangement. Tribune reverted to fortnightly publication. The drift to party orthodoxy was halted abruptly.

It seems that it was at this time that Foot and Bruce (who was Bevan's Parliamentary Private Secretary) and economists Dudley Seers and Tom Balogh began to attend regularly. All that can be said about these comings and goings is that the intervening period had produced rifts on the left-over question of the Korean war, NATO and the 'consolidation' politics of the Morrison-Attlee leadership. It is known that Ian Mikardo resigned the editorial board of Tribune in the Spring of 1949 immediately after the 'rented pages' agreement, and Foot, elected to the NEC and appointed Tribune editor the previous year, supported the western alliance. It is also known that Swingler publicly backed Mikardo against Foot.[6] But the growing threat of war in the autumn of 1950 jolted the left as a whole. Even those like Brockway who had not voted with the magnificent two (Emrys Hughes and S. O. Davies) against the Korean War now began to alert the movement to the threat of widening conflict.[7] So the autumn of 1950 saw the return of the Keep Left prodigal sons to Group meetings. Simultaneously Swingler stopped attending and George Wigg resigned for a time in January.

An indication of the tensions within the group is to be found in the following,

> 'That this group deplores the deterioration in the behaviour towards one another at meetings of the group of some of its members (who are, and ought to continue to be un-named),

and urges a return to its best standards of good behaviour, tolerance, friendliness and good comradeship.'[8]

This resolution was passed unanimously in December 1950, and it seems safe to assume that prior to its passing there had been a certain amount of bad behaviour, intolerance, unfriendliness and lack of comradeship!

The Korean War was undoubtedly the source of all the reverberations and tensions within the Left. Even though Keep Left supported the commitment to assist the USA in Korea[9] in July 1950, long discussions on the war continued and the group was forced to arrange meetings during the recess.[10] Group members were given the responsibility of lobbying Harold Wilson, Aneurin Bevan and government leaders on the issue of a peace initiative and a letter, dated 19th July, reveals the seriousness with which group decisions were taken,

'Dear Ni,
The Keep Left group has been talking about the Far East situation, and we would like to exchange some ideas with you.
Could you fix a time within the next few days for Jim Johnson, Tom Horabin and I to come along and have a few minutes with you?
My telephone number is TRAfalgar . . .
Yours sincerely,
Mik.'[11]

The summer of 1950 saw the first Brains Trusts. This proposal was made at the 25th July meeting[12] and it was later agreed to advertise it in Tribune and the New Statesman. On September 12th after the recess, there was a long discussion on MP's impressions, on the feeling in the constituencies over the issue of the wage freeze and the Korean War. The economists in the group were asked to 'begin studying the effect of increased expenditure on armaments in the national economy'. One result of this was confidential Group Paper No. 82 'A Socialist Plan for Fair Shares Under Rearmament' which was produced in the new year.

The Expanded Keep Left Group

The Margate Brains Trust was so successful it was suggested 'it might be useful to hold several each year.' Accordingly a Brains Trust Tour was arranged for the weekend of December 10–12 covering Rugby, Coventry, Leek, Blackburn and Oldham. The Brains Trust bandwagon had started to roll. Mikardo reported the receipt of a number of parliamentary candidates' requests to become associated with the group but it was decided this would be impracticable. It would make the group unwieldy.[13] In November Richard Acland 'reported that he had attended a meeting convened by George Thomas, which had been arranged since the return to the House of Ungoed Thomas, who was alarmed at the apathy of the Labour members. Acland reported that the Thomas group 'intended contacting the commandos.'[14] Later apparently the entire 'Thomas group' were 'invited to join the commandos'.[15]

The expanded Keep Left group was now beginning to become a pole of attraction for the left of the PLP.[16] The success of the Brains Trusts gave the group a vitality which arose from living contact with the activists in the ranks of the constituency parties. Keep Left had feelers out to the constituency activists and it was lobbying those leftwingers in the government and state apparatus who were now becoming more sensitive to the political consequences of the Korean war and the rearmament programme but who, up to this point, had remained in the government. This is what makes the Keep Left group worthy of study. Leslie Hunter's verdict that the group was 'dying' until it 'captured' the rebel three ministers[17] is almost the reverse of what, in fact, was the case. The Keep Left Group whilst small, divided on some issues and wielding little influence on the government was beginning to tap some of the rebellious vitality of the ranks. In this sense it was the rebels (who had gone along with the government up until April 1951) who 'captured' Keep Left, which had a better, though far from blemish-free record of criticism.

No meetings were held in the recess during Christmas 1950 due to the visit of Crossman and Mikardo to Israel.[18] but in January when the group met again the issue of Keep Left's relations with Ministers was raised by none other than Attlee.

On 29th January the following letter from the Prime Minister ended a series of exchanges between the Group and No. 10.

'My Dear Mikardo,
You will have received Moyle's acknowledgement of your letter of January the 23rd. I made no suggestion against the members of your Group, but I had that week had two instances of serious leakages when Ministers had talked to groups of Members in confidence. A particularly bad one was that which occurred after the meeting which Bevin and I had with the Foreign Affairs Group. I therefore considered it inadvisable for the time being to have other meetings with members on the subject. The decision had no reference to the membership of any Group, but was general. I wish members of the Party would realise that, if they want full information, they must reciprocatee by respecting confidence. I have no doubt that you and your colleagues do.
Yours sincerely,
C. R. Attlee.'[19]

Extensive discussion papers by Seers and Balogh occupied Group members in February and March 1951. The problems to which they addressed themselves paralleled the agonising inside the Cabinet.[20] Harold Wilson was said to have been 'favourable' towards Balogh's proposals.[21]

The Public Bevanite Group

The minutes of the Group meeting for 13th March refer to a 'report on Contacts with Ministers re Group Paper 82' (Fair Shares Under Rearmament). This means that Keep Left had been in contact with Ministers for some months leading up to the crisis. They had lobbied, circulated papers and kept open lines of communication. The presence of Bevan's secretary in the group strengthened those connections whilst Foot was in constant touch with Bevan's wife Jennie Lee through the Tribune editorial board. Foot suggests that Bevan was ultra-secretive, and kept his Privy Councillor's oath.

'. . . while he was in the government, no interchange occurred between him and any left wing groups in Parliament. The Keep Left group had offered the most consistent

> and coherent criticisms of government policy and several of its lines of criticism had coincided with or overlapped Bevan's in the Cabinet'.[22]

The Attlee letter and the testimony of Foot imply that collective responsibility was not at any point breached, but that the Prime Minister was clearly anxious on this point. Michael Foot's account of his own and the Keep Left group's role in the process of political differentiation is modest to say the least, if not self-effacing.

Hunter claims it was Harold Davies who persuaded the Group to approach the three ex-Ministers[23] but a great deal of contact had already been established by this late stage. Even then Bevan 'by no means rushed to accept the offer' since 'he had his own platform in Tribune from which he could address the rank and file of the party. He did not need a small and uninfluential group to disseminate his ideas' and 'he could have done all he wished without the formal apparatus of the group'.[24] Whilst there is a great deal of truth in this statement it does rather beg the question of why the leading personnel of Keep Left became leaders of the Labour Party and the chief Ministers of Labour governments a decade or so later. This fact indicates that there was more to the Keep Left Group historically than whether or not individual members of it needed the group, or were using it for their own purposes.[25]

Andrew Roth confirms the contact between Keep Left and Ministers,

> 'Early in 1951 Bevan and to a lesser extent Wilson, began to discuss their positions with leading members of the Keep Left group without necessarily agreeing on tactics.'[26]

and indeed on the biggest tactical question of all—resignation, Crossman was to have the first of many disagreements with Bevan.

> 'Crossman and others were opposed to the April resignations of Bevan, Wilson and Freeman on tactical grounds.'[27]

The rebels were welcomed nevertheless. All three attended on April 26th 1951, along with Driberg, Delargy, Will Griffiths,

Jennie Lee, Tim Mackay. From this historic meeting there were some notable unexplained absences—Brockway, Stephen Swingler and Tom Williams, whilst George Wigg returned to the group from his January resignation, at the following meeting.

The Bevanite group proper really begins here. The members at this historic meeting were,[28]

Richard Acland (KL)	John Freeman
Aneurin Bevan	Will Griffiths
Barbara Castle (KL)	Leslie Hale (KL)
Dick Crossman (KL)	Jennie Lee
Harold Davies (KL)	Tim Mackay
Hugh Delargy	Ian Mikardo (KL)
Tom Driberg	Harold Wilson
Michael Foot (KL)	

Seven of the fifteen present were either authors of the Keep Left manifestos or members of the group prior to the influx of the Bevanites. The chair was held by Keep Lefter Ian Mikardo. Jo Richardson who had been secretary of the Keep Left group since Mikardo's election to the NEC the previous October, became the secretary to the Bevanites. The minutes began at square one again, and minute number four discloses that whilst the matter of the group's name was discussed, and several suggestions were made, nothing was decided. The term 'Bevanite' was beginning to be used in parliamentary circles in relation to those who sympathised with the former Minister of Labour,[29] but not in relation to the group. Fear of a split and the still fresh memory of Zilliacus's expulsion was one reason why the Keep Left was not renamed,[30] and so the term 'Bevanites' began to prevail, even though the man after whom they were named had a poor attendance record.

The first meeting discussed 'matters inherited from the Keep Left Group'—amongst them the organisation of increasingly popular Brains Trusts, and the question of economic advisers.[31] For the rest of 1951 and beyond the Group grappled with a series of complex inter-related problems for which very little recognition has been given them by critics such as Coates who reduces Bevanism to mere 'parliamentary manoeuvring'.[32] These problems can be categorised as follows,

a) The degree of breadth and exclusiveness of the group at parliamentary level,

b) The working out of policy questions *without impinging on the sovereignty of conference.*

c) The public propaganda of the group and its relations with the ranks.

It is not being suggested here that the Bevanite group at any time solved these problems, merely that it addressed itself to them in a very serious manner, with much agonising and thought, and that therefore the charge of parliamentary manoeuvring is shallow and unworthy. Any group of socialists in the Labour Party seeking a path forward would need ponder just such questions and examine the Bevanites' record. Cautious recruitment went on through 1951. Each new suggested MP was discussed in terms of suitability by the group.[33] Not all of those suggested were actually contacted. Group supporters were given the responsibility of discussing with prospective members. The first substantial inflow followed the April 26th meeting. Nine hard core Bevanites joined simultaneously on 30th April,[34] but thereafter recruitment proceeded with great circumspection. One important recruit was Lord Faringdon.[35] Meetings took place in the summer recess. Bevan's frequent absences did not dampen enthusiasm.[36] Harold Wilson succeeded Mikardo as group Chairman later in the year. Ten specialist groups were set up for the consideration of policy. The lists of these groups were circulated in November, by which time the process of policy formulation was becoming well established. But in the matter of organisation a surprising degree of cohesion and centralised control is evident in the remarkable document 'A Plan for Mutual Aid. Group Paper No. 12.' The first signs of such a plan were the appearance of a map of the constituencies where *group members* had small majorities, drawn up for the purpose of working out tours and itineraries for speaking engagements, whereby members would assist each other in propaganda work and Brains Trusts.[37] Paper No. 13 appeared on 28th July and contained details of the daily movements of each of those group members involved in the campaign of meetings. The document was marked 'confidential' and called for members to help in converting the arrangements into 'a time schedule covering the whole 19 nights of the campaign which will show where every member is, on what day, and when he is away from his constituency.'[38] Andrew Roth has emphasised how beneficial such campaigns were for Harold Wilson personally due to Huyton being a very marginal seat at the time, but this ought not to blind us to the fact that the plan for mutual aid was *exclusive to group members*. The Bevanites, in what was to become an election year, concentrated all their energies on their *own members'* marginal constituencies and not marginal Labour seats in general. And in doing so they planned to harness the energies of 'friends' outside the parliamentary party.[39] Perhaps as a reaction to this tightness of organisation and the concern at the loss of the election (in which Bevanite marginals did very much better than other Labour marginals) a discussion opened in the late autumn on the nature of the group. Majority opinion appeared to favour the need for a larger, cohesive but non-exclusive group. Such a view was perhaps the natural outcome of the election which had transformed the perspective from one of capturing the leadership of a governing party, to one of preparation, over some years, for a Labour victory in which more Labour MPs might be won over to the Bevanite views on policy. Benn Levy produced a memorandum for group discussion which partially echoed these sentiments,

> 'The result of the General Election and of the voting at Scarborough must involve a completely new view of the functions of "Keep Left" inside the Labour Party. Both these events have shown that we no longer represent minority opinion, save in the Trade Union oligarchy and possibly in the Parliamentary party. It would be folly therefore to continue an exclusiveness which in fact gives the appearance of a minority clique. Nothing could be more damaging.'

Levy proposed 'the next stage of evolution for Keep Left' was to expand to at least 100-strong and to develop policies for future Labour parliaments.[40] Jennie Lee and Fenner Brockway too wanted a larger group. Argument appears to have been sharp at some points but it was finally decided that the group should continue to expand slowly in ones and twos, and that from time to time there should be meetings open to all PLP members on specific subjects. The first of these was to be Balogh speaking on the economic situation in November. The plan for rapid expansion to a hundred, even if it had been possible, held dangers of precipitating a split by challenging the authority of the party itself, and all realised that this was undesirable. The solution was the occasional 'open' meeting to demonstrate the group's non-exclusiveness.

However on the part of Bevan and Wilson there was even some discussion about rejoining the front bench, and giving up work on a Keep Left policy statement in January 1952. This was talking non-exclusiveness to extremes and would have made nonsense of the 'Bevanite' grouping's very existence.[41] The policy statement in question was the successor to *One Way Only* which had sold 100,000 copies during the summer and autumn,[42] and *Going Our Way*, in great demand just prior to the announcement of the election. The manner in which these policy documents were produced is further strong evidence of substantial group planning and control.

One Way Only was planned at a May group meeting. The outline was discussed and sections of it allotted to those with relevant expertise in foreign, economic and domestic policy. Foot agreed to publish it as part of a 'Tribune' series.[43] Later the draft synopsis was discussed.[44] When it was ready, careful plans for the press conference announcing it were drawn up.[45] This care in the presentation of the public propaganda of the group does not suggest a casual coterie of parliamentary friends but a serious political formation fully aware of its popular support in the party ranks, meeting the need for policy discussion at all levels of the movement. Likewise in its conduct of internal policy formulation there was a high degree of organisation, preparation and deliberation. On December 14th and 15th there took place what can only be called a conference of the parliamentary Bevanite group at Buscott Park, home of Lord Faringdon. It lasted two days and included the reading of detailed policy papers. Wilson delivered a 3,500-word paper as if 'for a Cabinet Committee'.[46] Crossman read one on Anglo-American relations, and Bevan was detailed to lead the summing up at the end of the second day. The Buscott Park conference was attended by 23 Bevanites and came to certain definite decisions. Due to the aggravation of the economic crisis by the deepening war in Korea, it was now considered that even the 'One Way Only' proposals were out of date, and therefore a new pamphlet would need to be out by March, 1952.[47] Wilson and Mikardo were to set up a subcommittee to produce a draft for discussion on 28th January. Balogh and Crossman would produce a paper on dollar aid. Mikardo and Brockway would write one on contacts with French socialists.

Despite this rigorous co-ordination of its activities the group did not seek to restrict Bevanite candidatures for the NEC. This was left open with some dissenting voices.[48] Nor were there any restrictions placed on those who might seek to serve on the Shadow Cabinet.[49]

Other matters which occupied the group's time in this period were appointing spokesmen to put the group line in parliamentary debates[50] and discovering the leanings of Labour candidates in bye elections.[51] There were also discussions with the 'General Council of the Victory for Socialism group'[52] and advice to Konni Zilliacus on how to get back into the Labour Party. The fact that both VFS and Zilliacus took the initiative in these overtures indicates the central position the Bevanites had now assumed in relation to other left tendencies. Nor did the group neglect its links with the wider movement. Sheffield engineers requested more Bevanite speakers after Wilson had addressed a private conference of AEU members there. But care was taken to check with AEU headquarters and the Sheffield City Labour Party before Bevan agreed to do a public meeting.[53]

A perpetual problem was press publicity. Tribune and the New Statesman were always accessible through Michael Foot and Richard Crossman respectively, but the group needed the coverage of mass circulation newspapers. Several of the Bevanites had access to Hugh Massingham of the Observer. Driberg wrote regularly for the Sunday Reynolds News and Crossman also had lines open to the Sunday Pictorial.[54] The Bevanites had done enough between April 1951 and March 1952 to convince the old guard union leaders and the PLP right wing that they constituted a serious threat to their dominance of the movement. They at least were in no doubt as to the effectiveness of Bevanite organisation, especially after 30th November

1951 when Desmond Donnelly began leaking group information to Hugh Dalton.[55]

After the press had spotlighted a plan 'to grab the Socialist leadership' in February[56] TGWU chief Deakin announced 'The trade unions will not be misled by the Tribune group of politicians who seek a short cut to the leadership of the party'.[57] On 5th March came the '57 varieties'[58] rebellion in the Defence debate when the Bevanites were joined in their abstention on the official opposition amendment by a combination of pacifists and non-Bevanite left critics. More Bevanite baiting from the Daily Herald prefaced the fateful 19th March meeting of the PLP, which reimposed standing orders for the first time since the landslide victory of 1945 had rendered them unnecessary. This step marked a turning point in the history of the Bevanite group and, in a broader sense, in the post-war history of the Labour Party. The Group was well aware of the impending crisis at the beginning of March when they took a decision to encourage constituency parties to send in resolutions condemning the Daily Herald's attack (at the time the Herald was the official Labour paper with the TUC holding 49 per cent of the shares).

The 'Open' Bevanite Group under Standing Orders

It was at the 19th March meeting that Charles Pannell made his allegation of 'a special group within the party, organised, secret, and with their own whips on'.[59] In this charge lay the seeds of the 'party within a party'[60] dispute which escalated in the Autumn.

There had been 'special groups' before of course. Keep Left was one such group. No one had suggested expelling it or curtailing its activities. However the charge that the Bevanites had their own whips (which really was not at any time the case) was almost as damning. Needless to say no evidence for this was ever brought forward. Certainly the '57 varieties' rebellion could hardly be cited as the handiwork of Bevanite whips.

At the time in question between twenty and twenty-five were meeting on a regular weekly basis[61] with Bevan himself the most notable truant. Indeed at this time he and Wilson considered winding up work on a new policy pamphlet. Bevan was certainly against exclusiveness in the group and he more than anyone disliked 'the cliqueyness of a closely knit group such as Ian Mikardo delighted in organising.'[62]

At the 11th March meeting, the plan of the right wing party leaders had been to demand not only the reimposition of *strict* standing orders but a signed acceptance of them by the fifty seven. They believed that only a handful would refuse to sign and that the recalcitrant minority instead of all 57, could be expelled.[63]

In the event a 'moderate' amendment was carried 162–73 which contained a milder interpretation of standing orders.[64] One week later the 1945 resolution suspending standing orders was revoked. Under these, mere suspension was the penalty for persistent disobedience to party decisions. However the vote in the PLP on 11th March was significant in that moderate opinion led, in this case, by Strauss, Strachey and Kenneth Younger had prevailed *by the grace of the unions.* Crossman claimed that Attlee

> 'complete misjudged the attitude of the unions which realistically assess the strength of Bevanism in the rank and file. Attlee's support was exclusively middle class at the meeting.'[65]

Crossman noted down the names of the leading Gaitskellite new thinkers who had voted with the losing right-wing minority on 11th March. Roth claims that Tom O'Brien of Cinema Technicians helped turn the tide at the meeting and that he was 'sensitive to the Bevanite ferment among union militants'. Perhaps this PLP meeting provides a more reliable guide to the essence of the Bevanites' struggle than the still popular mythology of Bevanite constituencies against stalwart trades unionism. One very important consequence of the re-imposition of standing orders has been highlighted by Leslie Hunter—

> 'Held in check by the standing orders in the Commons the Bevanites concentrated on extra-parliamentary activity . . . and so came into head-on collision with the leaders of the big trades unions'.[66]

Whilst too much could be read into this observation it remains a fact that within a few months of the PLP gag

Michael Foot launched an amazingly transformed weekly 'Tribune' with a campaigning Industrial reporter in Ian Aitken (now of the Guardian), which gave trades union news the edge over book reviews for the first time, and won for the paper its biggest ever circulation figures. Soon Deakin was being tackled at the dock gates. None of this may have been consciously worked out, but it was undoubtedly one of the practical effects of the PLP vote. Certainly the minutes of the group give little evidence of such a clearly-arrived-at alternative strategy. The vote, after all, was a blow and for some weeks the group was reeling from the effects. The argument about its nature and functioning took on a sharper tone. Geoffrey Bing thought suspension of the group might be considered 'before it was suspended for them'.[67] On 20th March the group considered the PLP ruling but came to no decision. But it did launch a campaign for resolutions from CLPs and trade union branches.[68] Five days later the question of new members being admitted was deferred in the absence of Bevan. It was now almost a year since the resignations of the three, and it appeared that the man most insensitive to the group's fortunes was Bevan himself. It was not until 10th April that he decided to attend and then only in a vain attempt to persuade his followers to be less exclusive. On 22nd April a Geoffrey Bing memorandum[69] proposed 'throwing open' the group to like-minded people. This, objectors warned, would make it impossible to plan Brains Trusts, tactics at PLP meetings and to have secretaries and minutes. What transpired was a compromise which kept the group in being with minutes, secretaries, and tactical discussions as before, but which threw itself open once a week (Tuesdays at 1.30).[70] This arrangement was more a result of difficulties in getting notice board permission from the Sergeant at Arms.[71] It certainly did not resolve the question in the Group and cut no ice at all with the party establishment.

But the group was as tight as ever. Potential recruits were being graded at group meetings in late April as 'commended' and 'highly commended'. Lord Silkin was 'dropped for non-attendance'.[72] The group began to campaign strongly on the issue of the bombing of the Yalu river power stations. It demanded a delay in German rearmament. Immediate membership and attendance picked up sharply. No less than thirty attended on 24th June—even Bevan was there.[73]

At this meeting the idea of a looser association named 'Labour Forum' was mooted at the same time as new Group sub-committees were announced to take charge of the different areas of work! And one of these, the Brains Trust Sub-Committee was inundated with CLP requests for Brains Trusts. On 1st July there were 32 in attendance discussing, amongst other things, sales of the planned weekly Tribune. Still more lists of contacts were being considered on 15th July. Meanwhile Bevan's book *In Place of Fear* was a 'huge publishing success.'[74] It was hardly surprising therefore that an enterprising journalist with an eye for a story should discover 'a party within a party'. On 5th August A. J. Cummings quoted this allegation in a News Chronicle article.

> 'Last week R. R. Stokes, Labour MP for Ipswich and Lord Privy Seal in the last government condemned the Bevanites as "a party within a party".'[75]

The article went on to say,

> 'The Bevanites hold regular meetings to decide their party line, quite independently of the official party meetings . . . They have organised a travelling circus which tours the constituencies crusading for the Bevanite slogans and attacking the official leadership. One notable performance at Birmingham Town Hall last March excluded all the Birmingham MPs except one—Mr Julius Silverman that irrepressible left winger . . . A Shadow Cabinet has been set up consisting of Mr Bevan (Prime Minister), Mr Crossman (Foreign Secretary), and Mr Freeman (Minister Without Portfolio).
>
> Messrs Bing and Mikardo are the back room organisers with Mr Ted Castle (husband of Barbara Castle MP and an ex-editor of Picture Post) as "national agent". Speeches in the House of Commons are allocated and formulated in advance.
>
> Their ready made propaganda organ is Tribune which circulates at special rates inside Constituency Labour Parties . . .'[76]

A storm now broke in the party. What had happened between March and August was that the PLP vote of 19th March had backfired on the right wing by forcing the Bevanites to engage, to a greater degree, in what might be called 'mass work' in the ranks. The Cummings article significantly notes three examples of extra parliamentary Bevanite activity as against only two at PLP level. Press speculation rumbled on during the run-up to party conference and after. Patrick Gordon Walker in a speech at Dorking alleged 'a deliberately organised party within a party'.[77] Lord Pakenham also used the same phrase, stating that the Bevanites 'concert their own line and choose their own spokesmen'.[78]

Hugh Cudlipp's Sunday Pictorial embraced the campaign with a front page leader demanding 'End the Bevan Myth'.[79] In September and October both Mikardo and Bevan accepted the challenge and replied in Tribune. Bevan argued that 'Mr Cummings of the News Chronicle drew upon his imagination —or a bad brief . . .' Bevan declared '. . . there never has been a word of truth in it'. But in his refutation he only *confimed what Cummings had said* denying only the conclusion, that these activities constituted proof of 'a party within a party'.

> 'Of course we have been holding group meetings. This is a normal feature of parliamentary activity. Some people hold weekly dinners which are of course attended by people of like mind, a function much too expensive for the rank and file of the party to afford. It was quite natural that when the three Ministers resigned they should consult with each other and with colleagues of similar disposition. To forbid this would make parliamentary life intolerable. The group heard papers read by economists and statistical experts, discussed the studied subjects so as to inform ourselves about the issues coming before parliament.
>
> Furthermore one of its most important functions was to organise Brains Trusts throughout the country for the purpose of Socialist education and also to promote the sales of Tribune and so help keep an independent Socialist Press alive.
>
> Dozens of constituency parties can testify to the value of

these Brains Trusts for promotion Socialist propaganda and for attracting large audiences (and revenue) . . .'[80]

The point at issue therefore was whether all the activities which both sides agreed were taking place constituted an embryonic *party*. It might have assisted to consider the Bevanites as a faction within the Labour Party, but this was after all a living battle between left and right and the correct academic term to describe the Bevanite formation was not relevant to the combatants. But the Labour Party had tolerated the ILP as a 'party within a party' for many years and to this day has affiliated to it the Co-operative party, some of whose members have politics almost indistinguishable from the Communist Party. What made the 'party within a party' controversy in the autumn of 1952 unique was that it took place at a time when the ranks of the party were still pressing forward strongly against the party-union bureaucracy, as the Brains Trust attendances and the Morecambe 'coup' on the NEC clearly prove.

At the Labour Party conference on 1st October, Deakin as fraternal delegate from the TUC attacked the 'Tribune Organisation'. He demanded,

'Let them get rid of their whips; dismiss their business managers and conform to the party Constitution . . . Let them cease the vicious attacks they have launched upon those with whom they disagree, abandon their vituperation and their carping criticism which appears regularly in Tribune'.[81]

The man who had been instrumental in terminating the Transport House-Tribune agreement two years earlier, and who now saw the paper flourishing as never before, had returned to the attack. J. P. W. Mallalieu was noticeably more accommodating in public than Bevan had been.

'Gaitskell will, I think, accept my personal word that the Bevanites have never had whips, never had a business manager, never had a campaign manager, that they have never thought of appointing such functionaries and that therefore they cannot dismiss them even when advised to do so by Arthur. I'm sure Gaitskell will dismiss such Transport and Generalisations.'[82]

But despite these public denials many Group members *were* anxious to reduce the group's cohesiveness. This may have been recognition that there was an element of truth in the right wing's allegations, or it may have been an understandable weakening under the pressure of a truly formidable press barrage.

Crossman wrote in his diary on the 1st August, *before* the Cummings article had appeared,

> 'The new Tribune may get the Group out of a serious difficulty. If, as we have all agreed, three or four of us are to stand for the Parliamentary Committee it will really be impossible for the Bevanite group to go on as at present. Four members of the Parliamentary Committee could not possibly report back to the group outside without violating the principle of Collective Responsibility. However we might perhaps change the nature of the group with an organisation connected with Tribune affairs generally and *stop it being a strict group in its present form.*'[83]
>
> (*my emphasis—MJ*)

Crossman in this same entry believed Brains Trusts could be re-named 'Tribune Brains Trusts', so that 'we could get away from this word "Bevanite"'! Here writes a man who is very well aware that the danger lies in the fact that the Bevanite group is *not purely a parliamentary coterie.* The 'seriousness' of the situation, for Crossman, lay in the Group's having become a channel whereby the strength and vitality of the mass movement was able to find expression at the highest levels of the *party* and the *parliamentary apparatus.* How to separate the two: that was his problem. The right wing sensed this danger too, hence their extreme sensitivity on the issue.

However, attempts at forestalling the press onslaught and the right wing offensive proved of no avail. The Bevanites took six of the seven seats in the constituency section of the NEC at the Morecambe conference, confirming the worst fears of the Gaitskell-Deakin wing. At Stalybridge on 5th October Gaitskell alleged that one-sixth of the constituency party delegates had appeared to be 'Communist or Communist inspired'[84]. This wild allegation took no account of the Cominform's portrayal of Bevanism as a cunning manoeuvre on the part of the right wing (owing to the former Labour Minister's admiration for Tito's Yugoslavia). Indeed, the Slansky trial that same autumn had ingeniously 'implicated' Crossman in the Titoist plot which Slansky was supposed to have organised. Since this was the regular weekly diet on which Communist Party members were being nourished in their party information bulletin World News and Views, then even if a sixth of the delegates had been Communists, it would not have helped the Bevanites greatly in their NEC victory.[85]

But in the atmosphere of the time, such fine points carried little weight. It was after all the middle of the McCarthy period. The right wing could weave amalgams of Bevanites with Communists just as readily as the Soviet Communists could invent plots between Bevanites, Titoists and fascists. As late as 1955 Gaitskell, in a private conversation with Crossman, discerned 'extraordinary parallels between Nye and Adolf Hitler'.[86]

Between Deakin's conference request for the banning of the group and the PLP meeting of 23rd October the press inquisition against the 'party within a party' relentlessly built up, with the Manchester Guardian making the pace.[87] Williamson of the Municipal Workers and Party Secretary Morgan Phillips (ironically, later, himself censured by the Gaitskellites!) added their voices. Fresh from victory at Morecambe the Bevanites began to buckle under the enormous strain imposed upon them by these manoeuvres.

The Clandestine Bevanite Group

With scant regard for democracy within his own group Bevan was about to announce its dissolution without consulting its membership! Jennie Lee 'slightly embarassedly' told Dick Crossman in a telephone conversation on 13th October,

> 'that Nye was composing an article for Tribune announcing the dissolution of the Group. However she seemed quite eager that I should come in this very evening while he is writing it but I fancy some other members of the group will have to be consulted too . . .'[88]

Foot, Wilson, Mikardo and Crossman debated for three and a half hours that evening whether to abolish a group that had not officially existed since March 19th, or whether to 'throw it open' for a second time. Bevan was for throwing it open so that everybody could attend 'and see for themselves the ridiculousness of the stories which have been told about it.'[89] Crossman and Mikardo resisted this proposition initially arguing it would discard the victory at Morecambe. Bevan however became 'very angry',

> 'to continue the group now is to perpetuate the schism . . . if you were to continue the group in these conditions and I were leader I would have you expelled. The group is intolerable.'

These private sentiments were very different to those Bevan was expressing publicly in Tribune, and seem not far short of a personal admission *that the Bevanite group did represent a party within a party.*

The group now demanded a tactics meeting, since many of them sensed, correctly, that they were being left out in the cold. Nonetheless the decision to throw open the group, which amounted to a conscious retreat before the party leadership's offensive, was taken *before* the group assembled on 15th October. Articles by Bevan (in Tribune) and Crossman (in the New Statesman) were already in type. Luckily for the conspirators the group endorsed Bevan's view, even though when the first new 'open meeting' took place on 21st October only four outsiders turned up. Attlee still was not satisfied. He rejected the 'open group' idea. At the PLP meeting which imposed the ban on 23rd October he seemed to confirm Bevan's private view.

> 'You can argue a lot about Groups, but they're like the elephant. I may not be able to define one, but I know one when I see one . . . what I disapprove of is an omnicompetent group like the ILP used to be'[90]

Clandestine activity now began. But Crossman had some pertinent diary comments summarising the period leading up to the ban.

> 'For the twelve months up to Morecambe, Bevanism, since it was not banned by Attlee, was considered quite alright and the party was having the best of both worlds with the

dynamic left free to be dynamic and the right not permitted to curb the left. Now the whole atmosphere has changed. *The really resolute Bevanites in the constituencies think the disbandment of the group is parliamentary tit-for-tat and are anxious lest the Bevanites will betray them by not fighting.* The right wingers have now raised their heads and said "so it was a conspiracy after all" . . . *I suspect the whole of party life has suddenly removed except in solid Bevanite areas.*'[91] (*my emphasis—MJ*)

His next entry (28th October) contains details of the group meeting. There was only one item on the agenda—disbandment. It was quickly decided to obey the party's ruling, but to establish a new amorphous set up with no minutes, no secretaries. This disbandment of the group was to be issued in a press statement held back for Tribune's convenience. 'Really' said Crossman 'Tribune is getting a confounded nuisance'.[92] With such sentiments did some of the parliamentary Bevanites begin the process of disengaging themselves from the Bevanism below. Much later Wilson was to echo these sentiments when he declared that Bevanism 'could well do without Tribune'.[93] How close Labour was to a split in that autumn of 1952 is not easy to assess but Bevan was probably right when he said in Tribune 'the task of maintaining the unity of Labour falls primarily on the Left'.[94] Had the Bevanites not complied with the PLPs ruling and continued with the organisation as it had been since 19th March, the trade union chiefs and the party hierarchy could hardly have ignored the rebuff. The Bevanites decision was a turning point. Henceforth the group led an existence of clandestine meetings and private lunches. Over a period of many months this had two effects. Firstly the leading Bevanites became remote from the rest of the parliamentary group—leading eventually to the rift between the centre-left Bevanites led by Crossman and Wilson who differentiated themselves out of the mainstream Bevanite current; and secondly, it presented obstacles to the organisation of work in the party and union ranks.

One feature worthy of special note in this clandestine period of Bevanism is that whilst the parliamentary group languished, and eventually disintegrated as a cohesive group formation, the mass work and propaganda side of the group flourished as never before. This latter aspect of Bevanism took the form of *increased Brains Trust activity in 1953* followed by a *drive into the unions in the course of 1954*. But even in this period the links between the parliamentary group and the extra-parliamentary wing were never completely broken. The forward thrust of the left in the party continued throughout the fifties and the early sixties, even in periods of heavy electoral defeat for Labour such as 1959–61. There was a muted, molecular development after 1957. This was enough to carry the former Bevanites into the leadership of the party within a decade of the movement's high point, enabling them to form governments when the disastrous years of Gaitskell's leadership had been eclipsed by the Profumo scandal.

The First and Second Eleven

There were no contingency plans when the ban was imposed. The group went through an extremely critical period for some months in the winter of 1952–53, but a clear pattern of organisation eventually emerged. The Bevanites adapted to the ban by splitting their activities into two fields covered by a 'first eleven' and a 'second eleven'. The first eleven consisted of parliamentary Bevanites meeting clandestinely at weekly lunches at Crossman's house. The second eleven contained the most organisation-conscious of the parliamentary Bevanites, meeting regularly with the Tribunite activists and propagandists for the organisation of mass work. Thus the parliamentary and extra-parliamentary facets of the work were structurally separate but linked by the presence of the old Bevanite organisation experts, Mikardo chief amongst them. This differentiation took some months to evolve. On November 25th the group met at dinner and considered the 'rapid disintegration' that had occurred. Crossman captures the mood,[95]

> 'The absence of a weekly discussion means that the members no longer thought things out with a common mind. How are we to cope with this . . .?'

One solution was the appointment of six 'scoutmasters' to contact six or seven other Bevanite MPs on a regular basis.

This arrangement was adopted but the parliamentary group shrank as Foot describes,

'So over the next few years a much attenuated Bevanite group—six members of the Executive, Bevan himself, Crossman, Driberg, Castle, Mikardo, Wilson plus the journalists who kept in contact with Tribune and the New Statesman, Jennie Lee, John Freeman, J. P. W. Mallalieu and myself—assembled every Tuesday lunchtime while Parliament was sitting, at Dick Crossman's house at 9 Vincent Square . . .'[96]

In the early months Bevan's tour of India did not help matters, and Crossman noted that the group was languishing in his absence. But it revived on his return. The extra-parliamentary work did not falter, but took on *new momentum* in the Spring of 1953. This suggests that some informal but highly effective second eleven arrangement may have already been taking shape. Tribune circulation manager at this time, Peggy Duff, explains how the second eleven worked and developed . . .

'In the beginning it was an informal group but it gradually became more formal and more important *as the heat on the first eleven increased.* After the famous resolution was passed by the Parliamentary Labour Party . . . the Second XI was *promoted*. From 1954 on certainly it met regularly once a month, kept minutes of its proceedings, established sub-committees and took in a few MPs to provide a link with the House. It even organised occasional social gatherings, usually at Lord Faringdon's house at Buscott Park . . .'[97] (*my emphasis—MJ*).

The 'promotion' of the Second Eleven *after* the ban is clear indication that the informal meetings were already in existence before it. And from this account it is evident that as the first eleven became attenuated and ceased minute taking, the second eleven grew from informal to formal status with minute taking and committee structures by 1954. One set of minutes of the second eleven dated 22nd September[98] reveals the personnel involved. Present at this meeting were Mikardo, Crossman, Bing and Jennie Lee, all of them old Bevanites and part of the 'link' of which Duff has spoken. Also present were Ben Parkin and Hugh Jenkins, who had more frequently been associated with VFS in the past, and who were not, at this stage, MPs. Other key personnel present were Ian Aitken, Tribune industrial reporter; Bob Edwards, Tribune editor; Peggy Duff, Tribune circulation manager; journalist Terry Lancaster and Bevanite secretary Jo Richardson. This is what the second eleven was looking like by late 1954 when the Tribune drive into dockland and the unions was just beginning.

Duff says that amongst the second eleven's activities were the manning of four important sub-committees—on elections to compile lists of constituencies and possible candidates; on contacts, to discover co-thinkers; on policy and propaganda; and on conferences. Other MPs who frequently attended were Foot, Castle, Freeman, Swingler and Harold Davies. Stan Orme and Albert Booth were also members, as were Ralph Miliband and Ted Castle. The selection of Bevanite sympathisers to get on to the candidates lists was an important part of these proceedings. In a private interview Castle expanded on the second eleven's work.

> 'Most of the second eleven's activities were secret but I think our antagonists guessed its existence. We did make a number of attempts to create a rank and file base. For instance on one occasion we invited Mr Bedford, Secretary of the London Co-operative Party to a second eleven meeting. This association might have given us the opportunity for a London organisation . . . We also considered working through the Union of Democratic Control and Ben Parkin was our connection here . . .'[99]

On the formation of the second eleven Ted Castle says this—

> 'The second eleven actually took form at a Labour Party meeting during the Margate conference of 1953. We held the meeting in a downstairs room and all manner of lefts came along, MPs and others . . . The second eleven met regularly on Sunday afternoons in people's flats—our Highgate flat or Jo Richardson's place in Hornsey. We discussed at one time the scope for changes in our organisation due to our widening impact on the party. As I recall there were

no formal channels of communication between us and the first eleven although of course Jo Richardson was "secretary" to both the first and the second eleven. And of course the second eleven also worked hard for the party in electioneering . . . Our problem was how we could get the unions to reflect what was going on in the party . . . but always Aneurin had a real fear of causing a split in the party. You see none of us could ever forget the effect of the split of 1931 and the terrible consequences for the party.'[100]

What is established from these excerpts of Duff, Foot and Castle is not that the second eleven amounted to any formidable organisational apparatus but that Bevanism *did not die organisationally* after October 1952, that it carried on clandestine work in a systematic determined way despite the bans of the party machine, and that its extra-parliamentary wing became *stronger after the ban.* Proof of this and of the deep concern it caused to the right wing was the incredible attempt to ban the Brains Trusts in the Spring of 1953. The second eleven itself certainly continued its activities into the summer of 1956 when, on the authority of Peggy Duff, 'word came from Harold Wilson that the existence of the second XI had been observed. He told Barbara who told Ted that the NEC was proposing to take action against them.'[101]

Brains Trusts

The Brains Trust movement was a remarkable phenomenon. It was no mere series of political meetings. It has been established that the first took place in the autumn of 1950 under the auspices of Keep Left and on the initiative of Ian Mikardo. From this time until well into 1954 and beyond they continued. In 1953 the demand for them was 'insatiable', according to Peggy Duff . . .

> 'As 1954 dawned Tribune announced that it had held its 150th Brains Trust and that forty parties were still waiting.'[102]

Paul Foot has described the movement as 'a massive apparatus of Brains Trusts held at the rate of four or five a week'.[103] Eventually there was hardly a constituency where one had not been held. Nor were they confined to the industrial heartlands of the working class—even places like Banbury and Chichester held successful Brains Trusts. But in London, Liverpool, Sheffield and the main centres they were huge affairs with thousands involved rather than hundreds. The London meetings were sometimes all ticket. Entry was not restricted to party members.

> 'The Brains Trusts were popular because they brought not one good speaker but four or five and they allowed for audience participation. The chaps on the floor joined in and could argue in a series of supplementary questions with the team on the platform.'[104]

Why should people turn up in such great numbers on Saturday afternoons and Sunday evenings in Co-operative halls, Labour clubs and schools? Partly it can be explained by the fact that this was not yet the era of television as far as millions of workers were concerned. There was a compelling desire to discuss, to air the problems of the movement after the defeat of the first ever majority Labour government. It may be that such a ferment of discussion has not been equalled in the movement. But this mood in the working class also sheds light on what some people have considered the organisational 'weakness' of Bevanism. In one sense even the second eleven's attempts at creating a grass roots organisation was *superfluous*. The Brains Trusts showed that what was needed was discussion, and that to facilitate this, very little in the way of sophisticated organisation was required. The structure of the Labour Party and its heavy pre-occupation with business at General Management Committee meetings combined with the tight scheduling of conference agendas makes far-reaching and prolonged discussion difficult, if not impossible. The Brains Trusts were a response to the needs for discussion of world and national issues that did not interfere with the day-to-day running of their party and its business affairs. All that was required was for the Bevanite activists who ran many of the constituencies to contact the second eleven organisers, and from then on the local party organisations would lay on the meetings and advertising. The Bevanites used the *existing party machinery* in the localities. At *that* level there was no need of 'a party within a party.'

Since Bevanism was a mass current rooted in the ready-organised party mass, such additional organisation as was required was decidedly *simple.* Here is an example of the general political rule—the greater the involvement of the mass, the less, and the less complex, the organisation required to give it expression. (Hence the formidable bureaucracy in sectarian formations insulated from the mass movement.) The party hierarchy's allegation that the group were 'a party within a party' obscures the fact that Bevanism was a mass current in the party ranks, by spotlighting the organisational requirements of the Bevanite MPs.

Strangely enough this view is augmented both by Foot, himself a Bevanite, and Bevanism's critics such as David Coates, *both* of whom are anxious to affirm the modesty and innocence of Bevanite organisation, and both of whom would deny that there was a 'party within a party'.

NOTES

1. For example see *British Social Democracy* (p. 185) by David Howell, Croom Helm, London 1976. Even in this balanced review of Labour history we find the following,
'Some attempts were made to organise within the constituencies but essentially the left's grass roots activities never extended beyond the holding of "Brains Trusts", which provided a platform for virtuosity, but little scope for influence over events.' And on p. 189 . . . 'Some of the reasons for failure were highly specific. The personalisation of disputes that followed inexorably from the domination of the left by articulate, forceful spokesmen diverted attention from the work of policy reappraisal. The difficulties of reaching agreement within an army of individualists have already been noted. These were exacerbated by the liking of some left wingers for elaborate tactical manoeuvres, and in contrast, by the distaste of others for any collective work.'
See also, Coates, *op. cit.* (p. 193–95)
2. *The Class Struggle in Parliament* (p. 102) by Eric Heffer, Victor Gollancz, London 1973.
Heffer argues that the modern Tribune group can usually put a clear line at PLP meetings,
'The Tribune Group today is very different from the Bevanite

group of yesteryear. The Bevanites were mainly academics with a few trade unionists. They had slender links with the trade union movement.'

3. This phrase, later used by A. J. Cummings of the News Chronicle on Tuesday, 5th August 1952 was parodied by Tom Driberg who described the Bevanites at one point as 'a smoking room within a smoking room'. Charles Pannell MP used it just prior to the March 1951 meeting of the PLP which reimposed Standing Orders.
4. *Harold Wilson, Yorkshire Walter Mitty* (p. 160) by Andrew Roth, McDonald & Jones, London 1977.
5. These minutes are in the possession of Jo Richardson, MP, formerly secretary to Ian Mikardo and also to the Keep Left and Bevanite groups. Copies of the minutes are in the possession of Andrew Roth of 'Parliamentary Profiles' an information service on parliament and MPs. The author was given access to Mr Roth's copies of the minutes and copies of selected entries from the unpublished Crossman diaries.
6. Tribune letter, 27.5.49, 'Keep Keep Left' by Stephen Swingler.
7. Brockway as a leading speaker at a VFS conference demanded the withdrawal of troops from Korea.
8. Keep Left minutes, 14.12.50.
9. Minute 197 of the Keep Left Group reports a long discussion on Korea resulting in assurances which the Group would seek from the P.M. It accepted however 'That we are committed to help the USA . . .' 4.7.50.
10. Keep Left Minute 205, 25th July, 1950.
11. Letter attached to minutes of 25th July Keep Left meeting.
12. Keep Left minute, 206, 25th July, 1950.
13. Keep Left minutes 6 & 7 October meeting. This meeting also decided that Jo Richardson should replace Ian Mikardo as Group Secretary since the latter's election to the NEC.
14. Keep Left minute 247, 28.11.50.
15. Keep Left minute 255 (ii), 5.12.50.
16. A letter from VFS in New Statesman, 24.2.51, says that VFS 'like the Socialist Europe Group we are prepared to sink our identities in any wider movement which may be formed to do the job more effectively.'
17. Leslie Hunter, *The Road to Brighton Pier,* (p. 42).
18. Keep Left, Minute 259, 12.12.50.
19. Letter attached to Keep Left minutes of 30th January 1951 and Minute 279 of the 31st January meeting.
20. Tom Balogh wrote Keep Left paper No. 80 in February, (itself an indication of the amount of discussion papers that had been produced in four years of the Group's existence) on the forthcoming budget. Seers is believed to have been the author of 'A Socialist Plan for Fair Shares under Rearmament' Paper 82 produced in March 1951.

21. Sunday Times, 25.3.51.
22. Foot, *op. cit. Vol. II*, (p. 434–44).
23. Hunter, *op. cit.* (p. 42).
24. as above, p. 43.
25. Roth, p. 141.
26. Roth, *op. cit.* (p. 140).
27. Roth, *op. cit.* (p. 140).
28. Keep Left, Minutes, 26.4.51.
29. Foot, *op. cit. Vol II*, p. 343.
30. Roth, *op. cit.* p. 144.
31. Thomas Balogh and Dudley Seers performed this role. They had joined with Foot five months earlier.
32. Coates, *op. cit.* p. 190.
33. Roth, *op. cit.* p. 151.
34. Bevanite Minutes, 30th April, 1951.
35. Bevanite Minutes, 26th September, 1951.
36. The secretary at one point inserted an ironic exclamation mark next to Bevan's name under 'apologies'.
37. Bevanite Minutes, 24th July, 1951.
38. Bevanite Minutes, 28.7.51 and 7.8.51.
39. A. J. P. Taylor was named as one to be approached.
40. Memorandum attached to Bevanite Minutes 30.10.51. The name of Levy is appended by hand.
41. Roth, *op. cit.* (p. 156) and Crossman's unpublished diaries for Monday, 21.1.52.
42. Tribune, 10.10.52.
43. Roth, *op. cit.* (p. 143).
44. Bevanite Minutes, 28.5.51.
45. Bevanite Minutes, 12.6.51.
46. Roth, *op. cit.* (p. 152).
47. Undated memorandum of the minutes of the Bevanite Group in the Roth papers. It appears to be December or March, and contains the 'decisions of the conference'.
48. Roth, *op. cit.* (p. 146).
49. Crossman's unpublished diaries entry for 30.10.51, in the Roth papers.
50. Bevanite Minutes, 24.7.51.
51. Bevanite Minutes, 10.7.51. Carmichael and Will Griffiths were entrusted with this task.
52. Bevanite Minutes, 12.9.51.
53. Roth, *op. cit.* (p. 151).
54. Roth, *op. cit.* (p. 143).
55. Foot, *op. cit. Vol II* (p. 358 Footnote).
56. Foot, *op. cit. Vol III* (p. 359) for details.
57. as above.
58. For details see below 'The Politics of Bevanism'.
59. Foot, *op. cit. Vol II* (p. 372).
60. Roth maintains that this phrase was first used by Pannell at

the PLP meeting of 19th March. But A. J. Cummings used it in August in the News Chronicle. See Roth, *op. cit.* (p. 159). This is a much more serious allegation than the phrase 'special group' which Foot uses in his Volume II. But it would not be the first time the press has rediscovered a piece of old news and re-presented it. Certainly the 'party within a party' row blew up in August.

61. Bevanite Group minutes, January and February, 1952.
62. Crossman's unpublished diaries, 10.4.52. Roth papers. Also quoted in Roth, *op. cit.* (p. 160).
63. Roth, *op. cit.* (p. 159). He quotes the iron rule that only rebellions of less than ten are punishable.
64. 'Such standing orders as will make it obligatory on all members to carry out decisions of the parliamentary party, taking into account the traditional conscience clause'. Roth, *op. cit.* (p. 159) quotes from this resolution.
65. Crossman Diary, 11.3.52, Roth papers.
66. Hunter, *op. cit.* (p. 52).
67. Roth, *op. cit.* (p. 160).
68. Bevanite minutes, 20.3.52.
69. Memorandum attached to Bevanite minutes, 22.4.52.
70. Crossman unpublished diaries, 10.4.52, Roth papers.
71. Bevanite minutes, 1.4.52.
72. Bevanite minutes, 29.4.52.
73. Bevanite minutes, 24.6.52.
74. Foot, *op. cit.* (p. 347). See below p. 305 footnote 22: 37,000 copies were sold.
75. News Chronicle, 5.8.52.
76. News Chronicle, 5.8.52.
77. Duff, *op. cit.* (p. 53). The author claims that Walker used it first and that Cummings took it up from Walker.
78. Tribune, 15.8.52.
79. Duff, *op. cit.* (p. 53).
80. Tribune, 17.10.52.
81. Tribune, 10.10.52.
82. Footnote in Foot, *op. cit. Vol. II* (p. 474).
83. Crossman's unpublished diaries, 13.10.52, Roth papers.
84. Ibid.
85. Roth, *op. cit.* (p. 170). Foot emphasises that 'One Way Only' was denounced 'as an imperialist war cry in Moscow'.
86. Crossman unpublished diaries, 27th October, 1952.
87. Foot, *op. cit.* (p. 384 footnote).
88. Crossman diaries quoted in Foot, *op. cit.* (p. 450).
89. Times, 6.10.52, quoting from his speech the previous day. Quoted in Foot, *op. cit.* (p. 383).
90. Roth, *op. cit.* (p. 170).
91. Crossman's unpublished diaries, 27.10.52. Roth papers.
92. Crossman unpublished diaries, 28.10.52. Roth papers.

93. Foot, *op. cit. Vol. II* (p. 454) quoting from Crossman's unpublished diaries.
94. Tribune, 17.10.52.
95. Crossman unpublished diaries, 26th November, 1952. Roth papers.
96. Foot, *op. cit. Vol. II* (p. 457).
97. *Left, Left, Left* by Peggy Duff (p. 46) Allison & Busby, London 1971.
98. These minutes are extensive and are in Jo Richardson MP's private papers. The photocopy of this one set are in the papers of Mr Andrew Roth, who was kind enough to let me peruse them. Access to the remainder proved not possible.
99. Private interview with Lord Castle. See Appendix 3 of the author's doctoral thesis.
100. Private interview with Lord Castle.
101. Duff, *op. cit.* (p. 47).
102. Duff, *op. cit.* (pps. 46–7).
103. Duff, *op. cit.* (pps. 46–7) quoting 'The Politics of Harold Wilson' by Paul Foot.
104. Duff, *op. cit.* (pps. 46–7).

Chapter Seven

The Inquisition of Bevanism

Why did the witch hunt against the Bevanites intensify *after the ban*? With 'the party within a party' disbanded the inquisition ought to have lost its purpose. Yet from 1953 onwards, the right wing embarked on an even more concerted offensive. They now turned their attention to the Brains Trusts. Of course escalation is in the nature of inquisition, but there was more than hysteria involved. The party mass was using the existing party machinery to deliberate on the vital world issues of the day. This brought the mass into conflict with the party bureaucracy. British Labour was attempting to seize hold of *its* organisation, that *it* had created. For bureaucratic officialdom 'the party' *is the apparatus*, which appears to them to have sprung from the foreheads of the party professionals. In the midst of this 'party' officialdom now perceived another, a 'party within a party' which threatened its security and the structural links and channels it had formalised with the *state bureaucracy* at government level.[1] For the party activists however the party is *themselves*. Finding obstacles springing up before them from 1948 onwards the party mass began to assert itself against bureaucracy which, as Gaitskell's budget demonstrated to them, had started to claw back some of the gains of the previous period.

Above all, the movement needed to debate and interpret world political events. To discover why the budget had cut their Health Service, they needed to examine the arms programme. This in turn brought them to examine the nature of the Korean War, the reasons for the Chinese revolution, and the whole matrix of world politics and world economy to some degree. The Brains Trusts were vital to this process of clarification. The party bureaucracy moved against them. The struggle now became the more general one of *democratic rights* within the movement, without which there can be no development of programme and policy.

As early as December 1952 there seems to have been an attempt to interfere with these meetings. Bevan, Wilson and A. J. Irvine were booked to speak at the Liverpool stadium but permission to hold the rally was suddenly withdrawn by the Directors. 'An enemy hath done this' wrote Harold Wilson in Tribune, and the paper's editor asked Liverpool MP Bessie Braddock if she would care to comment as other MPs in the City had done.[2] An alternative mass meeting was held in Birkenhead on the afternoon of Sunday, 1st February. There was now a veritable explosion of Brains Trusts. Tribune was obliged to introduce a special advertising category for them in January, and, later, bought a campaign van to promote sales at the rallies.[3] The May meeting at which the cash was raised to purchase this asset is indicative of the time. The Princess Theatre was hired and the meeting was billed as 'Keep Left for Peace'. On the platform were Castle, Foot, Crossman and Mallalieu. The sub-heading of the discussion was 'What is the meaning of the changes in Russia'. Within a fortnight the money had been raised.

Central to Transport House's investigation of the Brains Trusts was the sensitivity of the Trades Union leaders to Tribune's warnings of a 'Labour-TUC Split'.[4] On January 16th the paper had expressed the view that the Conservative party was bent on wooing the TUC from its traditional allegiances, and that the union leaders were encouraging the 'seduction' by their obvious hostility to the proceedings at Morecambe. This same edition strongly criticised steel union leader Lincoln Evans for accepting a knighthood from the Conservative administration at the very moment when the denationalisation of the Steel industry was on the agenda for the current parliamentary session.

In warning of the dangers of a split Tribune was doing little more than affirming what General Secretary Morgan Phillips had himself implied in an article in 'Fact' a few weeks earlier which had asserted,

> 'Unfortunately there are a number of people inside the Labour Party who have fallen very heavily for the bait

which the anti-Labour press has carefully prepared. They accept without question that there is a fundamental difference of policy in our party.'

For this Morgan Phillips was censured by his right wing colleagues on the NEC by 15–6,[5] on the initiative of the Deakin trade union 'bloc'. Now the NEC moved against the Brains Trusts as revenge upon Tribune.

Democratic Rights and the Witch Hunt

The pressure of the inquisition against the Bevanites mounted from this time on. From the right wing's point of view allegations of fellow travelling were easier to make now that the British Communist Party gradually edged away from early Cominform denunciations of Bevanism, and oriented instead towards a popular-front style campaign with the Labour left on the issue of German rearmament in the course of 1953–54. Not only the Bevanites, but the Trotskyists too, came under increasing pressure as a result of their modest success in establishing Socialist Outlook as a weekly.

A reading of the NEC minutes for 1953–54 discloses a long inventory of investigations, enquiries, expulsions and denunciations at all levels of the party from constituency to NEC and PLP level, and right across the board of the left-Bevanites, Communists and Trotskyists.

Simultaneously with the Brains Trust investigation, there was a row on the NEC about supposed press leakages concerning the findings of the organisational sub-committee. Mallalieu's name was prominent as a possible source of press information.[6] There was also an attack made on the Bevanites by William Lawther in the Daily Telegraph which epitomises the spirit of the times,

> 'The opinion of the Trades Unions is that the Bevanite activities are a deliberate attempt to undermine the leadership in the same way as Hitler and the Communists did. There is no difference whatever between them.'[7]

The press leakages affair erupted again on the NEC in the Spring of 1954. A lengthy appendix on press leakages accompanied the 24th March minutes. The party leadership was angry that information regarding the views of trade union leaders expressed privately at NEC meetings was finding its way to the press! In particular, the fact that Tiffin of the TGWU along with Gooch of the Agricultural Workers and Irwin of the ETU had opposed German rearmament proved most embarrassing for the Deakin 'bloc' in this the crucial year for the resolving of the issue in the Labour Party.[8]

There was a denunciation of two Labour MPs for attending an international meeting on German Rearmament in Paris, and an attempt by Mikardo to suspend the minute until the people concerned had had a chance to state their case was defeated.[9] Material of the Union of Democratic Control was closely scrutinised by the NEC[10] because Bevan and leading Bevanites had joined forces with the UDC to present a petition to parliament on June 15th. The fourth investigation at this same NEC was one into Northampton CLP.

The minutes for 28th April reveal why the NEC was so agitated. No less than 152 CLPs were listed as having passed resolutions opposing German Rearmament. Many demanded a special conference. Thus press stories disclosing divisions in the union camp on the NEC were vital. The NEC took legal counsel and in May the lawyers reported,

> 'We are of the opinion that as matters now stand no action can be taken to prevent such disclosures as are referred to in our instructions. We are of this opinion on the ground that there is nothing in the facts before us which could justify a Court holding that a member of the National Executive Committee is under any legal obligation, express or implied, not to disclose matters that occur in the course of the Committee's deliberations.'[11]

The only course the lawyers could devise was the amending of the party Constitution to render NEC deliberations secret. This could not be done, but on 18th May a special meeting of the NEC was called on the subject of party unity and collective responsibility of NEC members. Here the right wing secured a resolution making majority NEC decisions binding on members of the Committee unless otherwise specified. A further resolution moved by Chairman Wilfrid Burke, and seconded by Bevan, reminding members of their responsibility to conference and the need to combine freedom of action within certain limits received only seven votes as against twenty for the former.[12] But at the following meeting some relaxation of the rule was permitted for the duration of the German rearmament debate.[13]

However in July six members of the NEC who had published the Tribune pamphlet *It Need Not Happen* opposing German Rearmament were deemed to have violated the meaning and intention of the 26th May resolution on collective respossibility.[14] At these squalid sessions of the NEC the Bevanites not only defended their own democratic rights, but those of others in the party. Bevan moved and Crossman seconded the reference back on the proscription of Socialist Outlook (former paper of the Socialist Fellowship), which was by now entirely controlled by the Trotskyists. The reference back was lost by 14–9. In the appendix attached to the NEC's minutes the evidence about the existence of a clandestine Trotskyist party within the Labour Party and the profiles of the leading Trotskyists were taken en bloc and quoted from the Communist Party members weekly news service, World News and Views. It was largely on this Communist Party evidence that the Trotskyists were proscribed. The same appendix noted that Mr John Lawrence was no longer associated with the Outlook.

Now that the British Communist Party were concentrating all of their energies on the German Rearmament question, and therefore assiduously wooing the Bevanites, the weekly Socialist Outlook was an obstacle to the new popular front. It warned about the campaign's degeneration into an anti-German exercise which ignored the issue of British armament programmes. But whereas the Communist Party joined the right wing's witch hunt against Trotskyists in the middle of the McCarthy period, the Bevanites stood firm and resolutely defended the Socialist Outlook. Resolutions from 119 Labour parties opposed the NEC ban. Only one, Leeds North East, congratulated the NEC. Now, since the Trotskyists could be counted in tens at this stage, it is clear that the Bevanite ranks in the constituencies were solidly behind the Bevanite leaders on the NEC in defending the rights of Trotskyists to publish their newspaper in the Labour Party. *The Communist Party by contrast opposed the Trotskyists as resolutely as they had denounced the Bevanites only a few years earlier.* Leeds North East CLP and World News were the only people who could take satisfaction from the closure of Socialist Outlook.

Since by now the Bevanite second eleven was functioning complete with minutes and secretary, the NEC's move against the Trotskyists was not lost on them. The issue of rights of all tendencies to put their views in the party had become a vital one for the movement. Since the Communist Party's apparatus was entirely separate from the Labour Party, they perhaps could afford to be supple and engage in duplicity on matters of principle. But the Bevanites could not. The banning of their organisation, the moves against the Brains Trusts and Tribune had all served to steel the Bevanites on the issue of democratic rights within the party. Michael Foot denounced the ban in Tribune and the 'new tinpot Torquemadas' who were leading the witch hunt. A protest meeting at the Holborn Hall was arranged at which Foot and New Statesman Editor, Kingsley Martin, spoke, along with the editors of Peace News and Co-op News. At this meeting Foot declared that those who had received letters from Transport House demanding loyalty oaths should refuse to sign them,

> 'We cannot allow this to go on, and free controversy and free newspapers to be stamped out of existence . . . The great men who built this movement would be ashamed of documents such as this.'[15]

However, expulsions went ahead. In November the NEC heard appeals against expulsions from Trotskyists in Nottingham and Exeter. There were NEC enquiries into East Islington and Norwood Labour Parties. Reams of evidence and material came before the NEC members at meeting after meeting.[16] But whilst the matter of principle was a crucial one, the Trotskyists themselves were of only peripheral concern in this campaign. Their expulsion and proscription were a preface to the attempt at a final solution to the Bevanite problem. Now came the assault on Tribune in the late autumn of 1954, followed in March 1955 by the attempt to expel Bevan from the Labour party. German Rearmament had been narrowly carried at conference that year. Seven MPs had the whip withdrawn for a rearguard gesture in voting against the nine power agreement. It was no longer German Rearmament that was the battleground but *dockland* and the issue of democratic rights of dockers to join a trade union of their own choosing.

The origins of the dispute went back to August. In Hull there was a strike over the dangerous methods of unloading grain. TGWU ('white') union members, disgruntled at their leaders' refusal to grant recognition and the officials' instructions to the men to return to work, walked out of the TGWU and joined the smaller NASD ('blue') union. Recruitment to the 'Blue' from the 'White' gathered pace in the Northern ports. In October the Blue union's call for a strike against compulsory overtime drew a big response from White members especially in the TGWU's London stronghold. From here on, the inter-union dispute became a TUC and eventually a legal matter, extending over eighteen months. But behind the appearance of a dispute between two unions there lay the essential struggle of the ranks to free themselves of a bureaucratic, remote, right wing union leadership epitomised by the very Arthur Deakin who was determined to rid the Labour Party of Bevan and Bevanism.

The compulsory overtime issue had undertones of the '1305' dispute during Bevan's period at the Ministry of Labour. Once again the mass movement, and more precisely the dockers, were asserting the course and tempo of the Bevanites' struggle. The docks dispute of 1954 is the *very essence of the Bevanites' struggle* against party and union bureaucracy, the right of trades unionists and party members to assert control over *their* unions, *their* party, *their* leaders. Tribune backed the Blue, and the right of dockers to join a union of their own choosing. Sales reached an all time high in October and November 1954. Aitken was a first-class industrial reporter and the paper turned resolutely towards dockers, engineers, busmen and railwaymen, all of whom were involved in disputes during 1954 in a growing wave of militancy in industry. The TUC urged on by Deakin, expelled the NASD. Simultaneously the NEC attacked Tribune. On October 27th within hours of the TUC's ejection of the Blue, the NEC passed a motion of censure on Tribune and sent an ominous letter to the three members of the paper's editorial board—Jennie Lee, J. P. W. Mallalieu and Michael Foot, inviting their comments. Tribune's crime was that it had ridiculed Deakin in 'Slander on the Dockers' after he had foolishly asserted that the strike was Communist inspired, even though the dockers knew that King Street was extremely hostile to the Blue's activities.

The NEC's letter asked Tribune 'How do you reconcile your attacks on the leadership of the TGWU with your membership of the Party?' Bevan warned Attlee that if the three editorial board members were expelled, he, Bevan, would have to be expelled too. Crossman and Wilson 'did not relish the controversy'.[17] 'Bevanism cannot do without Bevan' said Wilson 'but it could do without Tribune'.[18]

Tribune replied to the NEC in a 6,000-word statement and extended the debate from a discussion of the dock strike to the principles of free speech within the Party. It reminded all concerned that the origin of the Transport and General Workers Union itself lay in a revolt led by Ben Tillet, Tom Mann and others against an older trade union leadership which had become inadequate to the needs of a new age.[19] Tribune's reply was reproduced as a pamphlet *The Case for Freedom—an Answer to Morgan Phillips and the NEC* which had a very large sale in dockland.

Percy Cudlipp reported at this time that 'certain powerful leaders of the TUC want to see disciplinary action taken against Tribune and the leaders of the hard core of Bevanites expelled'.[20] But the NEC climbed down after Tribune's spirited reply, warning 'similar conduct in future will compel the Executive to take action'.[21]

War between Tribune and the right wing on the NEC did not abate. The Docks crisis gave way to the expulsion crisis of March 1955. The minutes of the NEC for 15th December dealt once more with the exchange of correspondence between the committee and Tribune. NEC secretary, Alice Bacon, was also embroiled in another parallel skirmish with the paper. Miss Bacon tendered her resignation as a member of the Organisation sub-committee of the NEC,

> '. . . because it appeared "to be impossible to act as a member of the committee without being singled out for attacks in Tribune and misrepresentation in other papers".'[22]

Yet another NEC letter was dispatched to Tribune complaining at the description of Miss Bacon as 'Chairman of the travelling tribunal searching out Trotskyists in local parties'.[23] The offending Tribune article had dubbed her 'Busy Bacon'. It deplored 'the enormous extension of the power of bureaucracy within the party' and demanded an immediate end to the purge, and the readmission of the expelled Trotskyists.[24] In January 1955 the warring continued. Barbara Castle was taken to task over the remarks made at a Brains Trust in Deal, Kent, in which she had alleged 'dirty dealings behind the scenes at Scarborough' where conference had accepted German Rearmament. (Conference had been presented with an extreme composite resolution, and the Woodworkers union switched their vote, flouting the decision of their own conference.) At Deal Mrs Castle and other panel members also protested at the withdrawal of the whip from Sidney Silverman and his co-thinkers after the November vote on the nine power agreement.[25] At the NEC the May resolution on majority decisions was read out by the Chairman, and Morrison moved a censure vote on Mrs Castle which was carried 16–5. Then the NEC moved on to consider enquiries into Saltcoats, Maesteg and Norwood Labour parties. Norwood was to completely reorganise and 'a close watch' was to be kept on the activities of the Labour Publishing Society, publishers of the defunct Socialist Outlook.

The Expulsion Crisis

The climax of this protracted war against the left was the barely credible attempt to expel Aneurin Bevan, not just from the PLP but from the Labour Party itself in March 1955. The international setting was the fall of the Mendes France government, the ousting of Malenkov by Bulganin in Russia and the worsening Formosa crisis—all of which took place in January and February of 1955. The German Rearmament vote had been won at party Congress and the Bevanites had abstained on the nine power agreement on a European Defence Community Agreement in November. The docks dispute continued to stoke up enmity between Deakin and the Bevanites. The Deakin wing may have felt that the Bevanites had 'cheated their executioners'[26] by failing to vote with the Silverman seven in November, as the British Communist Party had advised.[27] But another opportunity for expulsion soon presented itself as the H-bomb testing controversy became the main item on the agenda at Bevanite meetings in Crossman's house at Vincent Square. Bevan had already sought, in January, a commitment from Attlee to press for a meeting of the great powers. And this was no more than the April 5th, 1954 resolution carried unanimously by the House, had proposed. Having failed to sway Attlee from the influence of the Gaitskellites, Bevan himself took the issue into the PLP. On 10th February his proposal demanding progress towards summit talks went down by 93–70, but a further resolution along the same lines, initiated by Strachey and the moderates, secured over a hundred signatures and was placed on the order paper. When Bevan pressed for time to debate the motion this was construed by the silent front bench opposition as a further challenge to Attlee's authority. A week later the PLP rebuked Bevan 132–72.[28]

American and Soviet testing of H-bombs was soon to be augmented by British tests. Labour's attitude to testing and manufacturing of nuclear weapons would have to be clearly spelt out. Neither the apathy of Labour's front bench, nor the continued ambiguity of Bevanite thinking on the nuclear deterrent could continue much longer.

The Vincent Square discussions produced a paper, written jointly by Crossman and George Wigg, which set out the case for acceptance of the nuclear deterrent. This, it was argued, would make possible the abolition of conscription and substantial reductions in the conventional arms programme. On the other hand, the document spelt out that renunciation of the bomb undoubtedly means renunciation of the western alliance—neutrality. The Crossman-Wigg thesis was in effect reminding the group that they could well be on the path back to *Keep Left* which first laid down the policy of neutrality from both 'camps'.

On Wednesday, 2nd March the Bevanites left their meeting to go to the House of Commons with 'no common view of their own, and having agreed on no tactic to deal with the niceties of the defence debate'.[29] The situation thus had all the ingredients of disaster tinged with tragedy—a delicate world situation, a party leadership unwilling to take up the challenge to the government, a right wing stung by Bevanite activities in Tribune and on the docks, a Bevanite leadership without policy or tactics on the issue to be debated. Only the steadfastness of Labour's ranks and a switched vote on the NEC saved Labour from an historic split. In the debate in the Commons Bevan threatened not to vote unless his own front bench clarified the position of the official opposition amendment. Did they mean that 'a conventional attack would draw a nuclear response, that the west would be the first to resort to nuclear weapons . . .?'[30] Then the following key words of his speech revived the controversy about whether the Bevanites were a party within a party,

> 'If we cannot have the lead from *them*, let us give the lead ourselves.'[31]

Whether or not Bevan meant by 'them' the Conservatives or his own front bench depended very largely on the angle from which one viewed the sweep of Bevan's arm gesture. But the consequences of the words and gesture were not at all ambiguous. The right wing unfurled the plans for Bevan's expulsion, and proceeded vigorously. Bevan and 62 other Labour MPs abstained on the amendment and that was proof enough for the Deakin-Gaitskell wing.

The expulsion crisis timetable reads as follows:

Wednesday 2 March	Bevan and 62 Labour MPs abstain on the opposition amendment to the Defence White Paper.
Sunday 6 March	Bevan falls ill with 'flu.
Monday 7 March	Shadow Cabinet vote 9–4 to recommend whip withdrawal from Bevan, with a clear inference that expulsion by the NEC could follow.
Wednesday 9 March	Special PLP meeting to consider the Shadow Cabinet's proposal postponed due to Bevan's ill health.
Wednesday 16 March	Special PLP meeting convenes. The moderate censure motion is defeated 138–124. The Whip withdrawal motion is passed 141–112.

Tuesday 22 March	Bevan threatens a breach of privilege case if the NEC tries to influence his future conduct as an MP.
Wednesday 23 March	As a consequence of the privilege threat, Attlee moves a compromise—a special sub-Committee to enquire into the case and report back. This is passed 14–13.
Tuesday 29 March	A sub-Committee of the NEC seeks assurances on (a) attacks on party and union leaders, (b) majority decisions, (c) *the existence of an organised group within the party with its own press.* Bevan presents his statement. The decision is referred back to the NEC.
Wednesday 30 March	By 15–10 NEC condemns Bevan and warns of drastic action for future offences. Expulsion is avoided.

Two aspects of the expulsion crisis are worthy of special note —the inflexible determination of the Deakinites to expel Bevan in the full knowledge that a split might ensure, and *the overwhelming opposition of the party ranks to such a split.*

The most incongruous aspects can be dealt with first. The Shadow Cabinet and the PLP quickly adopted a position on summit talks only marginally different from the man they sought to expel; and they pursued this resolution simultaneously as the expulsion campaign proceeded. Furthermore at no time did the party leadership contemplate expelling the other 62 abstainers. Whilst tactically sensible this was neither logical nor just. It would appear that the right wing still viewed the affair through the densely smoked lenses of parliamentary manoeuvring, blithely unaware that the pinnacles on which they were operating rested on the broad base of the mass movement outside parliament. It was this movement which was Bevan's strength. So whilst the Deakinites appeared to hold all the trump cards it was Bevan who won the battle to stay in the party. The democratic will of the mass movement prevailed over bureaucratic vote lobbying.

Crossman's diary discloses the shallow, even petty motives

of the expulsion lobby,[32] and their incomprehension of the deeper class forces at work.

Gaitskell in a conversation with Crossman confided,

> 'Bevanism is *and only is* a conspiracy to seize the leadership for Aneurin Bevan. It is a conspiracy because it has the three essentials of conspiracy, a leader in Bevan, an organisation run by Mikardo, and a newspaper run by Foot'. (*my emphasis—MJ*).

When Crossman challenged this, Gaitskell indicated that he really believed that Bevanite organisation was 'widespread in the constituencies'. He confided that Tribune, even though its circulation was not large, was 'the single most important factor which our people on the right complain of'. That the line between exaggeration and self deception in Gaitskell was fine indeed, is illustrated by his comparison of Bevan to Adolf Hitler in this same conversation. But distasteful or not, venom and poor judgement were now an objective element in the expulsion crisis. Hindsight could lead one to conclude that the affair was a storm in a teacup, but what Gaitskell's motives reveal is not how superficial the policy differences were between himself and Bevan, but how close Labour was to a split. No social democrat could seek accommodation within his own party to someone he considers to be alike to Adolf Hitler.

The Deakinites were determined and no less blind to the historic significance of a split than their parliamentary collaborators. The tough union chief's voice was audible in the words of George Brown (sponsored by his own union) at Belper on March 6th shortly after the Shadow Cabinet vote. Brown called on the party to 'clear up once and for all this question of the leadership . . .' and to stop the breaking of majority decisions.

> 'To stop it now . . . may cause some problems and trouble. But not to deal with it now will only shore up still greater trouble in the future'.[33]

Brown and Hartley Shawcross were the most prominent in the expulsion campaign. The press generally behaved like a pack running on ahead of the hunt. The Economist urged,

'To falter now . . . would be to concede moral victory to Mr Bevan'.[34]

Without being explicit, the Shadow Cabinet had given the PLP the firm impression that there would be a collective resignation if their recommendation were not sanctioned.[35] From the outset then a serious split seemed a distinct possibility. Publicly Deakin called on Attlee to give a 'very, very clear lead',[36] but at a private meeting at the St Ermin's hotel on Monday 21st March, just before the NEC meeting, he warned Gaitskell that in the event of wavering on expulsion the unions 'might have to consider their relations with the party'.[37] This was a marked change from his speech at party conference in 1953. Then he had asserted,

> 'I am certain there is no trade union affiliated to the Party which would for one moment consider disaffiliation of divorcement from this Party'.[38]

Nothing in Deakin's past record suggests that he would have premeditated a rupture between unions and party. Indeed he had been very loyal to Labour in office, whilst always a staunch opponent of any suggestion of a national wages policy. Yet his stubbornness on the Bevan expulsion crisis could have set in motion the relentless machinery of such a rift. Certainly factional meetings had been taking place at the St Ermin's hotel for some time, apparently, in the guise of agency service meetings. Gaitskell admitted this much in his confidential discussion at Vincent Square. Whether or not this was the 'organisation' which Deakin had promised would be set up to counteract that of the Bevanites[39] is not clear, but Bevanism was a frequent topic of discussion at St Ermin's hotel. At these meetings it was being asked by 'many of our big backers why we hadn't acted three years ago,'[40] at the time of the standing orders crisis in October 1952.

It is necessary therefore to underline that in the Bevan expulsion crisis historic questions were on the agenda, irrespective of the intentions of the dramatis personae—a split within the party as evidenced by the threat of collective resignation of the shadow cabinet, and the possibility of a split between the unions and the party. All this amid continuing allegations of a party within a party. The expulsion crisis was not solely about the career of Aneurin Bevan.[41]

The mass movement certainly understood this. Its response was massive, overwhelming. Bevan's illness, strangely, gave additional time for the opinion of the movement to be marshalled, expressed and delivered to the expulsionists in no uncertain manner.

On March 29th the NEC sub-committee met and was circularised with the official list of parties which had remitted telegrams and letters protesting at the withdrawal of the whip, which meant they certainly opposed expulsion. One hundred and fifty-one Labour parties were on the list, as were protests from Tom O'Brien's Cinematograph union and the AEU.[42] But this was by no means the full extent of the opposition. The South Wales NUM supported Bevan and called for a national conference of the Labour Party to be summoned immediately. District Committees of the AEU in Manchester, Birmingham and Leeds added their weight to their national leadership's own protest. The NUR executive came out against expulsion.[43] Margate CLP decided to call a conference of constituency parties 'in order that the rank and file can let their leaders know their views on the action taken against Mr Bevan,'[44] and on March 20th Croydon Labour Party sent out letters to all constituency parties asking them to support the Croydon proposal to amend the constitution to permit a congress of CLPs. The Margate proposal alarmed Morgan Phillips who declared that,

> 'it appeared to be an attempt to form a party within a party.'[45]

He added that the NEC would be seriously concerned if the conference actually assembled. The Sunday Times warned of the dangers of a new party emerging at a later date,

> 'The *hidden, distant* danger is this, that from the division of Labour a new left wing crypto Communist Party might arise, and, in the long run might become the alternative government, the nature of our system being to squeeze out the middle party.'[46]

The Sunday Times might have taken comfort if it had been

known that such a prospect was as alarming to Harry Pollitt as it appeared to the editors. Pollitt called for 'the most formidable (campaign) we have yet seen inside the Labour movement.'[47] But it needed no rallying cry from him. Wherever Labour gatherings were in progress during March there were attempts to move emergency resolutions. There was uproar at a meeting of the Scottish Council of the Labour Party in Glasgow when the Chairman refused to accept such a resolution.[48] The annual meeting of the Cheshire and Lancashire Regional Council of the party in Manchester witnessed similar scenes. On March 19th Will Griffiths had telephoned Stan Orme, a delegate to the conference and arranged that the Deakinite chairman should be moved from the chair if he refused to accept a resolution on the Bevan expulsion.[49]

Wilson had agreed beforehand to take the chair if the resolution proved successful, but it was narrowly defeated. It happened that the groundswell for Bevan coincided with some adverse decisions for the right wing in local parties picking new candidates after the new constituency boundary changes. In Birmingham the Ladywood constituency selected November rebel Victor Yates (who held the division) in preference to Woodrow Wyatt. Edith Summerskill was rejected by Fulham Labour Party and Elaine Burton by Coventry South. (This party had even called a special meeting to consider Mrs Burton's support for the whip withdrawal.)[50] The party ranks were asserting their will over the right wing who were now 'going through hell in the constituencies'.[51] This only made Gaitskell more determined on expulsion.

And yet it did not happen. Bevan had made it absolutely clear at the PLP meeting,

> 'whatever you do now I am not going out to form a new party'.[52]

The plan for a national conference of constituency parties did not get off the ground perhaps for the very reason that the ranks felt it might have led in the direction of a split. No, the voice of the movement was clear and united. 'Don't expel Bevan. No split!' At home, at the Commons, and at party headquarters Attlee found bulging postbags awaiting him with the movement's verdict on expulsion.

At this point of time splits began to develop in the ranks of the expulsion lobby. Attlee was also swayed by the opinion of legal counsel on the privilege issue which Bevan had raised. Tiffin was wavering. But finally it was the vote of Mrs Jean Mann on the executive which saved the day for Labour. The sub-committee elicited a statement from Bevan in which the issue underlying the entire affair was clearly spelt out,

> 'The sense of democracy in a political party is to enable the argument to proceed while at the same time maintaining the effectiveness of the party in action.'[53]

In a sense this principle, rather than any programme, policy or organisation, is what Bevanism was all about. In the sub-committee he had said that he had no responsibility for Tribune or its Brains Trusts but that they performed a useful service to the movement. Certainly this was no mere appeasing statement. He had never been a tight organisation man. The editing of Tribune and the running of the Brains Trusts had never been his responsibility as such.

Elected to parliament in 1929, Bevan understood better than many of the '1945' Labour MPs the effect of the split of 1931. It, too, was a split engineered by the right, albeit in very different circumstances, for which the working class had to foot the bill. Even if Bevan had wanted to form a new party which he most certainly did not, he knew also the enormous fund of loyalty that the party commanded in the ranks and amongst Labour voters who were not even members. It would have been a most damaging split. And nobody understood that better than the ranks themselves.

Of the two crises of the fifties which might have precipitated a split—October 1952 and March 1955—the latter was unquestionably the most critical. A split was closer at that time than at any time since 1931—a fact which has been given scant consideration by Labour historians.[54] It is far simpler and more 'logical' to examine the programme of Bevanism and that of the party itself and conclude that there was not sufficient grounds for a split. But politics does not live by the rules of logic or philosophers would have been kings many centuries ago.

The expulsion crisis was the more serious of the two because the Parliamentary Bevanites had, to all intents and purposes, given up the offending 'party within a party' in October 1952, and had been reduced to a lunchtime circle without any clarity or policy on the issue which precipitated the expulsion moves. In 1952 the Bevanites could climb down. *In 1955 they had nothing to climb down from.* Extra-parliamentary Bevanism was not the creature of Bevan. It was not his property to do with what he would. He could no more control that than the class struggle itself. Hence, his statement to the NEC at the end of the affair was entirely truthful. Yet at the same time Bevan *truly did represent this movement*—not entirely in programme, not in policy, not in organisation, and not perfectly, but he did represent it *in spirit*. When the right sought to exorcise this offending spirit they met the material force of the mass movement.

Amidst the turmoil one development of great portent for the future may have been overlooked—the emergence of the centre left.

The Centre Left

In the vote on the defence white paper there were a number of notable defections from the Bevanite camp—Wilson, Freeman, Crossman, Swingler, Hale and Delargy had voted with the official leadership. Indeed the very fact that Crossman should have invited Gaitskell for a 'secret drink' on the eve of the fateful NEC meeting reveals the degree to which bridge building was proceeding on the 'right' wing of the Bevanites. Later in the year Crossman was to go further in backing Gaitskell for the leadership, whilst in the lunch debates he was already examining the 'benefits' that might accrue to the left as a result of embracing nuclear defence strategy. And here we see an intriguing process unfolding—the beginnings of the evolution of the party rebels of the fifties into the Cabinet Ministers of the sixties. The first sign of the decomposition of parliamentary Bevanism was the public defection of Donnelly at the 1954 conference, although no Bevanite departed as dishonourably as he, and he had been tale-bearing for some time before that.

At the time of the expulsion crisis itself Crossman in the New Statesman went as far as to describe Gaitskell as 'the financial expert' and Bevan as the inspirer of the party's socialist faith. To Bevan, who had resigned the Cabinet precisely over the faulty financial expertise of the man who was now earnestly trying to expel him this was treachery. An exchange of correspondence illuminates the differences between the two men at this time. Crossman objected to four aspects of Bevan's behaviour—his resignation from the parliamentary committee, his decision to stand for Treasurer, his Tribune speech at Margate and finally the 'defence muddle'.[55] Crossman believed that Bevan's aim was 'fantastically over-ambitious' whereas his own was limited to restoring a 'proper balance between right and left in the party'. There was a sting in the tail however. Crossman closed with these words,

> 'Of course, if we still had a group, with group policy and group decisions, the whole situation would be different. But, possibly correctly, you set your face against this—and as a result each of us on each occasion has had to think and act for himself'.[56]

Here Crossman is excusing, justifying and explaining his behaviour in the expulsion crisis in a most disarming way. He puts the onus on Bevan for there not being a group with a policy and discipline. Whilst this was not entirely true Bevan was certainly not the most enthusiastic of group members, and in his NEC statement did not take responsibility for Tribune and its Brains Trusts. In other words Crossman is claiming to act in a Bevanite way, in the way Bevan himself was conducting affairs—as an individual responsible only to himself. But it is not entirely an honest presentation of the facts. After all the meeting with Gaitskell was *secret* and in the course of it Crossman was engaging in some quite conscious bridge building to the right. He confided to Gaitskell,

> 'that there was now a left of centre emerging which was not merely his (Bevan's) stooge'.[57]

By contrast in standing for Treasurer Bevan had begun to carry the struggle into the unions, to broaden it to a struggle against bureaucracy in general. This was not Crossman's way of working. When he spoke of groups he referred to influential enclaves of co-thinkers. Nor was this merely the difference between the 'intellectual' and the 'worker'. It represented a different attitude to the movement. Bevan was at home in the mass movement. Crossman was at home in a small group. Whatever Crossman's differences with Bevan, a vote for Gaitskell in the leadership contest was a vote for party strife. Mikardo attacked Crossman's decision in Tribune.[58]

In 1956 Crossman produced a paper on foreign affairs which came before the party's foreign affairs group in which he declared that it would be 'unrealistic' for Labour to scrap NATO, SEATO and other alliances.[59] In April 1957 Bevan accused Crossman of 'doing his usual turnabout'[60] on hearing that Crossman had favoured British H-tests in a speech in Germany. (And when the mass movement secured the historic vote for unilateral nuclear disarmament in 1960, it was Crossman along with Walter Padley who attempted to defuse the situation with the Crossman-Padley compromise plan.) The beginning of Crossman's defection therefore, in 1954–55, dates from the *growth of extra-parliamentary Bevanism* which was to escalate in the late fifties, and become transformed into the remarkable unilateralist movement. With such mass movements Crossman was never happy. Wilson too, began to take his distance from Bevanism. He stepped into Bevan's vacated seat in the Shadow Cabinet in 1954 and at the time of the NEC's clash with Tribune during the Blue union dispute in 1954–55, he stated that Bevanism could do without Tribune but not without Bevan. He clearly meant that extra-parliamentary Bevanism was becoming an embarrassment to *parliamentary* Bevanism. But extra-parliamentary Bevanism flourished in the end, even when Bevan himself had made peace with Gaitskell. At Brighton in 1957 Bevan was in conflict with Bevanism.

NOTES

1. See below. Sir Lincoln Evans accepted a knighthood as Steel was being de-nationalised.
2. Tribune, 4.1.53.

3. Tribune, 21.5.53.
4. Foot, *op. cit. Vol II*, quoting Tribune, 16.1.53.
5. Yorkshire Evening News 30.10.52, Lancashire Evening Post, 30.10.52. The NEC denied it at the time but all the indications point to it being true.
6. NEC minutes, 25.2.53.
7. Daily Telegraph, 29.1.53 quoted in NEC minutes, 25.2.53.
8. 14-page appendix on press leakages attached to minutes 24.3. 54.
9. NEC minutes, 28.4.54.
10. as above. UDC memorandum attached to minutes. Some fellow travellers were associated with it. See Appendix 8 of the author's doctoral thesis.
11. The opinion of Kenneth Diplock and Alan Orr, 29.4.54, considered by the NEC, 18.5.54.
12. NEC minutes, 18.5.54.
13. NEC minutes, 26.5.54.
14. NEC minutes, 28.7.54.
15. Socialist Outlook, 3.9.54.
16. NEC minutes, 24.11.54 appendix on enquiries and appeals against expulsions.
17. Foot, *op. cit. Vol II* (p. 454).
18. Foot, *op. cit. Vol II* (p. 454).
19. Foot, *op. cit. Vol II* (p. 454).
20. Duff, *op. cit.* (p. 65).
21. Letter attached to NEC minutes, 24.11.54. Sent to Tribune editorial board that day.
22. NEC minutes 15.12.54.
23. Letter appended to minutes of NEC 15.12.54 from Morgan Phillips to Tribune editorial board, Foot, Lee, Mallalieu.
24. Tribune, 26.11.54.
25. NEC minutes, 26.1.55.
26. Foot, *op. cit. Vol II* (p. 453).
27. World News, 16.10.54 'Defeat the nine power agreement'. The article called for 'the greatest development of mass pressure directed specifically towards Members of Parliament in preparation for the opening of parliament'.
28. Foot, *op. cit. Vol II* (p. 456).
29. Foot, *op. cit. Vol II* (p. 485).
30. Foot, *op. cit. Vol II* (p. 461).
31. Foot, *op. cit. Vol II* (p. 461).
32. Crossman's diary, 22.3.54 quoted by Foot *op. cit. Vol II* (p. 473–4 footnote).
33. The Times, 7.3.55.
34. The Economist, 19.3.55.
35. Foot, *op. cit.* (p. 470).
36. Foot, *op. cit.* (p. 473).
37. Foot, *op. cit.* (p. 473).

38. *Trade Union Leadership* by V. L. Allen, Longman, Green & Co., London, First edition (p. 153).
39. LP Conference 1954. Deakin's speech as fraternal delegate to LP from TUC.
40. Foot, *op. cit.* (p. 474). Footnote from Crossman diaries.
41. David Coates, *op. cit.* (p. 191). Coates seems to imply that the Left movement was a reflex of Bevan's career.
42. NEC minutes for 29.3.55 meeting, appendix dated 22.3.55 signed MP.
43. Peggy Duff, *op. cit.* (p. 71).
44. World News, 26.3.55.
45. Sunday Times, 21.3.55.
46. Sunday Times, 19.3.55.
47. World News, 26.3.55.
48. World News, 26.3.55.
49. Roth, *op. cit.* (p. 199).
50. World News, 26.3.55.
51. Gaitskell made a brief reference to this in his meeting with Crossman—recorded in Crossman diaries 22.3.55. See Foot, *op. cit. Vol II* (p. 474 footnote).
52. Foot, *op. cit. Vol II* (p. 471).
53. Foot, *op. cit. Vol II* (p. 488 footnote 1).
54. Perhaps the three week print strike which shut down the national press at the time of the expulsion crisis by denying much primary source material has contributed to this neglect.
55. Foot, *op. cit. Vol II* (p. 483).
56. Foot, *op. cit. Vol II* (p. 483).
57. Foot, *op. cit. Vol. II* (p. 483 footnote).
58. Tribune, 30.12.55.
59. New Statesman, 7.7.56, an article by Paul Johnson 'A Coexistence dialogue'.
60. Foot, *op. cit. Vol II* (p. 547).

Chapter Eight

King Street and the Bevanites

No study of the left movement can be complete without consideration of the attitude of the Communist Party of Great Britain (CPGB) towards it. Although a small party, with nothing remotely like the specific weight in domestic politics of a PCF or PCI, the CPGB has had, for a whole epoch, a measure of influence in the trade union machine from shop steward to national official level whilst never at any time with a mass following comparable to social democracy. It has always been the claim of the CPGB that it presents the only viable alternative to the reformism of the Labour Party, and it has no doubt been their belief that in the event of an historic disillusionment with the Labour Party the British working class would turn in the direction of King Street. *The Bevanite experience was therefore an interesting test of this perspective*, and also of the political tactics the CPGB might employ to win support from the leftward moving forces within the Labour Party. How did the CPGB measure up to the challenge of the Bevanite movement? What, if anything, did it gain? The relations between King Street and the Left in the Labour Party in the Bevanite period have never been very closely examined.

Since the broad direction of policy of the CPGB was very largely determined by international political requirements of the Kremlin a recapitulation of the main thrusts and changes of Soviet international strategy is a necessary preface to any review of CPGB policy.[1]

For the purposes of this study the period 1947–53 is called the *early Cominform period*, and from Stalin's death in 1953 to the dissolution of that organisation in April 1956—the *late Cominform period.* From October 1947 to April 1956 spans eight years and seven months. If we take Stalin's death as the turning point in March 1953, then five and a half years of the

Cominform, or *two-thirds* of its life was accounted for by the early Cominform 'line' or attitude to world politics, ultra-leftism, adventurism, intransigence combined with intensified domestic policing of the population. Only one-third of the Cominform's era is identified with attempts at detente and an easing of the Cold War on Moscow's part. Whilst the turn began before Stalin's death and continued long after it, March 1953 is a symbolic and appropriate date to mark the change in the Kremlin's approach. But this should not lead us to suppose for a moment that Stalinism was being phased out after 1953. Stalinism's entire history from its inception in the mid-twenties right up to the present day is marked by sharp twists and turns in both domestic and foreign policy, often closely intertwining.[2] The Cominform period is a recapitulation of these two opposing but combined traits of Stalinism, its 'tough' and 'tender' sides. The same Stalinists who collaborated with the Nazis in 1939 and signed pacts with Churchill and Roosevelt in the mid-forties, took part in their half of the Cold War against Truman and the West in 1947–48 and signed the Geneva agreement with the 'Western' powers in 1954.[3] Thus in the early Cominform period there are to be found references to peaceful co-existence and collaboration with the 'Western' powers, and in the late Cominform period relapses into the tough rhetoric of the Cold War. These differences in the Kremlin's approach are differences of degree and emphasis rather than differences in kind.

The CPGB, like all other Communist Parties, entered into a period of tough ultra-leftism from 1947 and was not to emerge from it until well into the fifties. The one apparent anomaly in our chronology was the appearance of 'The British Road To Socialism' in January 1951 with its mention of the parliamentary road to Socialism.[4] But this was something of an indulgence on the part of the Kremlin, for whom the British party was of minor strategic importance at the time; and to some extent it could also be viewed as kite-flying for the late Cominform emphasis on gradualism and peaceful co-existence. But the general features of the early and late Cominform period are nowhere more clearly revealed than in the particular approach of the CPGB to the Bevanite movement. And this in turn hinged to a large degree on the changing attitude of the

Kremlin to Tito's Yugoslavia, which held a constant fascination for the Bevanites.

The party's attitude to the Labour left was already in evidence at the time of the Keep Left revolt, which it described as a group in 'open support of the reactionaries of both parties'.[5]

King Street gave instant and unanimous approval to the Cominform's denunciation of Tito as a reactionary, in league with fascism and imperialism, even though for many party 'intellectuals' this involved a flat contradiction of all the praise they had heaped upon the Marshal only weeks earlier.[6] Party Secretary Harry Pollitt argued that men like Czech party leader Rudolf Slansky, who had duly denounced Tito, were not men who 'turn when Joe says turn'.[7] There followed Derek Kartun's 'Tito's Plot Against Europe'[8] and two years later James Klugmann's sublime piece of fiction *From Trotsky To Tito.*[9]

In the early Cominform period language that had not been heard since the 'third period' of 1929–34 came back into the King Street vocabulary in characterising social democrats of both left and right. Life was particularly difficult for the fellow travellers who had been practising deep entry into the Labour Party. John Platts Mills was expelled from the Labour Party in April 1948, as were Solley and Zilliacus in May 1949, and Lester Hutchinson shortly afterwards. Another Labour MP, P. Barstow joined the Communist Party in 1952. Platts Mills briefly led a 'Labour Independents' group in the Commons which stood against Labour with open CPGB support in the 1950 general election.[10]

The ostentatious exit of the more obvious fellow travellers from the Parliamentary Labour Party signalled a sharp change in the attitude of the CPGB to all social democrats. In the discussion preceding the party's twentieth Congress in February 1948 one contributor to the party's weekly news service World News and Views welcomed the 'shift to the left' in Pollitt's report but warned that the Attlee government would go 'even further in its treachery to the working class' and that it had given the 'final lesson' in Labour governments.[11] But the momentum of ultra-left denunciation of Labour, and the failure to discriminate between right and left within the Labour

Party did not really pick up until the latter months of 1948, and the CPGB's official policy remained one of working for a new government of the Left including Labour.[12]

During 1949 a series of front organisations were established—The World Peace Committee's British section, the British Peace Committee, and various new East European Friendship Associations which were to be strategic fields of activity for the party and those stalwart Labour MPs that still wished to be associated with the police states of Eastern Europe.[13] The CPGB's attitude to the Labour left could hardly have been improved by the special relationship between Transport House and Tribune, both of whom were resolute in defence of the rights of Social Democrats in these new 'People's Democracies'. But instead of aligning itself with the gathering forces of revolt in the Labour Party the CPGB became more strident in its attacks on social democracy—left and right. *The more the party opposed itself to the forward movement of the working class expressed through the Labour Party, and, more specifically, through Keep Left-Tribune current, the more marked was its decline in influence.* After one hundred candidates had been put up against Labour the crisis of the CPGB intensified.

> 'The result was disastrous; both Gallacher and Piratin, the sitting members were defeated, and as the "crypto-Communists" also disappeared, the party was deprived of representation in Parliament for the first time since 1935 . . . After this the real decline of the party had to be admitted. Communist bookshops all over the country were being forced to close for lack of custom, and the Daily Worker readership and advertising revenue slumped heavily.'[14]

The publication of the *British Road to Socialism* traditionally regarded as marking the CPGB's conversion to parliamentarism, did little to allay the suspicions of the social democratic mass. And even this document received a very 'tough' interpretation in the early Cominform period.[15] Whilst the party denied it contemplated the establishment of Soviet power, its alternative, the 'Peoples' Democracy' model of the Eastern European satellites, was every bit as 'Soviet' as the Soviet Union.[16] There is certainly no shortage of quotations from CPGB literature of the time denouncing 'the bourgeois theory of the state as an impartial apparatus'[17] and emphasising the need to 'smash all attempts to resist'.[18] Under Peoples' Democracy there was to be 'a new state apparatus . . . officered by men . . . from the ranks of the workers and peasants'.[19] Labour then, was part of 'the class enemy' and the pro-Labour press part of 'his main weapon'.[20] Nationalisation was being used by Labour 'to mask the reality of the growing reactionary character of state power . . .'[21] This was the tone of much of King Street's propaganda by 1951.[22] Bevanism was the CPGB's most serious problem for the next two years, until the denigration of Bevanism as a 'fake left' movement gave way, in 1954, to a more subtle approach.

The Daily Worker revelled in Bevan's difficulties prior to the resignations. It reported that, at the April Bermondsey meeting the Labour Minister 'defended the use of troops as blacklegs' in the dock strike. He had alleged that the dockers' actions were not democracy but anarchy.[23]

Immediately after the resignations the paper commented that the Cabinet crisis was due to 'American imposed rearmament and not to the overweening ambition or the deficient loyalty of Mr Aneurin Bevan . . .'[24] Nonetheless King Street was obliged to recognise the importance of the revolt, especially when the TUC General Council attacked the rebels.[25]

At the end of April the party rushed out a special pamphlet aimed at LP members[26] but the Party's Political Committee insisted that the resigning Ministers 'have presented no answer to the real issues confronting the Labour movement . . .'[27] Moscow was not satisfied even with this degree of coolness, and the new line that was to persist until 1953 was apparent in the report to the CPGB Political Committee of May 3rd,

> 'We should note the comments in "For a Lasting Peace" . . .[28] on the Bevan resignation, which pointed out that it arose from growing revolt in the Labour movement, and has brought into the open the split in the Labour government, but as far as Bevan is concerned *is a cunning manoeuvre for the purpose of deceiving the rank and file of the Labour Party*'.[29] (*My emphasis—MJ*).

Indeed an editorial in the journal of the Cominform went

further, declining even to use the word 'left' to describe Bevan and his supporters. Their 'manoeuvre' was merely an attempt by 'right wing Labour leaders' (this *included* Bevan) to 'split and disorganise the Labour movement'.[30] The CP began to look for the movement below which was, supposedly, undefiled by Bevanism.[31] It cited as evidence of this, the Socialist Fellowship Manchester conference, in which, as we have seen, the Trotskyists were playing a leading role.[32] The Daily Worker now began to reflect the tough Cominform line towards Bevanism. In its editorial on May 18th, entitled 'Mr Bevan's Blether' they accused him of using 'the usual scurrilous right wing language to condemn other critics'.[33]

In June, Communist Review was denouncing him as anti-Soviet[34] and it considered the Bevanite pamphlet *One Way Only* was

> 'far less clear, bold and class conscious than the foreign policy declaration of say, the AEU, NUR and ETU conferences . . . much of their analysis repeats the usual stale American-Tory-Transport House slanders about the Soviet Union'.[35]

This article conceded that the pamphlet was 'a valuable basis for discussion and united action'.[36] However the kind of activity envisaged was not the harmonious affair that might have implied. The Party sought only to 'use the situation to increase the sales and discussion of our own party programme'.[37]

Just at this time, in the summer of 1951, Bevan visited Yugoslavia. The Cominform moved quickly. Its journal commented,

> 'The worth of these "left" phrases becomes particularly clear from the single fact that at the present moment, Bevan is the guest of Tito, the spy and fascist.'[38]

This attitude of the Cominform marked a turn to a more virulent anti-Bevan tone in CP propaganda. Moscow feared the emergence of a new international 'centre' which might embrace dissidents like Tito, left social democrats like Bevan and perhaps even Mao.[39] Although it was only a small cloud on the horizon, Moscow was alive to this dangerous possibility. The re-formation of the Socialist International in August 1951 added to these fears.[40] Just how close the CPGB was to its 'third period' line of social-fascism[41] can be judged from this comment of Palme Dutt on the International's formation,

> 'Hitler, already, over a quarter of a century ago, chose the label "socialism" to describe his aims of war on the working class, on the Soviet Union, on the freedom of nations. Why should not the founders of the new Frankfurt International choose the title of "Democratic Socialism" to describe their aims of war on the countries of socialism and Peoples' Democracy . . .
> The resurrection of Axis fascism and of the pre-war Second International are two sides of a single American strategy.'[42]

As Stalin himself had put it in the thirties, social democracy and fascism were 'not antipodes but twins'. The Cominform dubbed the new organisation the 'police international'[43] no doubt to clearly distinguish it from their own. From this point onwards, the CPGB threw caution to the winds in an incredible campaign which drew together the anti-Tito campaign of the Cominform, the residual 'social fascist' theory of the thirties and anti-Trotskyism. The writings of the Yugoslavs Djilas, Kardelj and Pijade were described as a 'hotch-potch of Trotskyist phrases'.[44] Even Morgan Phillips and Sam Watson, two pillars of the orthodox Labour establishment were 'implicated' in a new world conspiracy by virtue of a five-hour meeting they had held with Tito and his Cabinet.[45] Social democrats, right and left, Titoites, Trotskyists, fascists and American imperialists were all in league, it was alleged. World News did not fail to note that Churchill's son-in-law Duncan Sandys also visited Tito.[46] The articles that appeared in Tribune[47] reporting Yugoslavia's bold experiments, and independent foreign policy, only 'confirmed' King Street's 'analysis'.

In November the CPGB published these fantasies in the form of a book by Klugmann, *From Trotsky to Tito.* It was withdrawn within five years. This book alleged that 'as the masses of the people turn away from Social Democracy [14 million voted Labour the very moment the book was coming out—MJ] reaction will turn to Titoism and all brands of pseudo-left demagogy as its main weapon of disruption.'[48] Bevanism, it suggested, was one such current, which concealed a right wing policy in left wing phrases![49]

The military aid agreement between Yugoslavia and the USA drove World News to publish Rumanian CP leader's call to 'overthrow the fascist dictatorship of the Tito gang'. The 'Tito clique', the appeal went on, combined its own theoretical efforts with 'Hitlerite economic ravings' and had established a 'Hitlerite order' in the economy under an 'Oberfuhrer'.[50] In December the CP revealed 'How the Titoites Work in Britain' with US intelligence, Trotskyists, and left social democrats.[51] The 'Titoite-Trotskyists' were supposed to have been sought out by the Bevanites whose plan was to hold on to the masses who were in the process of throwing off the long-established influence of social democracy. Social democracy was said to need left-sounding currents such as Bevanism to maintain their hold on the population. Finally Bevan had supposedly prepared the ground for Tito to establish an open link with Transport House. Thus ran the Klugmann theory.[52] The task the CP set itself was to 'divide the demagogues from those who genuinely are prepared to struggle.[53]

The party began the search for the 'genuine' left and reprimanded those in the CP who doubted its existence.[54] The search for the 'genuine' left was conducted throughout 1952. Anyone, even a former Labour Under Secretary,[55] who would say a few words against German Rearmament received more gratitude than Aneurin Bevan. The party press continued to demand struggle against the idea that socialism might be obtained through parliament;[56] to oppose the theory of the neutrality of the state, shared, it was argued, by both Bevan and Morrison;[57] and to underline the necessity of 'the people led by the working class to take power into their own hands.[58] The working class was urged not to rely on the parliamentary left but to use its industrial strength in addition to parliamentary representation.[59] Here the CPGB felt itself on strong ground. Bevan, it was argued, had,

> 'made clear his opposition to industrial action by the workers against the Tory cuts, and thus lined up with the dominant right wing leaders on this issue.'[60]

Isolation from the Bevanite current and electoral disaster drove the CPGB towards a perspective of industrial action. Even so 1952 was not especially noteworthy for industrial stoppages. In the pre-twenty-second conference discussion, industrial action to secure the defeat of the Conservatives was a popular theme.[61] Bevan's parliamentary perspectives were presented as part of a concerted operation by social democracy to contain the mass movement.

> 'Labour leaders from Bevan to Deakin have been pressed into service to condemn industrial action against the Tory cuts.'[62]

The unions were a favoured sphere of work because they were not considered Bevanite.

> 'The capitalist press is wholly misleading in describing the AEU policy as a Bevanite policy. It has little in common with Bevan whose limited stand is far far removed from this fighting AEU policy.'[63]

This prompted the party's leading propagandists to conclude,

> 'The terrible tragedy at this moment is that for all its fighting mood the Labour government is leaderless.'[64]

The CPGB members on the London Trades Council pursued this tough line by calling for a demonstration against Butler's cuts in March. The TUC reorganised the Trades Council, but not without considerable opposition even from the new reorganised Council.[65] A similar demonstration was well supported in the Rhondda. Syndicalism was now being counterposed to the 'parliamentarism' of *In Place of Fear*, a theme enthusiastically taken up by the Healy-Stanley wing of the Socialist Outlook.[66]

There can be little doubt that where the CPGB was involved in organising demonstrations against the Butler cuts, through positions they may have held in Union District Committees and Trades Councils, they experienced the enthusiasm of the mass movement for struggle. But the party had no justification to deduce from this that the ranks were not thoroughly pro-Labour in temperament, and very probably pro-Bevan.

After all 1952 was the run-up to Morecambe. Labour Party membership was rising steeply whilst CPGB membership fell by 9.5 per cent between 1950 and 1952.[67] Support for anti-Tory demonstrations in no way implied underwriting Soviet foreign policy as the CPGB might have wished.

The March 5th revolt of the fifty-seven Labour MPs against the Conservative Defence White Paper was treated to predictable cynicism. Nor did the pre-vote discussion satisfy the party. Whilst Bevan had come forward with a general criticism of American policy he also revealed 'his fear of the further development of the movement'.[68] The Cominform journal did not concede even this much to the former Minister. Its editorial the same week declared,

> 'The Right Wing Labour and Trade Union leaders—the Attlees, Morrisons, Deakins and Bevans are in deadly fear of the workers. They are panic-stricken because locomotive drivers have adopted a resolution calling for a general strike against the cuts . . . Bevan even refused to address a miners conference to discuss action against the cuts'.[69]

Here a militant syndicalist tone presents Bevan as a right winger, indistinguishable from his antagonists in the Labour Party struggle—Deakin and Morrison.

Labour's sweeping gains at the May elections did not alter the CP's line that Bevan was holding back the movement. J. R. Campbell reminded World News readers that the CP's 'British Road' was not purely parliamentary. Industrial action was needed to remove the Conservatives in 1952, he claimed, and Bevan was 'clutching at the coat tails of Uncle Sam'. Bevan's policy was 'not only in place of fear, but in place of socialism and common sense'.[70] George Matthews claimed Bevan's opposition to Government policy was purely verbal.[71] Whilst by August the party was compelled to recognise a significant development of the right wing's campaign against the Bevanites, it now claimed there was a danger that Labour movement could be deflected onto the discussion and argument around personalities instead of policies.[72]

A right wing group the 'Socialist Union' was formed in the Labour Party.[73] Tribune adopted its new campaigning format and went weekly in September.[74] At the Morecambe conference Bevanites won six out of the seven seats for the NEC's constituency section.[75]

In October Attlee's ban on party organisations was approved[76] and Gaitskell's Stalybridge speech opened a new right wing counter-offensive within the party.[77] None of this indicated a phoney war in the Labour Party, but the CPGB had no enthusiasm for the defence of the Bevanites at this stage. Indeed the party press appeared to be wishing to confirm Gaitskell's claim that a sixth of delegates to the LP conference were Communist or Communist inspired. 'Delegate after delegate . . . gave ample proof that they stood for something far to the left of the Bevanites'[78] said Peter Kerrigan on October 11th. The Political Committee report of October 3rd claimed that the main fight at Labour's conference was waged not by the principal figures in the Bevan group 'but by delegates from the CLPs and from progressive trades unions'.[79] This characterisation of Bevanism as a 'fake' left movement, fearful of industrial action, and in conspiracy with the right wing to hold back the mass movement below, continued throughout 1952 alongside the anti-Tito invective. For the CPGB the year began with the 'vigilance' campaign[80] and ended with the Slansky trial. The 'vigilance' campaign was an East European phenomenon in the main. Its object was the exposure of 'Titoite plots' and 'alternative centres grouping around their own adherents' in the CPs of the buffer states.[81] But the CPGB demanded 'Vigilance in Britain' also. 'Moral and personal weaknesses' of party members could be 'seized upon by the enemy'.[82]

At the party Congress in April, Pollitt declared, 'It isn't Aneurin Bevan that is developing this mass movement now manifesting itself . . . *Life and experience will prove, as so often before that such a united mass movement can never be developed under the leadership of anti-Soviet elements and admirers of Trotsky and Tito.*'[83] (emphasis in original report)

When *In Place of Fear* was published the same month, its attacks on totalitarianism, were dismissed as anti-communist. Emile Burns scoffed at the prediction that China would follow the rebellious example of Tito.[84] The book had been written during Bevan's visit to Yugoslavia the previous summer, and Bevan's projection of a Russian 'reformation' had certain similarities with Trotsky's perspective of a political revolution against Soviet bureaucracy. By November Tribune was getting a little tired of the CP's 'vigilance' and published a cartoon of Zilliacus, 'wanted—dangerous Fascist—Imperialist—Zionist—Trotskyist spy'![85] Mikardo parodying the CPGB wrote,

> 'It should always be borne in mind that our real enemies are not the Conservatives, or even the fascists but the so-called Social Democrats. Recently there has grown up an alliance between the so-called Social Democrats and the Titoist counter revolutionaries. Last year the capitalist Aneurin Bevan visited the imperialist Tito to concoct plans for a Titoist aggression against the peace loving democracies of Bulgaria and Rumania. Aneurin Bevan's real name is Al Bernstein, an American Jewish financier who speaks in a secret Welsh code'.[86]

The parody was very close to the reality of King Street's second-hand propaganda. In the Slansky indictment an international Jewish conspiracy *was* mentioned, and Zilliacus was 'implicated' along with the foreign Minister of Yugoslavia, Herbert Morrison and Richard Crossman in a Trotskyist-Titoist-Zionist plot![87]

Commenting on the sixth Congress of the Yugoslav party in November 1952 Klugmann, the party's theoretician, suggested that Tito's aim was 'to confuse the progressive, non-Communist left especially the left swinging movement in the Western Socialist and Labour Parties'.[88]

The CPGB was driven into ever more splendid isolation. Membership and sales of literature slumped. The Ridgeway demonstration in Paris jolted Moscow, and soon the French party gave the signal for some adjustment of line.[89] In September King Street theoretician, Palme Dutt, in his report to the Political Committee, permitted himself the indulgence of criticism on the lack of breadth in the 'Peace Movement'.[90] But it was the nineteenth Congress of the CPSU in October that confirmed the beginnings of a shift in Cominform tactics. Frustration of the 'Western' CPs may have played some part in this, but it was more likely that a section of the Soviet leadership was alarmed at the mood of revolt engendered by the collectivisation policy in the buffer states and sought a better understanding with the NATO powers, to preserve the division of Europe agreed upon in the post war treaties. But there is one anomaly here. The nineteenth Congress, which marked the modest beginning of the turn towards 'broad fronts' for peace and 'peaceful co-existence' was marked by the publication of an essentially ultra-left document—Stalin's *Economic Problems of Socialism in the USSR*.[91] The Generalissimo's book precluded the slightest possibility of a temporary or relative stabilisation of the capitalist world economy and projected imminent, catastrophic collapse.[92] This gloomy scenario was better suited to the tactic of unrelenting war on social democracy. It was Stalin's last indulgence, but party loyalists were repeating its inanities till as late as 1954, in the middle of a boom. Within five months of its publication the author was dead and the 'moderate' Khrushchev faction were walking the tightrope to power.

In November King Street was engaged in tentative 'self-criticism'. Pollitt addressing the EC of the Party on his return from Moscow confessed that the attempt to force the pace on the demand for a General Election had lost momentum and that the Conservative government had not been as ruthless as expected.[93] He therefore declared that,

> 'our full support will be given to every section of the Left in the Labour Party who desire changes in the policy and the leadership, however moderate they may be, that may lessen the grip of the USA on Britain . . .'[94]

Pollitt even defended Bevan against the right wing's allegation that the left had been responsible for Labour's failure to win the Wycombe by-election.[95] But these were only straws in a wind that did not really gather force until a good year later with the German Rearmament campaign. And even then, undercurrents of early Cominformism proved remarkably strong.

In the second quarter of 1953, 'self-criticism' became the vogue. It was the means by which the party leadership acclimatised the membership to the need for a change of line in keeping with the requirements of a new Soviet leadership. Even before Stalin's death Pollitt wrote a new article on the

Slansky trial which made no mention of a Bevanite-Titoite-Trotskyist amalgam.[96] His wife Marjorie Pollitt, fresh back from China, even ventured that sectarianism was 'the besetting sin' of the British party.[97] In February the party's chief admitted to underestimating the extent of the leftward moves of the rank and file of the Labour Party. The party had overplayed 'the danger of left manoeuvres'.[98]

Gollan repeated word for word Pollitt's statement that 'the small size of the party is the greatest obstacle to the achievement of our immediate and long term political aims'.[99] At an extended meeting of the EC, the committee 'quite deliberately put its own failings, weaknesses, faults and misdeeds first'.[100] William Lauchlin in March spoke of members who took 'cold blooded' decisions to keep people out of the CP,[101] and at a Glasgow rally 130 new members were claimed.[102] These moves betray the anxiety of the party leadership, no doubt prompted from Moscow,[103] to break out of its international isolation. But there was even a change in attitude towards the Conservatives. In April the party highlighted growing antagonisms between the UK and USA, and was delighted to note that 'the Tories are resisting attempts of the USA to force them into premature convertibility and . . . into European institutions dominated by the USA'.[104] At this stage the CP felt that the Tories would, in the last analysis, 'surrender' to Washington, but by May the 'real voice of Britain' was being expressed in parliament 'by Churchill and Attlee and by those demands for which we and the peace movement have been fighting so long and which have now gripped the masses of Britain.'[105] This kind of opportunism was too much for some leading Scottish members who resigned that summer.[106] In May the gains of Socialist-Communist left in the Italian local elections were cited as proof of what left unity might achieve.[107] Labour Monthly hailed this as a victory for 'the strategy of the united front, of co-operation in place of internecine strife and disruption'. 'Has all this no lesson for the Labour Party?' the Editor asked.[108] At the same time he lashed Labour for its 'anti-Soviet calumnies' and 'servile adulation of American imperialism' which he argued had handed the Tories victory in the Sunderland by-election.

This was indeed a difficult time for the leadership. The

entire party had been steeled in almost five years of intransigent ultra-leftism and were now required to unlearn all that they had learnt the day before. It was like riding two horses. The wild sectarian horse was little use for the delicate acrobatics of the broad front. Yet Stalin's 'Economic Problems' became compulsory reading in party branches. The 'Doctors' Plot' had all the promise of a new, anti-semitic purge. The Slansky trial generated furious controversy in the very broad Labour movement the party was supposed to be approaching with plans for joint activity. In some cases the older cadres who experienced the previous ultra-left zigzags of the third period and 1939–41 were being reinforced in sectarianism for the third time. The mentality of this layer within the party was not improved by vociferous social-democratic objections to Stalinist barbarism in Eastern Europe.

News of the CPSU nineteenth Congress only brought reminders from Tribune about the thirteen-year gap since the last one.[109] The CP's political committee was forced to denounce 'the right wing' (the CP's synonym for Labour MPs) for seeking to introduce a motion in parliament alleging the revival of anti-semitism in the Soviet Union[110] during the 'Doctors' Plot' affair. In March, when Stalin died, Michael Foot would insist on reminding Tribune readers of Stalin's support for Chiang Kai-shek, and how it had impeded the Chinese revolution.[111] How was the CPGB supposed to have a united front with people who raised such revisionist interpretations of history!

The mentality of the old guard is well illustrated by a Gallacher pamphlet on the Slansky trials[112] and by World News' comment that,

> 'Every man and woman in Britain will sleep more soundly at night because these conspiracies have been discovered in time . . . the uncovering of the present conspiracies may well prove to have been decisive in preventing a third world war from breaking out.'[113]

In the same article there were dark reminders of the Trotskyist and Bukharinist 'conspiracies' of the thirties, and allusions to others in Britain 'in the pay of the American imperialists . . . whom only the trial by a future Peoples' government of Britain will bring to light and deal with.' The post-Stalin thaw rocked King Street from April onwards and the release of the doctors 'wrongly arrested'[114] did not even bring a blush to the CP leaders' cheeks. Disgust with social democracy was further fuelled by reactions to the East Berlin uprising. When Gottwald died, a fortnight after Stalin, World News reminded its readers how he had foiled the abortive plot of the West and Social Democrats' in 1948 and 'merged' that party with his own Czechoslovak CP.[115] In April there were further 'revelations' about the 'arson' and 'wrecking' activities of the West German Social Democratic Party in East Berlin.[116] In June 'it was no accident' that 'the East Berlin "riots" and the Rosenberg execution together darkened a single week of history.' The rising 'met the needs of the US government.' (The demand for the legalisation of the Social Democratic Party was to the fore in East Berlin events.)

Labour expelled some members who had allowed themselves to be over-committed to some of the CP's 'peace front' activities. This was cited as evidence of the Labour leaders' unwillingness to engage in united action, and their 'capitulation' to American imperialism.[117] With such reasoning the CPGB was able to avoid a real united front campaign whilst at the same time advocating one. It was thus able, for some months, to proceed with the old sectarian line within an apparent tactic of seeking collaboration with social democracy. The 'blame' for the lack of unity could then be placed at Transport House's door. In the Spring of 1953 Labour obliged by expelling some peace campaigners and attacking the CP-dominated London Trades Council.[118] The CP answered allegations that it had been infiltrating the Labour Party, and declared its belief that 'the place of every worker . . . is inside the Communist Party' but 'our full support will be given to every section of the left inside the Labour Party which desires changes in the policy and the leadership'.[119] All of this had the effect of slowing down the turn to a veritable crawl.

Tito's visit to the UK in March did not assist. Nor did Jennie Lee's articles showing how Stalin had come to an agreement with Churchill in an attempt to decide the fate of Yugoslavia.[120] In August Bevan again visited Tito.[121] Tribune was full of admiration for the experiments in industrial democracy.[122] The summer of 1953 in fact witnessed the beginnings of a 'liberalisation' in the buffer states. Under the impact of the East German revolt Moscow slackened the reins a little, but Tito's experiments, which went much further in this respect, could not be countenanced.

The summer thus found the CP flaying around between rather empty demands for a united front, and reversions to 'social fascist' denunciations of Labour for non-compliance.[123] When Senator McCarthy attacked Attlee, Dutt found it a 'familiar irony'. Had not the Social Democratic leaders in Germany,

> 'refused a united front with the Communists against Hitler and imagined themselves safe in voting for Hitler in the Reichstag . . . only to find their turn came next'.[124]

Sixtieth birthday greetings to Walter Ulbricht occasioned similar remarks from Pollitt in early July.[125] Dutt denounced Labour's programme *Challenge to Britain* as a challenge to socialism. But still he called for a united front![126]

The Bevanites, as part of this social democracy, were therefore legitimate targets for continuing scepticism and hostility by these strange practitioners of the united front. In August Pollitt's indifference to the struggle in the Labour Party was expressed in the somewhat off-hand remark that its principal leaders were 'more interested in fighting each other than they are in fighting for what the workers want.'[127]

Figgins of the Railwaymen's union, who often gave voice to what the CP thought, rebuked the Bevanites in August's Labour Monthly. They were, he said, 'prisoners in the camp of their enemies' on the NEC. He demanded to know how they had voted on key policy issues. They were treading the path of compromise and were in a 'hopeless tangle'. They must 'admit their mistakes' and put forward 'a politically correct alternative policy'. He concluded that, compared with the NEC foreign policy 'Churchill is a revolutionary'.[128]

When in the late summer of 1953, Bevan made his second visit to Yugoslavia. Labour Monthly gave full vent to 'social fascism'. Labour's welfare state was 'disintegrating', its nationalisation only strengthened monopoly, and even its tax measures were supposed to have been derived from Bismarck,

Lloyd George and 'subsequently carried to an extreme height by Hitler'.[129] By November things had not improved. At the Labour Party Conference the CPGB would have it that Aneurin Bevan and Harold Wilson took the field against the progressive forces because they had opposed various resolutions on bank nationalisation.[130] Thus the CP ended up by attacking those they supposedly sought unity with.

The 'turn' had not come very far by the end of 1953. The party's fortunes were at a very low ebb.

NOTES

1. See Appendix 7 of the author's doctoral thesis: 'The British Road to Socialism—Two Versions'. Footnote 1 of this appendix contains material pointing to Stalin's personal involvement with the change in the CPGB's domestic strategy in the early fifties. See also pp. 17–24 of this study for comments on international Soviet strategy.
2. See same Appendix 7 for a fuller treatment.
3. Even today it would be foolish to say that because the PCI had advocated the historic compromise and 'Eurocommunist' parties embraced the parliamentary road that adventurism and the coup mentality have been foresworn. The experience of Portugal 1974–75 and the Communist party's involvement with the army officers there, its attempt to restrict the liberties of the Socialist party and the press, emphasises the need for caution. Likewise the Kremlin embraces intrigue, repression of national minorities and military adventurism on a grand scale in Africa today. None of this did they find in contradiction with the need for detente.
4. See Appendix 7 of the author's doctoral thesis for fuller treatment of the changing form of 'The British Road' and the changing emphasis given to the parliamentary road.
5. See p. 16 for the full quotation from World News 3.8.48.
6. Pelling, *The British Communist Party* op. cit. (p. 151).
7. Pelling, *op. cit.* (p. 149).
8. Pelling, *op. cit.* (p. 151).
9. Pelling, *op. cit.* (p. 151).
10. See CPGB election manifesto 1950 or excerpts in Appendix 7 of the author's doctoral thesis.
11. World News, 31.1.48. The letter came from a member of the Welwyn Garden City branch of the CPGB. A number of these

party members were expelled shortly afterwards for ultra-leftism! They were clearly regarded as 'Trotskyist' by some sections of the party (See World News, 17.1.48) but there appears to be little evidence that they were. Eric Heffer was one of the dissidents.

12. The new banner was hoisted by the French Communist Party in July 1947 with an attack on the idea of the 'Third Force' of the French Socialist Party (World News 10.7.48). By November the PCF were accusing the socialists of preparing the way 'directly for fascism' . . .

    'they personally use against the working class methods of police repression like those of the fascist regimes . . . This policy expresses the fundamental unity of the American Party of Blum and De Gaulle'.

    A French Communist Party's Central Committee called for vigilance 'to foil all provocateurs of the government, the fascists and the socialist leaders' (World News, 27.11.48). The British party had not gone quite that far, but the party theoretician, Palme Dutt, was making an amalgam between 'Mosley fascists, Toryism and the Labour government' by November in relation to colonial policy (World News 6.11.48). And as moves against Communists in the Civil Service and the expulsion of CP members who were full-time officials of the TGWU went ahead, the language became more strident.
13. See Appendix 9 to this volume. This analyses in great detail the voting behaviour of 121 left wing MPs on 14 key issues over ten years and presents them in the form of a grid making possible generalised conclusions about political leanings.
14. Pelling, *The British Communist Party* op. cit. (p. 163).
15. See Appendix 7 of the author's doctoral thesis for examples of ultra-leftism in the first edition of 'The British Road'.
16. See Appendix 7 of the author's doctoral thesis for further treatment of this subject.
17. Communist Review, April 1951, the CPGB theoretical journal.
18. World News, 7.4.51.
19. World News, 17.6.50, reprinted from 'For a Lasting Peace, For A Peoples' Democracy' (FALPFAPD) 26.6.50.
20. World News, 26.5.51.
21. Communist Review, May 1951.
22. Just how ultra-left the Cominform parties were may be judged from a perusal of an article by USA CP chief William Z. Foster (World News, 20.1.51). 'Wall Street is definitely driving towards the establishment of fascism in this country (USA)' said Foster. The Truman government was 'fascist minded' and 'fascist at heart'. The trades unions were not to be wiped out by one blow through the establishment of a Hitler-style labour front, but the same effect was to result from 'a thorough domestication of the Social Democratic (American brand) leadership in the trade

unions'. Another example of Cominform conformity is to be found in World News, 23.6.51, the CPGB was gallantly defending the genetic quackery of Lysenko, the Soviet biologist, and CP members in the AScW had succeeded in getting a report on the dispute published by that union.

23. Daily Worker, Wednesday, 4.4.51.
24. Daily Worker, 23.4.51.
25. Daily Worker, 26.4.51.
26. World News, 5.5.51.
27. Ibid.
28. 'For a Lasting Peace for a Peoples Democracy' the snappy title of the journal of the Cominform which circulated to all CPs. It was published in Bucharest, in many languages.
29. World News, 12.5.51.
30. 'For a Lasting Peace . . .' 11.5.51—front page editorial (rare for British news).
31. World News, 5.5.51.
32. See Chapter on the Socialist Fellowship.
33. Daily Worker, 18.5.51.
34. Communist Review, June 1951.
35. World News, 21.7.51. The unions mentioned in this piece were unions in which the CP was in a position to influence in respect of conference resolutions. The case of the ETU is celebrated.
36. World News, 21.7.51.
37. World News, 28.7.51.
38. 'For a Lasting Peace . . .' 27.7.51.
39. Klugmann, author of *Trotsky to Tito* quoted the US Information Service speculation on Mao becoming another Tito on 21.12.49. Time was to confirm this prediction at an interval of fourteen years.
40. World News, 18.8.51.
41. Stalin characterised Social Democracy in the period 1929–34 as Socialist in words but fascist in deeds—'Social Fascism'. Left social democrats were therefore 'left social fascists and social democracy was the twin of fascism.'
42. World News, 18.8.51.
43. World News, 18.8.51.
44. Communist Review, July 1951.
45. Communist Review, July 1951.
46. World News, 15.9.51.
47. Tribune, 20.9.51 'Tito and the West' by Jennie Lee.
48. *From Trotsky to Tito* James Klugmann, leading CP member (p. 199).
49. Ibid.
50. World News, 13.10.51, and 10.11.51.
51. World News, 1.12.51. Konni Zilliacus, Labour MP was one of the main targets of the CP. How they squared this with the fact that he had the whip withdrawn is a puzzle.

52. *From Trotsky to Tito*, James Klugmann, p. 195.
53. *Op. cit.*, p. 202.
54. It was suggested that Sidney Silverman, Desmond Donnelly and Ellis Smith (formerly Socialist Fellowship President) were possible candidates for collaboration because they had been demanding talks to ease international tension. But one piece of irony here is that, according to Foot, it was just about this time that Donnelly began leaking information about the Bevanite parliamentary group meetings to Dalton. The proof of this Foot discovered in Dalton's unpublished diaries. (Foot *op. cit. Vol II* p. 358 footnote). This fact reveals the shallow, if not dishonest, nature of the claim that Bevanites and right wing were in league. Indeed the CP themselves were closer to the right wing in their choice of 'genuine lefts'. For Donnelly was quickly to evolve into a mainstay of the right wing in the Labour Party.
    Another interesting aspect of the party's search for 'genuine lefts', who were not part of the Bevanite movement, was their discovery of Jack Stanley, moving spirit behind Socialist Outlook in which the Trotskyists, through editor John Lawrence, had a decisive sway. Stanley attended the Moscow Economic Conference in the Spring of 1952, as had Sidney Silverman. World News found Stanley's and Desmond Donnelly's comments on the Soviet Union at the Labour Party Conference in October, far more palatable than Bevan's critical remarks (World News 11.10.51).
    Stanley re-appeared in December as one of the sponsoring committee of the Moscow-inspired 'Congress for Peace' held in Vienna (World News 20.9.52). This Congress was for 'men and women of all views and faiths' yet World News could not have been unaware that Stanley was working closely with the Trotskyists, for Klugmann himself had documented how they had entered the Labour Party in 1948 to work in the left current (*From Trotsky to Tito*, p. 195). The question arises was the CP itself working inside that same current alongside the Trotskyists? For at the same time as they were praising Stanley, founder of Socialist Outlook, the CP was warning of Trotskyist influences in the left movement, (Communist Review, December, 1952). Another leader-writer for Socialist Outlook, and leader of the old Socialist Fellowship, was coming out with a line on the Bevanites, that was almost identical to the CPGB's. Writing to Tribune in March, 1952, Tom Braddock described the fifty-seven MPs voting against the Defence White Paper as 'the fifty seven varieties'. Their fight with the party leadership was 'just as much sham as is the one between the leadership and the Tory Party'. Braddock backed *Arthur Deakin*'s verdict that the defence vote was not an argument about principle (Tribune, 21.3.52).
55. World News, 23.2.52. Ernest Davies was the Under Secretary in question.

56. World News, 29.3.52. Emile Burns replying to criticism by party members that there were concessions to the parliamentary road in the party's attitude. See also World News, 29.3.52. Emile Burns.
57. World News, 8.3.52.
58. World News, 8.3.52. An article by A. Darwin 'Social Democracy & The State'. This same edition of World News carried an article by French CP leader Andre Marty in which he stated 'So the Socialist Party leaders (in France) are no longer content to hold back the mass movement for bread and peace and against Fascism; they are now trying to find pretexts to *get the fascists into the government.*'
59. World News, 29.3.52. Emile Burns. A view strongly propounded by G. Healy in Socialist Outlook.
60. World News, 8.3.52.
61. World News, 15.3.52 back page. Also World News 22.3.52.
62. World News, 29.3.52 and 3.5.52 pp. 196–8.
63. World News, 17.5.52, and 3.5.52.
64. World News, 1.11.52.
65. World News, 8.3.52.
66. Socialist Outlook, January and March, 1952. Socialist Outlook, 16.5.52, carried a review of *In Place of Fear* by John Lawrence which attacked Bevan's 'dynamic parliamentarism.'
67. *The British Communist Party*, Pelling, *op. cit.* (p. 192). CPGB membership according to its own EC reports was: 1950 (May) 38,853, 1952 (March) 35,124.
68. World News, 8.3.52.
69. For a Lasting Peace . . . 7.3.52.
70. World News, 10.5.52.
71. World News, 24.5.52.
72. World News, 23.8.52.
73. World News, 9.1.54, formed in Summer of 1952.
74. Tribune, 26.9.52.
75. *A Short History of the Labour Party*, Pelling, *op. cit.* (p. 110).
76. *A Short History of the Labour Party*, Pelling, *op. cit.* (p. 110).
77. Tribune, 10.10.52.
78. World News, 11.10.52.
79. as above.
80. World News, 5.1.52.
81. World News, 16.2.52.
82. World News, 15.3.52.
83. World News, 19.4.52. Report of the CP's 22nd Congress.
84. Communist Review, May 1952.
85. Tribune, 28.11.52.
86. Tribune, 28.11.52.
87. Socialist Outlook, 5.12.52. The issue of 28.11.52 quoted Mr A. Leonidov, a Soviet propagandist writing in the East German Neue Welt, that 'Tribune' was a 'two-faced centrist, Trotskyist splinter group'!

88. World News, 22.11.52.
89. The extent of the isolation of the Western CPs was more clearly revealed across the Channel. The disastrous Ridgeway demonstration resulted in a Gaullist-CRS attack on CP members, a series of police raids and the arrest of Communist leader Duclos. (See World News, 14.6.52.) In June the Americans bombed the Yalu and in November Eisenhower was elected President. The PCF was the first to sound the alarm and called for a 'correction' of its own 'sectarianism'. The strike wave to secure Duclos' release had been successful and, no doubt, the French party found the united action with others a refreshing change (World News, 5.7.52). All these changes were reported in World News.
90. World News, 4.10.52.
91. Reviewed at length in a series in the late Autumn of 1952 in World News.
92. World News, 31.3.53, p. 60 contains lengthy quotations on this theme.
93. World News, 15.11.52. The EC was held on November 9th.
94. as above.
95. as above.
96. World News, 3.1.53. This article appears to have been a premature attempt to 'disentangle' the Social Democrats and the left from their contrived 'involvement' in the Slansky case to enable the party to get a little closer to the left. Clearly this could not be done if the Bevanite left were 'implicated' in a plot against the East European states along with Tito 'the fascist and spy'.
97. World News, 3.1.53.
98. World News, 21.2.53.
99. World News, 21.2.53, Pollitt's report to the EC uses the selfsame wording as Gollan in World News, 28.2.53.
100. World News, 28.2.53, Gollan to extended EC meeting.
101. World News, 14.3.53, William Lauchlin at extended EC meeting.
102. World News, 21.3.53, Max Morris.
103. Because the PCF and PCI were engaged in the self-same manoeuvres when their leaders returned from Moscow.
104. World News, 11.4.53, J. R. Campbell.
105. World News, 25.7.53, PC meeting. This referred to Churchill's peace initiative of May 11th supported by Attlee on the 12th.
106. World News, 22.8.53 reporting August 6th Glasgow party meeting at which 545 backed the party, 34 backed its critics and 36 abstained. The rebels were Harry McShane, Hugh Savage and Alex Bernstein. This was a pale reflection of the Marty-Tillon revolt in the PCF at about the same time.
107. World News, 7.6.52.
108. Labour Monthly, July 1953.
109. Tribune,10.10.52.
110. World News, 7.3.53.

111. World News, 7.3.53.
112. Ibid.
113. World News, 18.4.53.
114. World News, 18.4.53.
115. World News, 21.3.53.
116. World News, 25.4.53.
117. World News, 4.7.53, and Labour Monthly, July 1953.
118. World News, 7.2.53, and Labour Monthly, February 1953. The Council had been disaffiliated by the TUC for its political activities.
119. World News, 3.1.53.
120. Tribune, 7.9.51.
121. Foot, *Vol II, op. cit.* (p. 406).
122. Tribune, 4.9.53.
123. The tactic of the united front was elaborated by the Communist International in the twenties. It was designed, specifically with Germany in mind, to unite working class parties on essential questions whilst recognising both the existence of separate parties and the rights of these parties to criticise each other. Its relevance is thus confined to those countries where *substantial working class support is aligned behind two parties. It has not the slightest relevance in Britain, where the Labour Party monopolises the support of the main forces of organised labour.* Nonetheless it is a slogan which remains popular with the Communist Party in its non-sectarian periods, and with small groups isolated from the mass movement.
124. Labour Monthly, June 1953.
125. World News, 4.7.53.
126. Labour Monthly, July 1953.
127. World News, 1.8.53.
128. Labour Monthly, August 1953.
129. Labour Monthly, September 1953.
130. Labour Monthly, November 1953. See also Dutt's arguments about 'right wing Labour's' programme having similarity with that of Mosley's in the thirties.

Chapter Nine

The Spirit of Geneva

Five key aspects of the political situation provide the framework for the consideration of relations between the Bevanites and the CPGB during 1954–55.

First among these were the tensions in South East Asia. In particular the struggle of the Vietnamese for national liberation and the overturn of the old social order, was part of the continuous process that produced the Chinese revolution of 1949. As such it represented a threat to the post-war settlements between the Kremlin and the West. This caused the Soviet leaders to accelerate their abandonment of Cold War intransigence, and to urgently seek rapprochement with the colonial powers in the Far East, France and Britain; to heal the breach which the Vietminh had opened up.

This was most vividly expressed in the French defeat at Dien Bien Phu which took place *in the middle of the Geneva conference between Britain, France, USA, China and the USSR.* The Soviet leaders, faced with the possibility of yet another Communist 'centre' outside of their control,[1] settled for the partition of Vietnam. The victorious Vietnamese communists thus began another 20-year long struggle to recoup that which they lost at Geneva. Secondly; the speed of the Kremlin's turn outpaced the CPGB, who, though ever willing, were tardy in keeping abreast, and weighed down with a cadre steeped in ultra-leftism. Indeed the party cadres were not the only ones to be left breathless. Washington found the new Soviet sweet-reasonableness difficult to adjust to, and Dulles' talk of 'agonising re-appraisals' and 'massive retaliation' seemed more in keeping with the late forties. Thus the United States was not party to the final Geneva settlement.

Thirdly, the decision of the Labour Party to send official delegations to Russia and China in the course of 1954 unleashed a wave of intemperate optimism throughout the movement, and especially amongst the Bevanite left, about the direction of the Chinese and Soviet dominated regimes and the nature of the new Kremlin leadership.

The left totally misconstrued the Russian moves towards rapprochement. *They saw in it what they wanted to see*—not a desperate bid to stem the growing revolt in Eastern Europe and South East Asia but a 'liberalisation' of Stalinism. The fourth aspect only compounded the Bevanites' confusion. The Khrushchevite wing of the Stalinist leadership began at this same juncture to make friendly overtures towards Tito's Yugoslavia. It was essential for Moscow to eliminate Belgrade as a possible centre of attraction for the states of Hungary, Poland, East Germany and Rumania, now in turmoil over forced collectivisation and centralised planning.[2] This meant patching up the quarrel of 1947, even to the point of Moscow eventually admitting responsibility for the rift. For his part, Tito began to tighten the reins within Yugoslavia. Bevan's friend Djilas, who had from October 1953 been intensifying his polemical struggle for the extension of the struggle for democracy and the withering away of the state in Yugoslavia,[3] was one of the first victims of Tito's new wave of repression, as was another of Bevan's friends, Vladimir Dedijer. It was being said by those in leading positions of authority in Yugoslavia that Djilas' political outlook exhibited the influence of Aneurin Bevan.[4] The strict limits to the 'direct democracy' and decentralisation of the 1950–53 experiments were now becoming apparent to those who had allowed superficial impressions to sway their judgement in the heady days of Tito's revolt.

> 'In harmony with Moscow, the Yugoslav party could more easily avoid ideological disintegration and justify its own dictatorship. Among the Soviet leaders, Tito saw in Khrushchev the best hope for influencing Russia's evolution, as well as for extending Yugoslav influence.'[5]

The Bevanites duly traded-in their illusions in Tito for a fresh set of illusions in the Khrushchev leadership.

The fifth element in Bevanite-CPGB relations was a domestic one—the development of widespread wages militancy and a deepening struggle against union bureaucracy, which gathered pace from the Autumn of 1954 onwards. In its modest, non-violent 'British' way this domestic struggle was related to the anti-bureaucratic struggles of Eastern Europe, even though it took place within the very different setting of a mature parliamentary democracy. The struggles of 1954–55 did more to upset the CPGB's strategy of courting the Bevanites than any other single factor. Because for all of King Street's talk about the ranks being to the left of the Bevanite leadership it was the leadership they were most anxious to woo. And their carefully rehearsed advances were constantly disrupted from below. But even this was nothing compared to the havoc later caused by the Hungarian and Polish events of 1956. In short it was the tempo of the class struggle in Britain, Eastern Europe and South East Asia which determined the fate both of the CPGB's strategy of a broad front with the Labour left and the fate of the Bevanites themselves.

In 1954 the familiar phrase that peppered the various CPGB reports and journals was 'the present small size of the party is the greatest obstacle to the successful achievement of both our immediate and long term goals'. This profound tautology was repeated by at least two party leaders in identical wording and appears to have been brought back from the USSR.[6] There were continuing frank admissions of the serious crisis in membership and sales of literature.[7] But by the end of the first quarter the party could claim to have halted the sharp slide in membership to some degree and to have modestly increased the sales of their paper World News.[8] The 'spirit of Geneva' and the German Rearmament campaign undoubtedly assisted here. The party put all its energies into these two campaigns in a concerted attempt to influence the parliamentary left. For example, in January 1953 Peter Zinkin had Bevan 'hobnobbing with the Egyptian dictator General Neguib' when he 'should have been out in the country helping to rouse the people' against the Rent Bill.[9] This was clearly a residual reflex of early cominformism. But on March 1st, it was announced that the USA now had the means of delivery of the H-bomb and that 'massive retaliation' to any aggressor was now possible. This, combined with the failure of the Berlin talks and moves towards a European Defence Community, to include a re-armed West Germany, alarmed the Soviet leadership; now the CPGB set about removing obstacles to the perspective of a broad front for peace. Their first task was the elimination of whatever Trotskyist influence that might exist on the Labour left.[10]

The period from January to April 1954 appears almost to be a struggle for the soul of Tribune between Stalinists and Trotskyists. Advertisement for the literature of both was stepped up considerably in the columns of the Bevanite paper. The latest statements of Soviet leaders, turned out as pamphlets, vied for custom with the writings of Leon Trotsky. Later whole page advertisements appeared advertising meetings of the British Soviet Friendship Society.[11] Book reviews of Deutscher's *The Prophet Unarmed* and Carr's *The Interregnum* written by Tribune's Richard Findlater, generated furious controversy. Lysenkoism, 'Socialist Realism' and the nature of the Chinese revolution were the subject matter of further book reviews which prompted complaining letters from CPGB supporters. When the review of Michael Padev's book *What Happens to Communists* revealed the nature of Stalin's purges and the fate of its victims, correspondents called for 'vigilance' against the likes of Bruce Bain.[12] One indignant correspondent added that 'right wingers' generally would have been 'liquidated by now in a true socialist society.'[13]

The Trotskyists who had been portrayed as little different from Social Democrats in the period 1948–53 were now characterised by the CPGB as wild 'left adventurers' as the party moved from its own wild adventurism to a new accommodation with Social Democracy.[14] The party's struggle for the new line staggered forward to the 23rd Congress in April with successes and setbacks. The Trotskyists were now out of action in the Tribune arena, preoccupied with the struggle to maintain the Outlook as a paper independent of the Bevanites, after the proscription. In Yorkshire a number of Labour Party members who had allowed themselves to become over-enamoured of the CPGB's peace groups and the Vienna Peace Congress were expelled by Transport House. Whilst Transport House showed no favouritism in this respect to Stalinists or Trotskyists, the Bevanites resolutely defended the expelled in both these cases.[15]

Nonetheless CPGB theoreticians were still proclaiming that Social Democrats could not be trusted to break up the state machine and that they would leave it untouched as they had done in 1945.[16] Complaints were to be heard that the CPGB was 'dissolving itself into the Labour Party'.[17] In March Pollitt published his *Open Letter to Members of the Labour Party* and his pamphlet *The People on the March.* In these tracts he made a clear appeal for unity in the struggle against German Rearmament. The party actually began publishing the texts of Bevanite parliamentary speeches, and despite the narrow defeats in the PLP in the Spring, Bevan was said to have won a moral victory. Special conferences were called on German Rearmament through the auspices of Peace Committees at local and national level with serious attempts to involve Bevanite MPs.[18]

The party's own propaganda gave a sharper edge to the *anti-German* aspects of the issue, drawing on a fund of anti-German feeling that had been accumulated in two world wars. At the same time they stressed the dangers of former Nazis acceding to influential command positions. Utilising these general fears and pandering to vulgar anti-teutonism was particularly objectionable in the light of the forthright opposition to German Rearmament by the German Social Democratic Party itself. Anti-German feeling was as strong in the Bevanite ranks as it was in the CPGB, where the collective guilt of the German people was an article of faith amongst many party members. This element in the campaign brought the Bevanites and King Street closer together. Virulently anti-German cartoons began to disgrace the pages of Tribune.[19] In its eagerness Tribune misquoted Chancellor Konrad Adenauer over the issue of Germany's eastern territories in the pamphlet *It Need Not Happen.* The Chancellor wrote to Tribune and secured an apology.[20]

At the CPGB Congress in 1954 Pollitt drove home his argument against the waverers. 'I am aware' he said, 'that we make many opportunist mistakes, but it is still our deep rooted sectarianism that is our principal weakness.'[21] The imperatives of Kremlin foreign policy were not to be denied by nostalgia for the tough 'left' line.

The Bevanites' wholesale immersion in the campaign against

German Rearmament gave some consolation to the CPGB leadership that even if they were not penetrating the left current, they were, on this issue, running alongside it for a change. The sharpness of Findlater and Padev on matters of Soviet history was more than offset, as the year wore on, by naïve credulity on the part of other Bevanites in their attitude to Eastern Europe. This was partly the result of the sudden popularity of the East-West trade campaign,[22] about which both Wilson and Mikardo had written favourably; partly to the Labour Party's decision to send official delegations to Moscow and Peking; and also to the popular front, on which the Kremlin had embarked throughout Europe to halt German rearmament.[23] It was assisted by anti-Americanism born of Dulles' verbal brinkmanship. The conciliatory tone within Tribune was launched in a series of extremely shallow, impressionistic articles by Mervyn Jones, a regular correspondent. He was challenged by the Chairman of the Czechoslovak Social Democratic Party-in-exile for the remark that he detected no police atmosphere in Czechoslovakia, and for his failure to mention the June 1953 demonstrations in Moravska Ostrava against the government's economic measures, which had resulted in the imprisonment of those whom he called 'Czech Bevanites'.[24]

When Djilas was dismissed from the Central Committee of the Yugoslav party Tribune was reluctant to pass judgement, referring to it as a 'family quarrel'. And whilst the Rumanian trials produced 'a sense of shock'[25] editor Bob Edwards managed to find words of praise for the 'new policy' of civil liberties which he detected in the USSR. He urged readers to take into account that the process of liberalisation must take generations.[26]

Tribune made no attempt to explain how the liberalisation process was being *reversed* in Yugoslavia. It simply reported a 'wave of intolerance' and issued a condemnation couched in pleading tones. Tribune's response to East European developments was monitored in pain or pleasure, but seldom understanding.

Bevan himself was only marginally more qualified and circumspect in his judgements on Eastern Europe and China. On his return from the official visits even he showed greater reliance on personal impressions than on the grim omens of history. Whilst paying tribute to the Chinese revolution and the national struggle he advised their leaders not to dismiss social democratic ideas of freedom.[27] He put a question mark over Mao Tse Tung's judgement.[28] In his discussions with the Kremlin's new collective leadership he detected 'none of the stuffiness of the Stalin period'. Khrushchev was not another Stalin. Bevan found him 'jovial'.[29] And it is certainly a fact that Khrushchev complimented him on the pamphlet *It Need Not Happen*, which was something of an embarrassment considering the presence of Bevan's NEC antagonists.[30]

Ian Mikardo's enthusiasm for the new detente was recklessly enthusiastic. In the Autumn afterglow of the publication of Morgan Phillips' *East Meets West*,[31] he ventured a series of articles on Eastern Europe which had the victimised Social Democratic exiles gasping with disbelief. There was 'very little poverty in Red Hungary' he claimed. The Hungarians were 'happy in their work', and Mikardo boasted he was not a man who could be easily 'kidded'.[32]

He felt free to go where he pleased. In both Poland and Hungary he believed material standards were high considering the greater level of the social wage. The churches were full (even this last fact might have cast doubt that all was well in this atheistic state). A leader of the exiled Hungarian Socialist Party was scathing at Mikardo's gullibility.[33] Did he not know about compulsory labour? Arbitrarily fixed wage levels? High production quotas? Stakhanovism? Did he not know of the passive resistance of Hungarian workers because there were no genuinely free trades unions? Finally he asked Mikardo why he had failed to condemn the imprisonment of former trade union and socialist leaders in Hungary. No satisfactory answer was forthcoming.

The most charitable thing that can be said about articles by Mikardo and others is that they revealed a very shallow understanding of the extremely contradictory and internally unstable nature of the East European regimes. It was as if the Tribune articles condemning the earlier trials and defending Tito from Moscow's monstrous lies had never been written, or written by different people. Moral condemnation of the East European regimes co-existed with a superficial indulgence in this pragmatic approach that characterised the Bevanites' attitude to the non-capitalist states.

The CPGB leaders were no doubt confirmed in their view of the fickleness of left social democracy by these changing sentiments. King Street never questioned the twists and turns of Kremlin policy but they understood even less the gyrations which they induced in the Labour left. By the summer of 1954 however, King Street may have felt they were making some headway in their bid for 'left unity'. Gollan's book *The British State* gave emphasis to the peaceful road to socialism, and this was in line with social democratic thinking. Tribune for its part made friendly remarks in an editorial celebrating the twelfth anniversary of the Anglo-Soviet treaty.[34]

The hesitant, mistrustful, detente between the rulers of Eastern Europe and colonial South East Asia proceeded under the impetus of revolt and the awful realities of war in the newly arrived era of 'deliverable' Hydrogen bombs. Though the Berlin conference of February 1954 failed to produce a settlement in Europe, the French and British foreign ministers managed to get agreement in placing Indo-China on the agenda for the Geneva conference which began on 26th April.[35] The British and the Americans experienced simultaneous threats to their spheres of influence in Latin America. British troops were sent into British Guiana when the constitution was suspended, whilst some right wing generals with the assistance of the US Marines and CIA advisers[36] overthrew the government of Arbenz in Guatemala to restore the confiscated property of the United Fruit Company of America.

But the Vietnamese crisis required greater subtlety of approach. For the solution of this problem and the general questions concerning the big powers, the Geneva conference was convened. It was to mark a definitive turn in the relations between the USSR and the Western powers after the Cominform intermission of 1947–53.

What the Vietnamese had achieved over the French army, they could not sustain over the combined diplomatic efforts of the USSR, USA, UK, France and China. The conference effectively partitioned Vietnam and a new, more bitter, twenty-year struggle began. For the Bevanites the road to the new hell was paved with the 'best' of intentions—peaceful settlement, negotiations and collaboration between East and West. And in the working out of the process the Bevan-Nehru axis was to provide an essential bridge between Moscow, Peking and the more conciliatory western powers. India was one of the three nations of the Supervisory Commission. What is more, the UK's role of the independent mediator, long advocated by the Bevanites, was the pivot of Geneva's 'success'.

Tribune was generous in its praise for Eden who was 'speaking for Britain' at Geneva, and making a 'genuine, sustained effort . . . to secure a negotiated settlement'.[37] Bevan's championing of Nehru was crowned by the success of the Delhi talks between Chou and Nehru. The latter viewed the machinations at Geneva in a favourable light and as a step on the road to the settlement of problems elsewhere. Meanwhile in the Washington talks Churchill expressed support for a policy of peaceful co-existence. This was the occasion of his speech asserting that 'jaw, jaw' was better than 'war, war'. The Communist Party commented favourably on Churchill's pronouncements and their front organisations were deeply involved in the Berlin 'World Peace Council' exercise, which called for pressure to secure a 'successful outcome' to the Geneva conference and in particular a peaceful settlement of the Indo China conflict.[38]

The CP in July noted, with satisfaction, the 'success' of the Geneva conference, and saw in it new hope for a European settlement, whilst at the same time they admitted the Viet Minh had made 'great concessions'.[39] In fact they had, with Soviet assistance, snatched defeat from the jaws of victory. The Bevanite leadership was drawn into this subtle embrace despite Bevan's declared opposition to SEATO—which had prompted his shadow cabinet resignation. The governments of India, Burma, Indonesia and Ceylon were no less opposed to SEATO, but this did not prevent their involvement in the overtures to Geneva. Indeed Nehru's acquiescence lent to the Geneva conference the aura of respectability derived from his status as leader of the 'non-aligned' nations, even though India did not participate directly. Nehru was the arch-representative of the very 'non-aligned' bloc whose authority the Bevanites sought to strengthen. Geneva was the very conference the Bevanites had been advocating for many months. All the

Bevanite pressure to get Eden to 'speak for Britain' resulted, in the last analysis, in negating the victory at Dien Bien Phu, partition and a new civil war. That was not how it appeared at the time. But that was the result.

The new climate, the 'spirit of Geneva', led to speculation as to whether there might now be the possibility of a German Geneva, with the resolution of the problems of European security and disarmament. This latter question had been discussed without any outcome at the London talks in May. The CPGB gratified by Bevan's 'progress', commented,

> 'The new Bevanite pamphlet *It Need Not Happen* (1/-, Tribune Publications) will also have the effect of strengthening opposition to EDC within the Labour Party. The fact that the pamphlet suggests that the Big Four conference should take the Soviet plan for a European Mutual Security Pact as a basis for negotiations means that the new Soviet proposals will have strong support from among the membership of the Labour Party'.[40]

German Rearmament became the major issue as the summer wore on. There were fifty-eight resolutions tabled on it for Labour Party conference. The Bevanite pamphlet received a huge sale. CPGB members were urged to sell Pollitt's pamphlet at Labour's regional German Rearmament conferences. When the French Assembly voted down the EDC, Britain was said, by the CPGB, to have become the centre of the stage in the anti-rearmament campaign.[41] There were calls for unity in action 'at local level'.[42] Feeling in the CLPs was particularly strong. The publication of Lord Russell of Liverpool's book *The Scourge of the Swastika* added to public controversy. Simultaneously Tribune produced a rather shabby article on the inherent militarism that was supposed to have permeated all aspects of German social life, including the position of the father in the German family structure!

Pollitt visited Russia shortly after the Transport House delegation. It seems reasonable to assume that he was briefed on the nature of the discussions, and he was certainly able to give a good report of the party's turn. The Communist Party's marshalling of their small but efficient trade union machine was indicated by the regular publication of tables in World

News, which gave the latest updated positions on the number of trade union votes committed on each plank of the party programme—East-West trade, against German Rearmament, for four-power talks, etc. The votes at union conferences would, of course, have an important bearing on the block vote at the Labour Party conference.

The confluence of Bevanite and CPGB campaigns on German rearmament produced a new, temporary alignment within the unions in the course of 1954. The changed attitude of King Street meant that the Bevanites were getting some additional wind in their sails. But it was not long before the Bevanites were fighting on two fronts again. In the Blue union dispute,[43] which erupted in the late autumn, Tribune took on the combined forces of the TGWU-Transport House bureaucracy and King Street. The very narrow limits of King Street's alignment with the Bevanites was fully revealed. For whereas the Bevanites enthusiastically welcomed the radicalisation of the ranks, the CPGB found itself under attack from Tribune for its attitude to the dockers' struggle. The CPGB, which only months earlier had been bracketing Bevanites with right wingers and the 'fascist' Tito, was now embarrassed to find itself opposing the Blue union along with Arthur Deakin!

The Communist Party's first response to the strike against compulsory overtime (it was the most important dock strike since 1926) was to call upon union leaders to rectify grievances. The TUC took the unprecedented step of denouncing the strike called by an officially recognised, affiliated union by its officially elected leadership. Arthur Deakin branded the NASD efforts as 'the spearhead of the communist drive for control of the ports.'[44] Not only was this patently at variance with what dockers knew to be the case, but it had the effect of sharpening the antagonisms between the Bevanites and the Communist Party, for the former were most anxious to dissociate themselves from this smear.[45] The CP was almost equally indignant for though their members in the White union belatedly backed the strike against compulsory overtime, they militantly campaigned against those dockers who were voting with their feet for the NASD. Tribune ridiculed the Deakin allegation in late October and published factual evidence to show that the Daily Worker had denounced the NASD in Hull causing a prominent CP docker to leave the party. This meant, they claimed, there were no further CP members on the NASD executive.[46]

'Deakin Aids Pollitt' ran the sub-head of Tribune's special supplement, and reply to the NEC.

> 'Harry Pollitt and his friends were slow in discovering what was happening on the docks. They jumped on the band-wagon long after it had started. Of course they do their best to exploit the situation. But Mr Pollitt's best thanks are due to Mr Deakin'.[47]

It was galling to be linked with Deakin in this way, for the Transport Workers leader was so unpopular with his members that he dared not accept an invitation to address them at an Albert Hall rally. The main thrust of CPGB propaganda in the dispute was the danger of 'breakaways'. But the NASD was no breakaway union such as the CPGB had itself engineered in 1928.[48] It was a bona fide union with a long history, and an affiliated TUC body. The charge that the NASD union was a 'breakaway' only assisted the Deakinites in their vendetta. Tribune reported the 'comical' sight of the CPGB members,

> 'in unity with full time TGWU officials for the first time in their lives . . . urging the workers not to break away.'[49]

The NASD was soon suspended from the TUC for failing to give a satisfactory explanation of why it had enrolled TGWU members in the northern ports, and being in breach of the Bridlington agreement. A Court of Enquiry attacked the 'Blue' union for causing a provision of the Dock Labour Scheme to be infringed. Behind this allegation was the question which was to become the subject of a High Court hearing—did the docker have the right to belong to a union of his own choice?[50]

This very important issue was again enthusiastically embraced by Tribune whilst the CPGB and Deakin continued to emphasise the 'breakaway' issue. The affair was doubly embarrassing for King Street because the Blue union dispute carried forward into 1955 to coincide with the climax of the right-left struggle in the Labour Party. It was not the time for any aspiring left winger to be associated with Deakin in any way for he was, at that very juncture, the man determined on Bevan's expulsion.

The October 27th 1954 vote of censure on Tribune was included in the text of an ominous letter which asked how the editorial reconciled their attacks on the TGWU leader with their membership of the Labour Party? The editorial board's three-page supplement reply received a massive sale on the docks. Tribune took on all comers—the TUC, NEC, CPGB and Fleet Street. They defended their entire record on the dockers' struggle and spoke out for the docker's right to choose his union.

Two rank and file dockers' conferences took place in the latter part of 1954—one called by the Blue union supporters and one by the Communists. Tribune decided to throw open its columns to both sides. Vic Marney put the CPGB's case for opposing support to the NASD, arguing that 'defection' would weaken the struggle within the TGWU against Deakin who could then continue to dominate the Labour movement through the block vote. Marney argued that the NASD had split the movement and that the right wing and the employers were 'laughing'. This line of reasoning could not, of course, explain the alarm of the TGWU chief and the NEC alike.[51] Dick Barrett, NASD leader, was scathing in his reply. He charged the CPGB members with 'scabbing' for their failure to be involved in NASD recognition strikes in the northern ports.[52] This was in line with Tribune's own criticisms of the CPGB-led TGWU Liaison Committee in London.[53] By July the following year Tribune denounced the 'unholy alliance' of the government, employers, the TGWU bureaucracy and the Communist Party. But it was not only in dockland that King Street-Bevanite relations were becoming strained, once more, in the late Autumn of 1954. Some of the old doubts about social democrats were creeping back into party propaganda. The loss of the German Rearmament vote at the TUC and at Scarborough, and the Bevanites' compliance with the whips' call for abstention on the nine-power agreement in November nourished early cominform prejudices about the essential unity of Bevanism and the right wing. The CPGB could indulge itself.[54] Unity between the Communist and Labour ranks was impossible, it was argued 'unless we combat Social Democratic ideas at every step'.[55] There were still 'some' on the left who took the 'Atlantic alliance and the cold war as their base', who would insist on stressing the 'idea of democracy' and who shared Fabian ideas with the right wing.[56]

Critical letters in Tribune reflected disappointment at the outcome of the German rearmament campaign.[57] World News had to face the fact that the Moscow conference on European Security would take place without the Western powers. The spirit of Geneva was wearing thin. The party condemned . . .

> 'the passivity of the top left group associated with Bevan. They had all the opportunity in the world to conduct a really powerful fight in parliament on German rearmament, but were satisfied with abstention'.[58]

Six Labour MPs who had voted against the agreement were described by the CPGB press as courageous men who had saved the honour of the Labour Party.[59] Michael Foot was quick to explain the reason for the abstention vote. There was, he said, a genuine fear of mass expulsions and a split, which had been strongly intimated by the party hierarchy. This, it was argued, would have given the right wing a party purged of the left-wing elements *just as the trades unions were becoming radicalised.*[60]

The CPGB was not satisfied. They were incapable of recognising the weight such arguments carried with the Labour left. This was because fundamentally they were indifferent to the struggles within the Labour Party except insofar as they might be put to use in the achievement of the CPGB's own strategic aims.[61] *To the extent that the Bevanites' struggle against German rearmament meshed with the needs of Soviet foreign policy, it received CPGB backing. But their interest in the movement's battles against union-party bureaucracy ended at this point,* as their attitude in the TGWU-NASD dispute betrays to some extent.[62]

In broad panorama 1955 was distinguished by the clear congealing of opposed alliances. SEATO and the Bagdad Pact (later CENTO) completed the structure of Western alliances whilst the Warsaw Pact came into being in May—without

Tito's Yugoslavia—a year before the East European deluge and the Suez adventure.

In Germany, as ever, the process was writ large with the formal conversion of the GFR and GDR as fully sovereign states, East following West.[63]

On the first day of the reassembling of parliament in January Bevan held a private meeting with Attlee in the quest for an initiative towards summit talks on the very question of Germany and the wider issue of atomic weapons. In February Bevan's PLP resolution to this effect was defeated despite the fact that a similar resolution had been passed almost a year earlier. Numerous articles in Tribune spelt out the same theme—the urgent need for talks. Then followed the abstention of the 62, the emergence of the centre-left and the expulsion crisis.[64]

The Bevanite sins of the previous November were now set aside by the CPGB. There was heavy advertising by front organisations in Tribune. The CPGB was strongly opposed to the expulsion attempt. World News clarified . . .

> 'We are not concerned with Mr Bevan as a person. We are deeply concerned with the attack on the left.'[65]

Pollitt called for the most formidable campaign yet against Bevan's expulsion, a plea which could only marginally have added to the welter of protest already under way in the trade union movement. Bevan was ever more outspoken for summit talks and, in February, was billed with Soper and Foot to address a rally 'Talk With Russia Now!'. He also spoke out against American bases in Britain.[66] Pollitt predicted a new popular front 'on a scale bigger than at any time since the pre-war days . . .'[67]

But the popular front never really materialised. As early as February the CPGB put behind them the cataclysmic economic prognosis of Stalin's 'Economic Problems' when they openly admitted their predictions of slump in 1954 were wrong.[68] Western capitalism was not the transitory phenomenon early Cominformism had supposed. Eisenhower, Adenaeur and Churchill-Eden seemed firmly in the saddle, the latter underlined by the increased Conservative majority of May 1955. CPGB propaganda now turned to winning the 'people' to put pressure on the (Conservative) government. In this operation the Bevanites were only one consideration.[69] By August one party spokesman found the Labour Party 'even lagging behind the Tories in the field of foreign policy.'[70] It was alleged that the right wing's domination of the Labour Party was maintained 'on the basis of anti-Sovietism and anti-communism' and that the Labour leaders were afraid of the effect of a relaxation of international tension on the internal situation of the party.[71] Nonetheless Tribune editor let slip the incautious remark that 'Stalinist policies have once more been *"decisively repudiated"*.' (my emphasis) on the occasion of the Austrian Peace Treaty. But the new Geneva talks in the summer produced no settlement. Bevan's verdict was that they merely held out some hope for agreement at the scheduled Foreign Ministers meeting in the autumn.[72]

The left's continuing enthusiasm for summit talks hinged to a great extent on the prospect of a real agreement: the CPGB's cultivation of the left rested on the extent to which the Bevanites could reconcile themselves to the barrenness of such meetings.

When the Russians announced troop reductions of 64,000 Bevan called on the Conservatives to 'match the Russians' sincerity' by reducing National Service, ending the Chinese embargo and removing Chiang from the Security Council.[73] But in September Bevan warned that peaceful co-existence 'must not mean the acceptance of the status quo' otherwise it would be 'the peace of the strong'.[74] Thus what the Soviet leaders wanted and what the left expected from international negotiations were two different things. The former wanted to reinforce hegemony over their sphere of influence along the lines of the 1954 Geneva agreement, whilst the left sought to freeze the struggle between the two 'camps' so that the struggle for social justice might proceed, conducted by those who were 'denied what is due to them'.[75]

All the greater then was the disillusionment and acrimony when the Foreign Ministers' conference ended in deadlock in November. Bevan put the major share of the blame on Macmillan and Dulles but insisted that Russia was also responsible. He was angry at the 'deception'. He detected a 'new shift in Russian policy' and asked why the Russians had drawn back. Russia 'should not have encouraged so many expectations if she did not intend them to be taken seriously'.[76] In December Bevan made clear his distaste for Khrushchev's boasting of Russia's new nuclear strength and the threats which had put him 'on the same level' as western sabre-rattlers.[77] He began to detect a 'second cold war'. Nonetheless, Bevan again seized on Molotov's offer to stop nuclear tests and called for the West to respond. All of this patient investigation of the multilateral avenue was a very important preparatory stage for the later development of *unilateralism*, which was born of total disillusionment with summit talks.

King Street relapsed into reaffirmations of the irreplaceable role of the CPGB in the Autumn of 1955. The Labour left had 'virtually abdicated' and 'Bevan himself had indulged in considerable anti-Soviet propaganda in the recent period.'[78]

In 1954 and 1955 the CPGB had begun the new orientation. At Moscow's behest they had engineered a turn towards a popular front. Whilst never gaining the confidence of the Labour left, they had drawn close to them over Geneva and German Rearmament. In contrast to the cold war period, they found some sections of the Tribune left quite capable of superficial flattering remarks about Eastern Europe.[79] It was gratifying. *But the movement of the ranks in dockland and the failure of summit talks in 1955 were the factors that disrupted their version of left unity.* Worse was to come however when the East European working class rose up in 1956 in an attempt to break the grip of the USSR on the buffer states. Meanwhile the CPGB departed the year 1955 with the rallying call 'Defend the Geneva Spirit!'[80]

NOTES

1. The Chinese too, were party to the Geneva Agreements, and it is possible that such thoughts may have crossed minds in Peking, although it seems more likely that security of China's own borders was a greater motivation.

2. *Fejto, A History of the Peoples' Democracies*, Penguin, London, 1974, (p. 362).
   'The technique of economic planning in the Peoples' Democracies after 1948 was based on the Soviet model, with its centralised decision making; priority for heavy industry; contempt for material incentives, and recourse to ethical and political motives . . .
   Initially the machinery seemed to function very efficiently. Between 1949 and 1953, the industrial production of the six Comecon countries rose by 114 per cent, and in certain countries like Hungary, where the ambitions of the planners knew no limits the results had been even more spectacular. Heavy industrial production increased fivefold; the engineering industry was seven times more productive in 1953 than 1938 . . .
   All these factors contributed to a fall in the standard of living, estimated at 20 per cent in Hungary in 1953 as compared with 1948 . . .
   The post Stalinist 'new course' set itself the task of correcting the most glaring mistakes, eliminating the symptoms rather than the organic faults of extreme centralisation. The steps taken during 1953–54 in the GDR, Hungary, Czechoslovakia and Poland were designed merely to raise the standard of living and slow the tempo of industrialisation . . .
   After Malenkov's fall—which also brought down Nagy in March 1955, before this reform could take effect, the old practices with a few minor modifications, were soon revived; and the 1956 rebellions were the price that had to be paid for this . . .'
3. Nevertheless collaboration at the highest level between the Labour Party and the Yugoslav Communists continued. (NEC minutes 28.9.55.) As late as this we find an 8-page document 'Forms of Co-operation Between Socialists' by Vellto Vlahovic of the Yugoslav League of Communists considered by the NEC. The Yugoslavs also had close links with the WFTU.
4. Foot, *Vol II, op. cit.* (p. 421).
5. Fejto, *op. cit.* (pp. 55–56).
6. World News, 21.2.53. Pollitt's report to the EC has the self-same wording as Gollan in World News, 28.2.53. (See above p. 213).
7. World News, 2.1.54, World News was very much a party newspaper, unlike the Daily Worker which was for more general propaganda. It was the successor to International Press Correspondence which ceased publication in 1940.
8. World News, 17.4.54.
9. World News, 23.1.54.
10. See page 182 of this volume. The minutes of the NEC of the Labour Party for 28.4.54 in which the proscription of Socialist Outlook was finalised clearly show that *evidence supplied by the CPGB was instrumental in securing the ban*. The minutes say . . .
    'Mr John Lawrence, until lately the editor, was organiser of

'the Revolutionary Communist Party [a Trotskyist organisation —MJ] in South Wales. Recently he resigned as editor, following a dispute about policy with Mr G. Healy, a member of the editorial board.'

According to 'World News', 20th March 1954,

'Mr Healy, is of course, one of the best known of pre-war Trotskyists, he was publisher of the Trotskyist journal Socialist Appeal in 1938, and one of its regular contributors, a member of the Executive Committee of the Workers' International League and a full time organiser of the Revolutionary Communist Party.'

Other contributors to Socialist Outlook named as members of the Revolutionary Communist Party included Mr H. Finch of Birmingham.

The NEC minutes went on . . .

'From complaints that have been received it seems evident that a Trotskyist organisation is functioning within the Labour Party . . .'

The NEC concluded,

'That persons associated in any way with the editing and sale of Socialist Outlook, or contributing to that journal are declared to be ineligible for membership of the Labour Party'.

The minutes neglect to inform whether the complaints received were from party branches. Considering that the Trotskyists were busy opposing the chauvinism surrounding the CPGB anti-German Rearmament campaign, it is entirely possible that the 'complaints' referred to came from fellow travellers, since the World News articles took express exception to the Trotskyists' opposition to the World Peace Council and the British Peace Council (World News, 20.3.54) the very front organisations which the CPGB was using to propagate the anti-German Rearmament campaign. The self-same meeting at which the Outlook was proscribed had before it yet another lengthy list of CLPs opposing German Rearmament.

The World News articles contained the names and curriculum vitae of every leading Trotskyist.

11. Tribune, 5.11.54.
12. He used the pen name Bruce Bain some of the time and was certainly the bane of King Street's life.
13. Tribune, 29.1.54. Padev meanwhile was challenged to a £100 wager for the actual names by an incredulous Stalinist correspondent. Padev accepted, supplied the names and requested the money to be sent to a charity for the publication of a complete book of the names of Stalin's victims. It would, he said, be a bulky document.
14. World News, 20.3.54.
15. See Tribune, 15.1.54, opposing the expulsion of lifelong Labour Party members Frank and Mary Smithson in Yorkshire.

16. World News, 17.4.54. James Klugmann reviewing John Gollan's book, *The British State*. See also World News 13.3.54.
17. World News, 3.4.54.
18. They should not be confused with the regional conferences called by the Labour Party to discuss German Rearmament. One such conference held later in the year (October 31st) was advertised in Tribune, 29.10.54. Ben Parkin and Fred Messer were two Labour MPs who obliged at local meetings. See Appendix 8 of the author's doctoral thesis for the Union of Democratic Control petition, an example of the kind of campaign for which the CPGB was calling.
19. Tribune, 9.4.54 depicted a slobbering Teutonic gorilla being handed a gun by Uncle Sam (John Bull it seems was not involved). The other must have gladdened the hearts of party members hankering for early-Cominformism, it pictured British social democrats dancing hand in hand with Nazis around a Maypole tree (Tribute, 30.4.54).
20. Tribune, 20.8.54. The CPGB clearly believed (and so did many Bevanites) that the West which included Adenauer, was anxious to conquer Eastern Germany. All the evidence however points to the conclusion that the division of Germany was in the long term best interests of Moscow, London, Paris and Washington.
21. World News, 24.4.54.
22. A key demand of the CPGB at the time.
23. Three Labour MPs attended the international conference against German Rearmament in Paris in March 1954—Jennie Lee, Hugh Delargy and William Warbey. This was undoubtedly a popular front exercise. Whereas the United Front was designed by the Communist International to unite working class parties for the purposes of common struggle on agreed issues, the popular front, pioneered by Stalin in the thirties, embraced all parties and movements (including bourgeois ones) against fascism.

    Apart from Social Democrats, others present at the Paris conference were the Italian and French Communists, Teracini, Casanova and Villon.

    But the Conference was dominated by non-socialist politicians, some of whom wrote to Tribune on March 26th, 1954, appending their names to a protest letter on German Rearmament. They were:
    Daladier and Forcinal of the French Radical Party;
    Pierre Lebon and Jacques Soustelle, URAS deputies;
    Edmond Michelet, Jacques Debu-Bridel, Michel de Pontbriand, Henry Torrs, Senators RPF;
    Henri Bouret, deputy MRP;
    and André Denis, deputy, Young Republic.

    One interesting side aspect of the German Rearmament campaign was that it produced a split in the Socialist Outlook coinciding almost exactly with the CPGB exposé and the Transport House proscription of the paper. John Lawrence and Tom Braddock resigned. Lawrence began writing regularly for Tribune from then on. Lawrence was a supporter of the Paris conference. He had been criticised in the letter columns of the Outlook for his tacit support for Molotov's proposals for a four-power deal on Germany. His critics were in favour of unconditional withdrawal of all troops from Germany East and West, and self-determination for Germany. Lawrence's editorials, by contrast, owed much to the 'Nazi Generals' propaganda used widely by the CPGB at this time.

24. Tribune, 26.3.54.
25. Tribune, 7.1.54.
26. Tribune, 7.1.54.
27. Tribune, 3.9.54.
28. Tribune, 15.10.54.
29. Tribune 24.9.54. See 1.8.54 and 8.8.54 for the series.
30. Foot, *Vol II, op. cit.* (p. 444). Khrushchev was fully aware of the divisions within the LP delegation. He expressed his inability to reconcile the Labour Party's good wishes with its support for the EDC. Bevan did not allow that line of discussion to develop for fear of an open row with his colleagues. This incident shows how assiduously the Soviet leaders were pursuing their courtship of the Bevanite left.
31. Advertised in Tribune, 26.11.54.
32. Tribune, 17.9.54. See footnote 2 above on falling living standards and heavy workloads in Cominform Hungary.
33. Tribune, 1.10.54.
34. Anglo-Soviet Alliance of 26th May, 1942. The treaty ruled out 'mutual aggrandisement for themselves' for both parties and Tribune totally neglected to point out that the Kremlin had broken this clause many times over—in Poland, Bessarabia, the Baltic States and many other places. What Tribune was celebrating therefore was very unclear. And it certainly was in flat contradiction to the paper's attitude of 1949 when NATO was formed.
35. Grenville, *op. cit.* (p. 440).
36. *Central America—A Nation Divided* by Ralph Lee Woodward Jnr. Oxford University Press, New York, 1976 (p. 234). 'The position of the Guatemalan delegation of the UN as well as official statements of the Guatemalan government suggested that, insofar as foreign policy was concerned, Guatemala had become a virtual Soviet satellite by 1954 . . . When Guatemalan exiles from Honduras, assisted by the United States Marine Corps and CIA advisers invaded the country the Guatemalan army refused to defend the government and the crisis ended quickly . . .'
37. Tribune.
38. World News.
39. World News, 31.7.54.
40. World News, 31.7.54.

41. World News, 26.6.54.
42. World News, 26.6.54.
43. See pp. 184–5 above.
44. Tribune, 12.11.54, 'A Slander on the Dockers'.
45. Tribune, 12.11.54, 'A Slander on the Dockers'.
46. Tribune later admitted an error. There was one CP member still on the NASD executive.
47. Tribune, 12.11.54, supplement, 'A Slander on the Dockers'.
48. See Pelling *The British Communist Party op. cit.* (p. 50). The CPGB controlled two unions in 1928 which they had split away from parent bodies—the United Mineworkers of Scotland and the United Clothing Workers—neither of which made much headway according to Pelling.
49. Tribune, 19.11.54. Ian Aitken.
50. In March 1955 Merseyside won a two-day strike against the local Dock Labour Board to break the 'White' closed shop. In May another strike failed to gain the blue representation on provincial joint port committees.
When the NASD, fearing TUC expulsion, offered to 'return' all recruited members a Liverpool docker, Francis Spring, took out an injunction preventing them from excluding him from membership. This was upheld in the High Court in March 1956. The dispute rumbled on to 1959 when the NASD was expelled. See Pelling *A History of British Trade Unions, op. cit.* (pp. 238–9).
51. Tribune, 31.12.54.
52. Tribune, 7.1.55.
53. The attitude of the Liaison Committee over the NASD representation strikes was described by Tribune as 'cagey' at first. And when the committee ordered the dockers back, Tribune alleged they were telling the NASD 'You're on your own'.
In July Tribune's lead story on the NASD declared 'You can't treat free men like cattle'.
54. The French assembly's ratification of the nine-power agreement had also undermined the value of an alliance with the Bevanites.
55. World News, 20.11.54.
56. World News, 20.11.54.
57. The party really had pulled out all the stops in the German Rearmament campaign despite the heavy loss of members since 1948. As well as concerting its trade union activity, its sympathisers were active in the Co-operative Party. There was a delegate conference on German rearmament called by the Political Committee of the Co-operative party and the Union of Democratic Control with Ben Parkin and Fred Messer in attendance. The Co-operative Party Congress registered a big vote against German rearmament and World News gave prominent coverage.
58. World News, 4.12.54. The article also argued . . . 'Before the parliamentary debate, the vote to support the nine power agree-

ments was only carried in the Parliamentary Labour Party by 124 votes to 73 . . . less than half the PLP voted for support of the Nine Power Agreements.'

59. World News, 27.11.54. The six included Nenni telegram rebels S. O. Davies, Sidney Silverman and Emrys Hughes, all of whom at some time had written for Labour Monthly and had been involved in one or more 'front' activities, as had another, Ernest Ferneyhough (See Grid, in appendix to this volume).
60. The Docks dispute took place at the time of a more general militancy on wages. This was recognised by Tribune in two articles by Ian Aitken—'Workers Demand a Bite of the Boom' 17.12.54, and 'A Share of the Boom' 29.10.54.
61. For example, see the attempt to embrace Conservative support for talks (World News, 14.5.55). Assistant General Secretary of the CPGB, George Matthews argued that in an H-Bomb war everybody would suffer. 'That is why the Communist Party appeals to all who want peace, irrespective of their normal party leanings.'
62. At this point the dormant Victory For Socialism sprang, inexplicably, to life. It invited all Tribune readers to a conference and published a pamphlet *In Pursuit of Peace*. A leading personality of VFS at the time was Hugh Jenkins. He was one of many who got involved in controversy with Tribune's literary correspondent Richard Findlater. Jenkins in line with the CPGB view, argued that there had been Nazi support for the German building workers strike in June 1953 (Tribune, 9.12.55). At the time of the Soviet invasion of Hungary Jenkins argued that the Soviet Union had 'the best excuse' for invasion, in a highly abstract argument which sounded suspiciously like an apology for Soviet action. (Tribune, 7.12.56).
63. It is possible that a wing of the Soviet leadership was toying with the idea of abandonment of the East German commitment, but there is insufficient evidence to say for sure. A few days after the East German uprising in 1953 Beria was overthrown 'on the pretext of having pursued a capitulatory policy . . . in March 1963 Khrushchev claimed that Beria and Malenkov had urged the East German party to abandon the GDR as a socialist state, and to renounce the building of socialism as an aim.' (Fejto, *op. cit.* p. 37) Malenkov was removed from his post in February 1954. Bevan, in Tribune 21.1.55, urged the 'western' powers to test out Russia's proposals for free elections in the whole of Germany, to see to what extent they were serious. In April 1953 plans for a Soviet-Austrian Treaty were announced, and Soviet occupation was to cease in eight months. This announcement lent some credence to Soviet sincerity on the German issue—although in the author's opinion the USSR could never have agreed to a unified Germany.
64. See p. 187–195 above.

65. World News, 19.3.55. See also, 26.3.55.
66. Tribune, 25.2.55. London Transport refused to advertise the rally and this caused some controversy.
67. World News, 19.3.55.
68. World News, 12.2.55.
69. An amusing aspect of this campaign was the drive to build the CPGB in small towns and rural areas, hardly strongholds of the Bevanite left.
70. World News, 12.8.55.
71. World News, 12.8.55.
72. Tribune, 29.7.55.
73. Tribune, 19.8.55.
74. Tribune, 16.9.55.
75. Tribune, 16.9.55.
76. Tribune, 25.11.55.
77. Tribune, 2.12.55.
78. World News, 16.12.55.
79. For example in January 1955 Tribune reported the forthcoming trials of Djilas and Dedijer in Yugoslavia under the title 'A Nation on trial', Tribune believed the trial 'promised to be fair' and would 'further enhance the reputation of Marshal Tito and his countrymen among their true friends'.

    But in June with the shameful trials over, Tribune's diplomatic reporter awarded two 'prizes'—one to Tito and one to Khrushchev for apologising to him at the time of the Soviet-Yugoslav detente.
80. World News, 26.11.55.

Chapter Ten

Bevanism, Stalinism and Eastern Europe, (1956-57)

The fundamental weakness of Bevanism lay not in its organisation, which was more than adequate to its perspectives; nor in its lack of a more radical domestic programme, the adoption of which would, in any case, have infringed the sovereignty of conference; nor its supposed failure to pursue the struggle within the trade unions; and Bevanism certainly did not lack political will, as its forthright struggle for democracy within the Labour Party testifies.

The above objections constitute a standard repertoire of criticism of left social democracy. And whilst they are, all of them, misplaced criticisms, they also manage to evade the true deficiency of the movement, so that justice is done neither to the strength nor weakness of Bevanism. Abstract reference to the Bevanites' 'theoretical lacunae'[1] begs the concrete question. In what aspects of political theory did Bevanism fall short? The author believes his answer to that question has yet to be found in any published text.

The Achilles heel of Bevanism found its highest expression in the personal tragedy of Aneurin Bevan at Brighton in 1957. It lay in the incomprehension of *the permanently and profoundly reactionary character of the Kremlin and its agencies in world politics*, combined with a failure to grasp *the enormous scale and significance for socialists of class and national struggles in Eastern Europe, and their essential unity with western struggles.*

To the extent that sections of the Bevanite movement resisted the Kremlin's advances they retained vitality and drive. To the extent that the Bevanite leaders responded, or conceded ground to the Kremlin, they were enfeebled, and finally, broken as leaders of the left.

By the logic of horse-sense this ought not to be. The horse-sense political spectrum equates communism with the Kremlin and places both to the left of social democracy. Moves towards the Kremlin are therefore 'moves to the left'. *Yet the closer Bevan approached to reconciliation with Gaitskell at Brighton, the closer he moved to the political positions advocated by the CPGB in foreign and defence policy.*[2] For this reason it is essential to trace, in the years of the decline of the Bevanite movement, 1956–57, the molecular progression of its attitude to developments in Eastern Europe and of its attitude to the apologists for the status quo in that quarter—the CPGB.

Nineteen fifty six was a tumultuous year. It devastated the Communist Party and exacted retribution from all who had failed to heed the warning of the East German uprising of 1953. Popular frontism still had the upper hand in the party's dealings with Labour.[3] Strong cues for the new line emanated from the PCF when it vainly proposed an electoral alliance with the Socialists and Radicals in the January elections. In Britain, Executive members openly mooted the popular front[4] and this found an echo when Sidney Silverman took up the theme in Tribune,[5] recalling the enthusiasm for the popular front in the thirties. Tribune was not enthusiastic.[6] But whilst King Street's motivation was external—the exigencies of the power struggle within the CPSU,[7] the Labour left did attempt a genuine appraisal of the state of the movement, its tasks and problems.[8] And despite the setbacks in the deputy leadership contest, the Treasurership contest and another Tribune financial crisis,[9] Bevan and his journal turned again to the mass movement with a series of highly successful rallies.[10] There was a new series of expulsions of leftwingers in London[11] as the Gaitskellites celebrated their victory. A repeat of the March 1955 expulsion crisis, with the right wing in a more advantageous position in the PLP appeared a distinct possibility. Bevan showed an awareness of this at the Birmingham rally when he called for 'accountability and freedom' in the party, and declared 'Labour must believe in freedom'.[12]

Having asserted that the surge from below was being blocked by all manner of bureaucratic distortions, he attacked Attlee's 'democratic secrecy',[13] adding 'But I am not a communist. I am a democratic socialist'.[14] Unimpressed by Bevan's campaign for free speech in the movement, and his opposition to bans and proscriptions, the CPGB, piqued, and in blithe ignorance of the imminent Khrushchev 'revelations', proclaimed that 'in one of his usual anti-Communist outbursts' Mr Bevan showed that 'he was completely in ignorance of the Communist Party's method and policy.'[15] The remark that the leader of Labour's left 'did not put forward a clear alternative socialist policy which would match the deep feelings of the mass of Labour Party members' drew Tribune's wrath.[16] 'John Marullus' ridiculed the procedures of the approaching CPGB Easter Congress. All decisions there would be stage-managed, as they had been in 1939 when Pollitt's own opposition to the Moscow line of 'imperialist war' was baulked by the direct intervention of the Kremlin. Marullus drew a parallel between the bureaucratic methods of King Street and the right wing.[17]

King Street's smug self-righteousness soon vanished. From February onwards the CPGB went reeling into protracted catastrophe—the secret speech, Poznan, Hungary, mass desertions and leadership changes. Tribune and the Trotskyists picked up defectors by the hundred.[18] The rickety superstructure of the CPGB collapsed in the Hungarian gale. And if many party members joined Labour, it was not because the Bevanites had any worked-out conception to the East European events, but because Labour, even under Gaitskell, provided a less oppressive framework for arriving at answers to these problems. The crisis of the CPGB was, however, only a small part of the wider crisis of the Kremlin's international apparatus. It might have been worse but for Tito and Togliatti, the fraying edges of Stalin's theoretical mantle. Moscow managed to convert them from a liability into an asset. For instance Tito's earlier projection of an international composed of Communist and Socialist parties[19] was taken up by the new Soviet leadership. The Soviet approach was, however, rejected by the Second International conference in the Spring of 1956,[20] although discussions with Labour leaders continued.

Articles by Togliatti, with vigorous emphasis on the peaceful transition to socialism, appeared frequently in the King Street press throughout 1956, and were an integral part of the courtship of social democracy. Whilst Togliatti's recent credentials were better suited to this operation, British CPGB leaders spoke with pride of the 'British Road to Socialism' having anticipated the now-popular parliamentary perspective.[21] Sectarianism now came under attack and the Labour Party question rose to number one on the agenda for general discussion. The Daily Worker called a 'Unity' conference in June[22] and the party's May Day theme was for a Labour-Communist majority in parliament.[23]

The CPGB still had a lot of ground to make up to convince the doubting social-democratic left that it was serious. Years of sneering anti-Bevanism and lying about Tito could not be dispelled overnight. And whilst the dramatic change in the party's attitude had some effect in the long run, *it was the changes in Russia itself*, and Russia's relations with Tito and the Second International that pulled more weight with left opinion.

At first the left were far more interested in the text of Khrushchev's speech, much of which confirmed what Trotskyists and social democrats had been saying for years about Stalin's regime, than they were in 'appeals for unity'. Though the speech was made in February it was not until June that King Street was forced to acknowledge the authenticity of the text, which appeared first in the non-socialist press.[24] Yet as early as March 2nd Tribune had asked why, after fifty visits to the USSR, Harry Pollitt was 'unable to tell us about any important development in Soviet policy until after it happened'. Tribune asked whether his journey was really necessary.[25] And the following week it wanted to know 'Will they take back the lies about Trotsky?' and 'would they now release imprisoned communists?'[26] Michael Foot, quoting Trotsky in a Tribune leader, demanded of the CPGB 'Do You Defend Murder?' He claimed that the Communist Party was close to complete demoralisation, and called on democratic socialists to show a new audacity because the ranks of the CPGB were not to blame for the sins of their leaders, and many of them had joined because of the 'timidity of the Labour Party and its compromises'. Making a somewhat lopsided analogy between Stalinist and domestic Labour bureaucracy, he asserted that many Labour leaders feared freedom too and that 'bureaucracy lies heavy on our own institutions'.[27] But ironically none of this prevented Tribune calling for a welcome to Bulganin and Khrushchev on their British visit.[28]

Despite Tribune's fraternal intentions, the visit further exacerbated Kremlin-Social Democratic relations. The Daily Worker alleged that Bevan and Gaitskell were involved in a 'cold war propaganda stunt' when the latter presented the Russian leaders with a list of still-imprisoned East European Social Democrats.[29]

Nonetheless behind these audacious thrusts against crisis-ridden Stalinism it is possible to detect a quite profound naïvety. The Soviet offer of a moratorium on H-tests in the Spring was seized upon over-enthusiastically by Donald Soper. He argued the offer should be taken up, for by so doing 'we shall be strengthening the best government Russia has had'![30] Bevan revealed the same over-estimation of the significance of Khrushchev's changes as a 'wholesale repudiation of Stalin' yet, somewhat inconsistently, noted that the new Soviet leaders were 'consolidating it in an ingrained habit of thought'. The Kremlin changes were not just another plot, he said.[31]

The Khrushchev speech was, indeed, no plot. But it was not sincere either. It left a great deal unsaid. And its delivery was certainly part of a new *strategy* in which the dissolution of the Cominform and the creation of the Warsaw Pact were further integral elements. Historical objectivity was not the purpose of the exercise. The Bevanites never seriously attempted an analysis of East European politics that might have explained the Kremlin's new course.[32] Bevan himself over-relied on personal impressions of Khrushchev, the man.

Typical was Bevan's comment on the dissolution of the Cominform. His article 'Farewell to the Trojan Horse' interpreted this as 'the abandonment of world revolution' as it was conceived by Lenin and Stalin. It would appear that the events in China in the twenties, Germany and Spain in the thirties, not to mention the Nazi-Soviet pact, had all failed to shake Bevan's belief in the Kremlin's attachment to world revolution. This was perhaps a quite common illusion on the Labour left, which viewed the Cominform as part of a European revolutionary strategy. Bevan argued that the existence of the Cominform had 'made it impossible to enter into any binding arrangements with other left parties'.[33] But no statement reveals his vulnerability more clearly than that published after the Poznan riots.[34] He spoke of the danger of conceiving of liberation in Eastern Europe as a war operation, for that could lead to *civil war* and foreign intervention. Yet the Russian foreigners had been intervening in Poland certainly since 1948 and for centuries before that.

> 'It is a lamentable fact that the rising in Poznan comes at a time when there is a real prospect of improvement of conditions throughout the Soviet world . . . I believe the relaxation, material and political, which is taking place among the Soviets, flows from a sense of greater self-confidence and from strength, not from weakness.'[35]

Bevan believed the political systems of the East needed 'antennae' which would enable the leaders 'to learn how what they were doing looked to their politically inarticulate followers'. What is instructive about this article is the clarity with which it shows Bevan's reliance upon the Khrushchev wing of the Soviet and East European ruling caste to steer the economy and political system *on behalf of* the people. This liberal wing would initiate the reforms. It would receive warning signals from its antennae. It was proceeding from strength. *In fact, throughout 1956 all the signs were pointing in the opposite direction. The Soviet leaders were in deep crisis.* Concessions were made and the people demanded more. Part of the truth was told and the people demanded the whole truth. The lid was lifted. The real cleansing force in Eastern Europe was welling up from the 'politically inarticulate followers'. Bevan had already begun travelling the road to Brighton, the road which would end with reliance on talks conducted by the Soviet leaders and the West as a means to ridding the world of H-bombs, rather than reliance upon the unilateralist movement that was soon to become a truly mass movement.

Poznan might have been sufficient warning. But it was not. One senses in Bevan's remarks regret ('it is lamentable') that the people of Eastern Europe were beginning to take their destiny into their own hands. The Trotskyists, who were regular guest writers for Tribune in 1956,[36] by contrast, drew strength and confidence from the Poznan events,[37] and pursued their old Stalinist enemies relentlessly. They and the Bevanites picked up some of the defecting intellectuals from around 'New Reasoner', the dissident Communist review.[38]

The crisis of the intellectuals was augmented by the crisis of the party's union cadre as 1956 wore on and the various struggles in the AEU and ETU unfolded.[39] The situation at mid-summer is well illustrated by this excerpt from a leading article by Michael Foot,

> 'Into this office comes a steady flow of letters from British Communists. Many are marked "not for publication" or are signed with pseudonyms or initials. We respect these devices while regretting the position within the Communist Party which they indicate.
>
> We know that Communists read Tribune despite the solemn warnings of their leaders because they find here a socialist interpretation of the doctrinal crisis through which they are passing.
>
> Some of these Communists tell us that they have left their party, either to join the Labour Party or to form an independent group. Others remain to reform the Communist Party. Communists who realise how their loyalty has been exploited must work out the future for themselves'.[40]

And yet the Bevanite movement was hardly in a state of readiness to receive the King Street defectors. It had passed its peak in the Labour Party by this time. It was no more clear about the situation in Eastern Europe than those who sought clarification, for, as we have seen, Bevan was as surprised and saddened by Poznan as many of them. This is what gives 1956 its unique flavour. For a time, anyone with ideas could get a hearing.[41] Previously isolated sects flourished. New tendencies and magazines suddenly appeared. People who would have shunned each other's company found themselves at the same discussion conferences. And all of this, not because of any profound social crisis in Britain, (where social democracy was in the middle of a thirteen-year trough in its fortunes and Conservatism three years from a landslide majority) but because of the pitch of the social crisis in Eastern Europe.

Bevanite-CP relations reached an all-time low when the Hungarian revolution broke out in November, immediately after new Polish upheavals. Peter Fryer, former Daily Worker reporter, whose Hungarian despatches had been spiked by his party chiefs, became a regular Tribune correspondent,[42] whilst maintaining the closest connection with the Trotskyists.[43] In November Tribune gleefully reported that CP members were resigning and joining the Labour Party.[44] John Marullus denounced Reg Birch's support for the Russian invasion, and reminded his readers,

> 'Not so many months ago Tribune had a quarrel with Mr Reg Birch of the AEU who had shown himself less enthusiastic than he pretended to be in favouring democracy in his own union.
>
> 'Now Mr Birch writes to the Daily Worker defending up to the hilt the bloody suppression in Hungary. And he does so in the name of democracy.'[45]

And when the Hungarian general strike began Tribune announced 'We back this Strike'.[46] 'Workers' Councils speak for Hungary' ran the headline of another article by Paul Ignotus.[47] Konni Zilliacus denounced the attack on the Workers' Councils, all the more significant since he declared himself a 'life-long friend of the Soviet Union' in the same piece.[48] Tribune took up the demand for a Labour delegation to attend the trial of Hungarian Workers' leaders.[49]

Simultaneously it was publishing Djilas' denunciation of Tito for ambivalence towards Soviet intervention in Hungary.[50] Jennie Lee went to cover the Djilas trial for Tribune and, in a major article defended the Yugoslav dissident.[51]

But if Bevanite disillusionment with Tito had taken five years, disenchantment with Khrushchev required a great deal less. In under a year emotions tumbled from enthusiasm in February to despair in December. The Bevanites never really anticipated the measures to which the Russian leaders would descend, basically because the depth of the social crisis in Eastern Europe eluded them. With such poor judgement, renewal of enthusiasm could never be precluded (and was to follow surely enough in as many months again). Both Bevan and Tribune totally misconstrued the meaning of the events of the Polish October. Though Tribune called on its readers to stand up and cheer the Poles, all *Gomulka* had achieved were concessions in return for an agreement that Soviet troops would remain in Poland for as long as NATO troops remained in West Germany. Yet this was interpreted on November 2nd as follows,

> 'The statement by the Soviet government which has followed the tremendous events in Poland and Hungary will rank—if it is sincerely implemented—as a charter of freedom for half of Europe.
> It defines as the new basis for relations between Russia and the former satellites "the principle of full equality, respect for territorial integrity, state independence and sovereignty, and non-interference in the domestic affairs of one another".
> It seems that the governments of Eastern Europe are to become once more masters in their own house, free to decide their industrial, agricultural . . . and foreign policies.
> This is great news. Democratic socialists will welcome it gladly. They will rejoice that at five minutes to twelve councils of wisdom and moderation have prevailed in Moscow.'[52]

Tribune's political wisdom was not enhanced by the inclusion of the insurance clause 'if it is sincerely implemented'. It quickly became apparent that 'wisdom' of Moscow consisted in its having neutralised Poland all the more thoroughly to deal with the Hungarian revolution. *Yet even in late November 1956 after the brutal repressions, Bevan was enthusiastic about Khrushchev's public gesture to withdraw troops from the buffer states if the moves were reciprocated in Western Europe.* In an article 'The Last Chance For Statesmanship' he pleaded,

> 'Is he (Khrushchev) saying something serious and so weighted with possibilities that we should not dismiss it'.[53]

Bevan's credulity with regard to Khrushchev is doubly surprising in the light of two major Soviet troop mobilisations in Poland and Hungary between 19–24th October,[54] and the full-scale, bloody invasion from November 4th onwards. Khrushchev's memoirs reveal that invasion was never in serious doubt. He confides that the Russians were 'completely indifferent' to Nagy's demands to withdraw, and that the initial withdrawal was largely tactical. A Chinese proposal to let the Hungarians deal with the situation themselves was taken up but eventually dropped because, 'someone warned of the danger that the working class might take a fancy to counter-revolution. The youth in Hungary were particularly susceptible.'[55]

Hence Marshall Konev, who said he required three days preparation, was told,

'Start getting ready. You'll hear from us when it's time to begin'.[56]

The new Polish leadership, whom Tribune had called upon readers to stand up and cheer, were even *consulted in advance* about the invasion plan. Gomulka and Cyrankiewicz were regarded by Khrushchev as an 'acceptable', 'trusted' leadership,

'We not only wanted to know the opinion of the Polish comrades before taking such a decisive step as sending troops into Budapest we also wanted the Polish comrades' response to be positive. We wanted their support.'[57]

Khrushchev does not say definitely that he got such support, but it seems the only possible conclusion. The Polish army was solidly behind Gomulka.[58] Polish opposition might just have halted the Russian's plans. Bevan's old friend, Marshal Tito, appears to have taken the invasion almost casually. When he asked Khrushchev when the invasion was to take place, the reply was 'soon'. Tito then invited Khrushchev to rest up for a few days in Yugoslavia first![59]

None of this could possibly have been known by the Bevanites at the time. Hence the almost pathetic request of Tribune on November 2nd for the West to 'respond' to the statement of the Soviet government of October 30th. The West was indeed 'responding'—but hardly in a manner the Bevanites would have found credible. Khrushchev, again, reveals the degree of confidentiality prevailing at the highest levels between East and West.

'While we were dealing with these problems, second echelon English and French diplomats in London and Paris met with our embassy people over a cup of coffee or a glass of wine and said "You seem to have some trouble on your hands in Poland and Hungary. We understand how it is.

> We're having some trouble of our own over in Egypt. Let's have a tacit understanding between us that you'll liquidate your difficulties by whatever means you see fit, and you won't interfere while we do the same".'[60]

This is not the only indication of collusion at the diplomatic level, and there is some evidence that the State Department recognised the 'legitimacy' of Soviet action in Hungary.[61]

If Khrushchev's testimony is to be believed, it means that the Soviet 'explanation of the Hungarian revolution as imperialist-inspired was not only a lie—but known to be a lie—at least by Khrushchev, who appears to have had these diplomatic reassurances beforehand. Thus the Russians, Gomulka, Tito, and very probably, the western powers all had advanced notice of the invasion. Even at the time Tribune was embarrassed by its own credulity, for when it was all over the paper acknowledged its weakness,

> 'when we thought the Russian government would keep its promise to leave Hungary, and suggested hopefully "West Must Respond to Russian Moves".'[62]

Nonetheless Bevan was clearly struck by the link between Suez and Hungary and asked whether the British decision to invade Suez spurred the Russians to enter Budapest. Michael Foot argues that Ministers knew Soviet tanks were moving westwards, through British intelligence. The decision to invade Suez 'released the Russians from their moral isolation'.[63]

If there had been a significant 'moderate' faction within the CPGB, there was sufficient sympathy on Bevan's part for the 'moderate' wing of East European Stalinism to have permitted a more amicable relationship between the Communists and the Labour left. But the British CP leadership was in thrall to Moscow, accepted its interpretations of the Poznan and Hungarian revolts,[64] stood by the repressions, stifled the discussion,[65] and witnessed the loss of almost one-third of its membership. Set against these momentous events the CPGB's attempts at 'unity' were puny, and could hardly be taken seriously. The Daily Worker 'unity' conference,[66] comparative studies of Labour and Communist Party programmes,[67] self-criticism for past sectarianism towards the left[68] were to no avail. If anything they alienated their own dissident members still further whilst not impressing anyone on the left. There was, however, talk of a new-found unity[69] within the Labour party itself, for in the midst of the turmoil and in the aftermath of the 'Law Not War' demonstration against the Suez invasion, Bevan had been elected Treasurer and was rapidly becoming the Labour Party's official spokesman on foreign affairs. Tribune's strength throughout 1956–57 lay hardly in political acumen, theoretical clarity or the steadfastness of its leadership. None of these showed up very well. Its attraction was its basic honesty, its readiness to provide a platform to all shades of left opinion and its sense of moral outrage when those in whom it placed credence revealed their cloven hooves —in a sense its own credulity which reflected the benign attitude of a working class not steeled in the harsh political realities of Eastern Europe. Tribune was an arena, a concourse area, a clearing house for ideas. No one could ignore it—the parliamentary left, the Communist Party, the Trotskyists—all utilised its columns. It mirrored accurately the turmoil of the period. And whilst it hoped for the emergence of a more liberal Stalinist leadership in the East, it continued to pursue the CPGB at home, following every new development in the party's crisis.[70]

The cruellest blow to King Street was Tribune's appointment of Peter Fryer[71] as its reporter at the Special Hammersmith Congress at Easter 1957, the very Congress where Fryer's own appeal was to be dealt with.[72] Fryer continued to monitor the progress of the dissident party members, in particular the Socialist Forum movement.[73] But he founded his own paper, *The Newsletter*[74] in May and the energies that might have been channelled into Tribune were now directed, in the main, at regrouping his former colleagues.

In the autumn of 1957 Foot's sympathetic review of Djilas' *The New Class* alleged that the Communists had lost the theoretical advantage of Social Democracy, Stalinism having caused theory to degenerate into 'puerile tautologies'. Soviet Communism had become 'one of the most brutal tyrannies the world has ever known'.[75] Tribune noted 'The Old Guard Lose Their Power' and drew a parallel between the declining influence of right wing TUC and Communist Party bureaucrats.[76] And yet despite the salt rubbed into King Street's wounds Tribune's own underlying theoretical weakness was strikingly apparent. Months after the tragic events in Poland we find Tribune urging 'Give Gomulka solid support'.[77] Ian Mikardo was undignified in his praise speaking about the 'terrific achievements' made in the space of a year,

> 'I call down blessings on Gomulka's head and strength to his elbow'.[78]

Even Bevan indulged in the hazardous pursuit of comparative demonology. Commenting on the visit of Gomulka to Tito he ventured there was 'far more freedom in Poland than in Yugoslavia, and that Djilas would not be in prison if he were in Poland.'[79] As if not to be outdone, Gomulka, a few weeks later, in October, postponed the Polish party's planned December conference, expelled half the party membership and denounced 'all liquidators, revisionists, dogmatic sectarians and organisers of groups with a line contrary to general party policy.'[80] Yet Tribune continued to speak glowingly of the 'bloodless' Polish revolution of 1956.[81] And, not six months after Hungary Ian Mikardo was writing that the Russian leader was 'sensitive to other peoples' ideas' though he 'makes decisions quickly and firmly'.[82] Two months before Molotov and Malenkov were unceremoniously expelled from the Central Committee the same writer was of the opinion that Khrushchev adhered 'firmly to the principle of collective leadership', and Raymond Fletcher argued 'with him (Khrushchev) we can do business'.[83] Fletcher believed,

> 'The pace of Soviet "liberalisation" will be settled partly by the intelligence and understanding shown in the West'.[84]

Underlying these ill-considered sentiments was a vulgarised 'withering away of the state' conception which Fletcher outlined in an article entitled 'Moscow's economic might make Kremlin bosses redundant'.[85] Liberalisation was seen as an irreversible process and a by-product of industrialisation, and therefore to impede Khrushchev was tantamount to blocking the path that historical progress had chosen. It was an idea which welded Hegelian fatalism to Fabian gradualism in the service of liberal Stalinism. At the same moment, some of the Tribune left 'discovered' Mao. Basil Davidson was enthusiastic about Mao's 'departures from Stalinism' and argued that some of the ideological and 'democratic' developments were 'The Biggest Thing Since Lenin'.[86]

Yet at a secret international conference of Communist Parties in Moscow in November, 1957, the first since the dissolution of the Cominform, Mao Tse Tung was taking the lead for a return to the old tough centralism, and the final declaration marked a tentative return to the 'camp versus camp' position of 1947–53![87]

The Bevanite left had not thought through the enormous implications of the revolutions of 1956. The articles of Mikardo, Fletcher, Davidson, Bevan and others betrays a deep yearning for an *understanding* with the undertakers of the Hungarian revolution, for a detente that would bring peace so that the 'irreversible' Fabian process of liberalisation in the East might proceed; so that democratic socialism might be established gradually there as they sought to establish it gradually in Britain. *And this desire to 'do business' with the Kremlin was important because it was a vital component of multilateralist thinking on the Hydrogen bomb, the issue which split Bevan from the Bevanite movement.*

In February 1957 Tribune urged the West to 'Say Yes to Shepilov'[88] who, as Soviet Foreign Minister, had put forward proposals for a Middle East peace settlement in answer to the Eisenhower declaration of military and economic aid to ward off the spread of Communism. Bevan, too, displayed some enthusiasm for these Soviet proposals.[89] In June, Tribune attacked the 'blind, stupid, obstinate' Western leaders for having made no response to the Soviet gestures, believing that such agreements 'could bring freedom' to the people of Hungary, Poland, and East Germany.[90]

Bevan wanted to turn the Socialist International towards the peoples of Eastern Europe[91] yet showed distinct impatience with the exiled Socialist party representatives within it.[92] In August he indulged in some anti-German rhetoric worthy of 1954, seeing within Germany 'elements more explosive than those which Hitler was able to exploit with such ferocious demagogy'.[93] The presentation of West Germany as the main threat to peace was, of course, a continuing theme of Soviet foreign policy as was Bevan's own preoccupation with an East-

West negotiated settlement. Notwithstanding his thoroughly democratic credentials and his abhorrence of dictatorship, Bevan was closer to Khrushchev than he knew. When the Soviet leader made a very tough speech in the East German parliament in August threatening that Europe would become 'a desert'[94] Bevan commented 'It is unfortunately a statement of fact and follows naturally from the Berlin declaration . . . Khrushchev is saying if you try to unify Germany by force this is what will happen. No Germany will be left either divided or united'.[95]

Yet Tribune and the Bevanites continued the pursuit of a possible 'neutral' belt in central Europe by negotiation.[96] The withdrawal of troops of both Warsaw pact and NATO from Europe and the creation of an atom-free zone, whilst a plausible aim in itself, was the vision which led them to the quagmire of peace through interminable and fruitless international negotiation. With some naïvety Tribune argued that if Khrushchev's plan was accepted 'rigid Stalinist dictatorships might collapse like ninepins. The Hungarians might gain by negotiation the free and neutral state for which they fought last year' and Communist states would be 'prey to democratic socialism'. 'Neutral countries . . . would crop up everywhere and escape from the tight compartments of the rival alliances . . . the Cold War would fade . . .'[97] If that were indeed the scenario why, then, should the Russians propose it: on 2nd October Polish Foreign Minister Rapacki unveiled the plan for a nuclear-free zone in the UN General Assembly, with one important difference, *that NATO and the East European Alliance would police it.*[98] Disengagement, as it came to be called, was quickly embraced by the Labour Party as a whole.

Here we see how an excellent idea is embraced by the advocates of the 'two camps' purged of its progressive content and decked out in the service of the continued division of Europe. Bevan's road to Brighton was smoothed by these subtle amendments and 'good intentions'. He saw the possibility of demilitarisation, withdrawal of the troops of both alliances, break-up of the buffer states' Stalinist tyrannies and social democratisation of Eastern Europe—*all to be achieved by international agreement between the architects of Yalta and Potsdam!*[99]

NOTES

1. Coates, *op. cit.* (p. 197). Chapter 7. 'The weakness of the Labour Left'. The criticisms made by Coates contain those listed above. The 'theoretical lacunae' of Bevanism are not specified.
2. Most often, when Bevanism was in conflict with the right wing it was also in conflict with the CPGB—at the time of the 1951 budget; during the special relationship with Tito-Yugoslavia; in the dockland struggle; in the campaign against bureaucracy in the ETU, and at the time of Hungary.
3. In the beginning of 1956 the Communist Party had a mild relapse into early Cominformist denunciations of the Bevanites. Maurice Dobb told Tribune he was 'saddened' to see Bevan laying the blame for the failure of Summit talks on the Russians when it had clearly been Dulles and Macmillan who had 'jettisoned the Geneva spirit'. Dobb argued 'the insane anti-Communist prejudice fostered by the cold war . . . has spread its infection even among the Labour left.' (Tribune, 6.1.56).
   The CPGB Economic Committee were predicting generalised slump again and in January, World News weekly column on events within the Labour Party shrank dramatically. The Labour Party was strongly attacked in the CPGB's resolution for its forthcoming 24th Congress. 'These leaders (the LP) are hostile to Marxism, to scientific socialism; they preach class collaboration, disarm the workers by preaching the neutrality of the state, more and more stress the need to defend capitalism and renounce even the aims of socialism.' (World News, 28.1.56).
4. World News, 14.1.56. A regular column 'Around the Districts' reveals the Trades Councils as the arena for the CPGB's unity campaigns.
5. Tribune, 13.1.56. Exactly in line with CPGB policy Sidney Silverman MP's article posed the question 'Why Not A Popular Front?' Silverman had been a willing participant in the Moscow Economic Conference of 1954 and sat on one of its committees, Bevan described him as 'fifty-one per cent pro-Soviet'—*Rebel in Parliament* (p. 128) by Emrys Hughes, Charles Skilton Ltd, London 1969. Lucien Weitz (Tribune 20.1.56) reported that recent international events had widened the gulf between French socialists and communists.
6. See Tribune's response, 13.4.56.
7. The light engineering faction of Malenkov had been defeated by the heavy engineering faction. One result was the new five-

year plan published by the Kremlin on 15.1.56. Ian Mikardo, incidentally, found the figures 'impressive and frightening' (Tribune 20.1.56) but not, apparently, questionable.

8. This attempt at stocktaking for the left was a series of articles by G. D. H. Cole, published in Tribune and beginning with 'What is Wrong with the Trade Unions?' on 30.12.55. Others in the series were 'The Fear of Communism'; 'Trade Unionists in Politics' which examined trade union-Labour Party relations; and 'Workers' Control in Industry'.
9. Michael Foot *Aneurin Bevan* Vol 2 (p. 500). Tribune on 10.2.56 increased its price by two pence.
10. These were announced in Tribune, 13.1.56. One was held at the Albert Hall Manchester on February 4th, and one at Birmingham on February 25th, and were described as 'regional conferences' and there was a 'great demand' for tickets. World News, 18.2.56, referred to Mr Bevan addressing '1,000 *delegates* at a Tribune conference in the Manchester region' (my emphasis). The same article noted the big increase in Bevan's vote in the deputy leadership contest in which James Griffiths won with 141, and Bevan increased his vote from 70 to 111.
11. Tribune, 17.2.56 announced nine expulsions in Peckham, three in Dulwich and twelve Councillors in Camberwell (Tribune 24.2.56). In one Peckham Ward eighty-five out of two hundred Labour Party members resigned in protest.
12. Tribune, 2.3.56. This coincided with reports of Khrushchev's 20th Congress speech.
13. Foot, *Vol II, op. cit.* (p. 503).
14. Foot, *Vol II, op. cit.* (p. 500).
15. Tribune, 10.2.56, quoting from the Daily Worker.
16. Tribune, 10.2.56. John Marullus. Like many sectarian groups today, the CPGB believed that the left had the authority to propose an 'alternative' to the democratically arrived-at decisions of Labour's conference.
17. Tribune, 10.2.56. John Marullus. See also Pelling (CP) *op. cit.* (p. 111).
18. The author was one.
19. Labour Party NEC minutes, 28.9.55. Appendix A—an 8-page article by Velkjo Vlahovic on the Yugoslav Communist Party originally published on 6–7 July was up for discussion. Entitled 'Forms of Co-operation Between Socialist Forces' it analysed relations between the Cominform and the Socialist International and saw them being replaced as follows . . . 'Future co-operation of socialist forces will move towards the most comprehensive and broadest association of all organisations, parties and movements fighting for socialism'.
20. Tribune, 9.3.56 reported that the British amendment (i.e. the Labour Party's) *not* to reject the Communists' overtures was defeated at the Socialist International Congress. The Congress

found the overtures 'not genuine' and provided 'no grounds for departing from the position taken by democratic socialism, which formally rejects any united front or any other form of political co-operation with the parties of dictatorship.'

21. See Appendix 7 of the author's doctoral thesis for the radically different versions of 'The British Road' from the early and late fifties. World News, 10.3.56 quoted Marx (in a black-edged box!) on the possibilities of peaceful transition to socialism and, 11.8.56, Engels (in another box) in similar vein.
22. World News, 19.5.56.
23. World News, 5.5.56.
24. Henry Pelling (CP) *op. cit.* notes a 24th Congress resolution regretting the fact there was no published text of Khrushchev's speech. World News, 30.6.56 reported a Political Committee (CPGB) statement what 'in the light of the unofficial text now published, which, in the absence of an official denial, may be regarded as more or less authentic, we reaffirm the general lines of the resolution of our EC of 13th May'. (In this resolution the criticisms of the 'cult of the individual' had been approved.) The circumstances surrounding the way the CPGB was 'informed' was highly embarrassing for the party leaders and tantamount almost to a snub.
25. Tribune, 2.3.56.
26. Tribune, 9.3.56.
27. Tribune, 30.3.56. In April (6.4.56) Tribune asked whether Pollitt and Gallacher knew the truth about Rajk and Slansky. On 13.4.56 a correspondent condemned the French CP's vote for Mollet's emergency measures in Algeria.
28. The AEU national committee unanimously invited both Soviet leaders to attend their sessions. Tribune, on the other hand, condemned the expulsion of five Motherwell councillors who had opposed inviting the Russians to a civil reception. No doubt, the paper remarked, the majority 'were hoping to make Khrushchev feel at home in a congenial atmosphere of purges and expulsions'! (Tribune, 23.5.56.)
29. Foot, *Vol II, op. cit.* (p. 505). The Daily Worker's version of events was challenged by Tribune 27.4.56. All the Labour leaders had done was to raise the question of what 'enemies of the people' were, and how guilt for such charges might be established.
30. Tribune, 27.4.56.
31. Tribune, 23.3.56.
32. During the NEC 'dinner' row, Tribune (27.4.56) alleged that George Brown was the main interrupter. Michael Foot *Vol II* (p. 505) says that Bevan was not worried by it and that good relations were established with Khrushchev soon after. Khrushchev's own comment at the time was, that if he lived in England, he would be a Conservative.

There was *some* discussion of Eastern Europe but it was extremely superficial. There was no analysis of the economies of the Comecon states. John Marullus (Tribune 4.5.56) in 'Six Points For Socialists' found economic advance 'impressive'; blamed 'western' *and* Soviet leaders for the Cold War; invested Labour with the task of preventing the 'final clash' between 'East' and 'West'; opposed silence on the infamies against human freedoms in Eastern Europe and *especially called for the release of Social Democrats.* An article (22.6.56) declared joint opposition to NATO and the Warsaw Pact.

33. Tribune, 27.4.56. 'Farewell to the Trojan Horse' by Aneurin Bevan.
34. Tribune, 6.7.56, it seems uncharacteristic of Bevan to credit leaders with greater wisdom than the movement, yet he did. Perhaps five years of relentless struggle had taken its toll.
35. Tribune, 6.7.56.
36. Tribune, 6.7.56. 'Will They Take Back The Lies About Trotsky' by G. Healy. William Gallacher (Tribune 6.4.56) former CPGB MP and Max Morris (Tribune 9.2.56) both complained of 'ultra-left' correspondents in Tribune.
37. Although, ironically, support for the Warsaw Pact was then, and remains for Gerard Healy's followers, a point of principle!
38. There is an interesting side aspect of the CPGB intellectuals revolt. Some, like historian Brian Pearce, were probing deeper and producing historical research papers on Communist history. Others, it seems, were reacting against King Street's turn towards broad fronts, and hankering after the 'tough' ultra-leftism of the Cominform Stalinist period. The former group left the Trotskyists within a year or two. The latter—Cliff Slaughter, Tom Kemp and others seemed to find in the Socialist Labour League what they had lost in the Communist Party of the Cominform. Here, they were repeating an experience of twenty years previously when Gerard Healy, himself a former Stalinist joined the Trotskyists after Stalin abandoned the 'third period' for the popular front against fascism.
39. Pelling, (CP) *op. cit.* p. 174. Leading trade unionists who resigned the CPGB were:
    Jack Grahl (FBU); Leo Keely (FBU); Les Cannon (ETU); Alex Moffat (Scots NUM).
40. Tribune, 9.7.56.
41. Trotskyists of every variety did very well out of 1956.
42. Especially from December onwards. Fryer's book, *Hungarian Tragedy* was most sympathetically reviewed in Tribune 14.12.56.
43. He was editor of the Trotskyist 'Newsletter'.
44. Tribune, 23.11.56.
45. Tribune, 16.11.56.
46. Tribune, 14.12.56.
47. Tribune, 14.12.56.

48. Tribune, 14.12.56.
49. Tribune, 21.12.56. Tribune's observant staff noticed a 'change of line' between the early and late editions of the Daily Worker of November 14. In Tribune 16.11.56 reported that the Daily Worker suggested Bevan himself ought to be part of a Labour Party delegation to Hungary to assess the situation. But in the second edition the names of Bevan and Morgan Phillips had vanished and was replaced by a proposal for an investigating team of 'workers'.
50. Tribune, 30.11.56.
51. Tribune, 21.12.56. Jennie Lee 'What Was the Real Crime of Djilas'.
52. Tribune, 2.11.56.
53. Tribune, 23.11.56 Aneurin Bevan 'The Last Chance for Statesmanship'.
54. Fetjo, *op. cit.* p. 104–8 and p. 120).
55. *Khrushchev Remembers Vol I* (p. 445–6) by Nikita S. Khrushchev, edited by Strobe Talbott, Penguin, London 1977.
56. Khrushchev, *op. cit.* (p. 447).
57. Khrushchev, *op. cit.* (p. 448).
58. Fetjo, *op. cit.* (p. 106) records Gomulka's firm commitment to the Warsaw Pact, and the USSR's strategic interests. P. 104 & 108 confirm army support for Gomulka.
59. Khrushchev, *op. cit.* (p. 450).
60. Khrushchev, *op. cit.* (p. 459).
61. The Warsaw Pact of May 14th 1955 is a Soviet version of the North Atlantic Treaty Organisation. Under the Pact's provisions Soviet troops have remained in Hungary, a member nation, to 'safeguard' her security. The view in the State Department is that there is little doubt that the troops have a right to be there. But the question might be raised about the legitimacy of their use to put down an internal revolution. Even this raised a problem however. Soviet troops are being used at the request of the Hungarian government. There is little effort in Washington to deny that United States forces abroad could be used in the same way if there were a communist-led revolution in, say, Italy. In 1944–45 for example, British troops at the request of the Athens government fought Communist rebels in Greece'.
    New York Times, 27.10.57 quoted in *The Hungarian Revolution*, p. 92, by Melvin J. Lasky, published by the Congress for Cultural Freedom, Secker and Warburg, London 1957.
62. Tribune, 28.12.56. They were making reference to the Soviet government's declaration of 30th October, 1956 quoted in Tribune, 2.11.56. See quotation above.
63. Michael Foot, *Aneurin Bevan, Vol II* (p.354).
64. World News, 7.7.56 and Daily Worker throughout November 1956.
65. The projected special conference was postponed to the follow-

ing Easter. In the summer of 1956 the CPGB leaders visited Moscow.

66. June 30th and July 1st. See World News, 7.7.56. See also Labour Monthly for October articles by Crossman on Socialist-Communist relations and Klugmann on *G. D. H. Cole and Unity.*
67. A comparative study of the official Labour Party programme 'Towards Equality' and the 'British Road', the CP's programme, contained in World News, 28.7.56.
68. World News, 17.3.56. John Eaton and A. MacLaren discussion letters. World News, 28.7.56, more discussion letters on the same topic.
69. Michael Foot, *Aneurin Bevan Vol II* (p. 557).
70. Tribune gave systematic coverage to the CP's crisis now at fever pitch, many of whose key figures had resigned. Tribune reported that the Daily Worker's assistant editor had moved a resolution on the CP executive condemning the first Russian intervention in Hungary (Tribune 4.1.57). The resolution had been backed by six EC members but opposed by the Pollitt, Gollan leadership. Peter Fryer, the former Daily Worker correspondent advertised a series of meetings for dissident CP members in the Spring (Tribune 4.1.57). Another Holborn Hall meeting heard demands for the lifting of the ban on factions in the CPGB (Tribune 1.2.57), whilst in Oxford Tribune reported expulsions from the student branch of the CP for 'Titoism' and 'Trotskyism' (25.1.57). Charlie Coutts, the CP's successor to Fryer in Hungary had his version of events strongly challenged (Tribune 25.1.57), whilst Tribune reminded readers of Khrushchev's comment that if he were English he would vote Conservative (Tribune 4.1.57). Bevan meanwhile visited Italy in February where he hoped for a re-alliance of the Socialist Party with Saragat's SDP as a result of the Venice conference. Nenni's Socialist Party was strongly critical of the USSR and he was now for 'disengagement', although some of the Nenni Socialists were opposed to the fusion. None of this was to the liking of the CP who had been patiently associating themselves with the Nenni socialists for some time.

    George Paloczi-Horvath and Paul Ignotus were two Hungarian socialists who kept up a continual attack in Tribune's columns. The latter wrote an open letter (Tribune 1.3.57) to George Marosan, a member of the Kadar puppet government in March. Numerous meetings on Hungary were advertised—notably one addressed by Anna Kethly a Hungarian SPD leader, which was organised by the London Labour Party with James Griffiths as main speaker. (Tribune 26.4.57).
71. Tribune, 22.3.57.
72. His appeal was rejected.
73. Tribune, 3.5.57 reported the Wortley Hall conference of dissident communists.

74. The Newsletter founded 10.5.57, with Trotskyist collaboration, later became the organ of the Socialist Labour League, which left the Labour Party some years later.
75. Tribune, 8.9.57 'Can the Communists Answer This Challenge', a review of Djilas' *The New Class* by Michael Foot.
76. Tribune, 13.9.57. Former CP member Llew Gardner, now writing for Tribune, harried the Scottish Miner's Executive, whose Stalinist-inspired report denied aggression by Soviet troops in Hungary!
77. Tribune, 5.1.57.
78. Tribune, 21.6.57. Ian Mikardo's report back from Poznan.
79. Tribune, 27.9.57. This article on the Tito-Gomulka meeting is an excellent example of the view that there is an irreversible process of liberalisation taking place in Eastern Europe. The NEC of the LP protested at the secret trial of Djilas (reported in Tribune 11.10.57) and Tribune added its support. Djilas was already serving three years, to which a further seven were added.
80. Daily Worker 26.10.57. The report alleged Gomulka was under fire from the old guard and those to Gomulka's left.
81. In Poznan the final figures were 54 dead, 300 wounded, 320 arrested. Fetjo, *op. cit.* (p. 66) quoting from Avanti, Rome, 8.7.56.
82. Tribune, 10.5.57.
83. Tribune, 12.7.57. Raymond Fletcher—*Behind the Kremlin Power Struggle*, Molotov resigned as foreign minister in June 1956. It was announced in July 1957 that he, Malenkov and Kaganovich had been expelled from the Presidium and the Central Committee for establishing an 'anti-party group'.
84. Tribune, 12.7.57.
85. Tribune, 11.1.57.
86. Tribune, 21.6.57. Basil Davidson 'This is the Biggest Thing Since Lenin'.
87. Fetjo, *op. cit.* p. 138–9.
88. Tribune, 15.2.57.
89. *Aneurin Bevan Vol II*, Michael Foot (p. 540). The proposed settlement involved the removal of foreign troops, an arms embargo and neutralisation of the area. Says Foot it 'echoed much of what he (Bevan) had been saying for weeks'.
90. Tribune, 14.6.57. Tribune complained that two weeks had gone by since the Russian offer, without a Western response.
91. Tribune, 12.7.57. The article is a mixture of excellent motives and ignoble suggestions. Bevan complained that the Socialist International's attitude was anti-Communist, reinforced by the presence of representatives of the exiled socialist parties from the Baltic states and from Eastern Europe. It was 'altogether natural that they looked upon everything that came from Russia with unrelieved hostility'. These exiled parties became 'increasingly out of touch with the countries of their origin, their

advice and policies are bound to lose any sense of contemporary values'. Bevan felt that the obstinacy of these exiles, many of whom had a much more realistic grasp of the deviousness and ruthlessness of both tough and tender Stalinists, stood in the way of rapprochement with the more 'liberal' wing of Eastern European Stalinism. Yet there are inconsistencies in Bevan's position at this time, for he concedes, in the same article, that Khrushchev's grip on the party machinery 'hardly seems to be a manifestation of an increasing democratisation in Russia'. The system 'can hardly be stable or worthy of imitation when leaders so recently venerated are one after another cast down from their high places'. 'If so much that rises to the surface in Communist countries commands so little respect what are we to guess about what lies behind and below?' He was optimistic about the international turning its face towards the East but naïve to suppose that Moscow would ever countenance the legalisation or even the toleration of Social Democrats in the East. This, the exiles understood far better than Bevan.

92. Tribune, 12.5.57.
93. Tribune, 2.8.57. Bevan was angry that the Berlin declaration of Britain, France, the USA and the FGR was designed to influence the West German elections against the Social Democrats. He feared the military revival of 'Germany' would make her once more 'the arbiter' of European destinies. In this article Bevan appeared to regard Germany as little better than fascist below the surface, a sentiment virulently strong in Moscow.
94. Tribune, 16.8.57. Bevan believed that Khrushchev had 'accepted the logic of the situation' (i.e. world destruction of international agreement) whereas the West had not. In this view of the world lies the seeds of his conversion to multilateralism. The destiny of mankind lay in the hands of the established leaderships of West and East.
95. Tribune, 16.8.57.
96. Tribune, 16.8.57 and 22.6.56, 'Get the Troops Out of Europe' was the lead story. It was enthusiastic about the Russian proposals which had been repeated via the vocal chords of Herr Grotewohl of East Germany.
97. Tribune, 16.8.57. This article displays remarkable naïvety. The Soviet leaders were to sign away their control of Eastern Europe which would fall into the lap of social democracy.
98. Foot, *op. cit. Vol II*, p. 555.
99. Tribune, 29.11.57.

Chapter Eleven

The Bevanites and the H-bomb

The revolutionary events in Eastern Europe laid bare two distinct, broad trends within the Bevanite movement, *already* apparent by 1956.

Michael Foot represented the majority feeling of the radical Bevanite ranks who were to become the mainstay of Labour unilateralism when he took the opportunity, in the course of the year, to pursue historical-theoretical questions raised by the Khrushchev speech and the Hungarian revolution, to sharpen the polemics against Stalinism.

By contrast, those like Bevan, whose scheme of a gradually emerging liberal Kremlin leadership was disrupted by events, approximated ever more closely to the multilateralist position of the official Labour leadership and the pro-Kremlin left—despite their distaste for totalitarianism. This observation entails putting back by a full year the genesis of Bevan's rupture with his movement. For the differences between Foot and Bevan over the H-bomb in Autumn 1957 were already implicit in their different attitudes to Eastern Europe. The Brighton debacle was not simply about 'defence' or 'the bomb'. It was about the means by which political problems of the division of Europe and the world into two 'camps' might be resolved—whether by the self-activity and initiative of the mass movement, or by the intrigues of the very architects of those divisions. The H-bomb question, being the most profound question of modern politics, in which is contained the very destiny of mankind only *dramatised and accentuated* these conflicting approaches. Atomic weapons and the two camps were born together.[1]

It was tragic but it really was not accidental, that, on this vital issue, Aneurin Bevan, who had so often been in conflict both with Labour's bureaucracy and the CPGB, found himself with substantially the same position as his former antagonists. Long before Brighton, Bevan's role as one of the drafters of the programme *Industry and Society* was the target of left criticism and he was increasingly being drawn into the party leadership. At the beginning of 1957 Bevan stood somewhere between the radical Bevanites represented by Foot, and the compromisers, Wilson and Crossman who had already taken their distance from Bevanism and unilateralism.

Bevan's visit to the USSR in the Autumn of 1957 was undertaken in his capacity as Labour spokesman of foreign affairs and his membership of the NEC. He arrived in Russia after discussions with Khrushchev's trusted Gomulka about Labour's plan for disengagement in Europe.[2] This in turn had been approved at a meeting of the Socialist International in Vienna, with Bevan himself present, *only days earlier*. It is therefore perhaps significant that Gomulka's foreign secretary Adam Rapacki should have unveiled, one month later, on Thursday, October 2nd, the day of the crucial vote on the Norwood unilateralist resolution, and forty-eight hours before the launch of the Sputnik,[3] a plan for a nuclear-free zone in Europe, jointly policed by NATO and the Warsaw Pact. Bevan's visit, in another sense, symbolised the gravitational pull, exerted from the Soviet bureaucracy, through the domestic Labour bureaucracy to the leadership of the Labour left. This influence had grown steadily since Stalin's death and the accession to power of Khrushchev. Even the Hungarian bloodbath did not diminish it. And it is worthy of note that Bevan 'suppressed his temptation to mention Hungary and Poland' in the course of his discussions with Khrushchev.[4]

Bevan's paper was, after all, a creature of the popular front in the thirties. Its post-war estrangement from the Communist left was attributable less to theoretical conviction of the reactionary nature of the Soviet state, than to the intransigent sectarianism of the Cominform, which precluded collaboration with all but the most thick-skinned fellow travellers. The lessons of the Nazi-Soviet pact before the war were being unlearned again at least by Bevan, although the Michael Foot wing of the movement remained extremely guarded in this respect. Bevan's Russian visit, his discussions in Poland and the launching of the Sputnik, confirmed him in the view of a world divided into two blocs with a neutral bloc trying to emerge between them. This neutral bloc would have to be established in Central Eastern Europe through negotiation. The new liberal Stalinist leaderships would assist the process, and this, he believed, might make possible further liberalisation along social democratic lines. The neutral centre bloc might then be in a position to restrain and moderate the superpowers who were on the threshold of push-button warfare capability. *British possession of the H-bomb became for Bevan, at that point, the key to the achievement of a negotiated peace.* Unilateralism became redundant for him.

In the last issue of Tribune before the Norwood vote Bevan put forward this view of Britain, and British Labour specifically,[5] as the broker for peace, the go-between of the two blocs. He asked 'are we Tories too, or have we the capacity to meet (the Russians) part of the way?'[6]

Throughout 1957 he moved steadily closer to the Russian position on international negotiations. And in Warsaw, in September, three weeks from conference, he denounced the Eisenhower doctrine to the delight of his Polish hosts and explained away 'certain undesirable aspects' of Poland's domestic situation as flowing from 'historical limitations' and not from 'Gomulka's own principles'.[7] This went beyond good manners. But just how far this fatal permissiveness towards the Kremlin went can be seen from a Tribune statement of December, which only goes to show that despite its unilateralism, the paper shared some of Bevan's presuppositions even after the Brighton conference. 'Since Stalin's death the most evil of (the Russians') actions was the suppression of the Hungarian revolution. But appalling as that policy was it was not proof of their unwillingness to reach serious international agreements'.[8]

But there can be no doubt that Bevan's position on unilateralism underwent a distinct clarification and transformation in the course of 1957. Tribune led a spirited campaign throughout the year. The Bermuda meeting in the Spring gave Presidential and Prime Ministerial[9] endorsement to continued testing. In April came more Soviet tests.[10] And there was the Christmas Island test carried through in the face of Japanese protest.[11] There were reports about biological effects of strontium and the increase in deformities in human and plant life not only in Tribune but in the press generally.[12] A PLP meeting in early April persuaded the Shadow Cabinet to drop its resolution on international agreement to stop tests, and to consider the demand from the floor of the specially convened meeting to suspend British tests pending an initiative on international agreement.[13] This resolution had clear unilateralist implications, and the Shadow Cabinet bearing in mind a 1956 conference resolution, 'bowed to the will of the back benchers'.[14] This was hailed by Tribune as a great victory for Labour's rank and file.[15] Bevan, in India at the time, made explicitly unilateralist comments which Foot considers to have been misconstrued through being taken out of context. But Bevan did say that the weapon was 'useless' and that there was 'no good purpose *at all* [my emphasis] in Britain also arming herself'[16] with it. And in a letter to his wife, Bevan accused Crossman of 'doing his usual turnabout'. He commented that Crossman had been 'reported as saying in Germany that he favours us making the bomb'. *The implication is, here, too, clearly that Bevan did not.*[17] He wrote in Tribune on May 15th that the H-bomb was not a deterrent.[18]

He addressed mass meetings on the question in the summer and Foot believes that Bevan caught the mood of the great audiences[19] which seems to suggest that he might have gone further than he intended in some of his speeches. In Cardiff at the miners' Gala he called for street demonstrations[20] if the government would not act. In Manchester he argued that Britain should say,

> 'We can make the H-bomb *but we are not going to make it. We believe that what the human race needs is leadership in the opposite direction and we are going to give it*'.[21]

That this was the most important issue in the Labour movement is evidenced by the fact that there were 127 resolutions in the 'disarmament' section at the Labour Party conference, the great majority of which were unilateralist.[22] At the beginning of August, in an editorial, Tribune called for the dismantling of 'our petty arsenal'.[23]

A review of Bevan's speeches and articles in the course of 1957 reveals a large number of statements and arguments with clear unilateralist implications, although some of these can be construed as rhetorical devices of taking arguments to their logical conclusion. Perhaps it was wrong of the unilateralists to have considered things Bevan said in debate with upholders of nuclear strategy as being concrete policy rather than abstract argument. But whatever was going on in Bevan's mind many unilateralists did regard him as one of them, almost as their spokesman. Tribune certainly was most often unilateralist.

Less than a fortnight before conference opened and long before CND was formed, five thousand people came to hear Mikardo, Castle and Greenwood address the H-bomb campaign committee demonstration in Trafalgar Square.[24]

What of the Communist Party's position on unilateralism? As in the case of Bevan some speculation took place about the CPGB having changed its line.[25] A review of King Street literature and leaders' comments on the subject during 1957 does not confirm this. The trouble is that unilateralists and multilateralists often said very similar things when leading up to their very different conclusions as to how nuclear weapons should be ended. Both denounced the physical effects on plants and human life; both demanded an end to tests 'now'; both used arguments about Britain needing to be first to take a moral lead; both favoured suspending tests 'immediately' pending something; both argued that H-bombs were 'no defence'.[26] It was therefore quite possible for the CPGB to *appear* to be saying the same things as the unilateralists and that is why it may have *appeared* to unilateralists that the party had changed its line at the time of the Brighton conference. The beauty of the Norwood resolution was its clarity. Although it lost the day in the voting, it won the battle for clarity. Bevan and the Communist Party, Tribune and the unilateralists, were all clear where everybody stood after the Norwood vote.

The CPGB began the year with a Daily Worker lobby of parliament,[27] laying great stress on the need for a European Security pact. But in February the party was not even calling for unilateral renunciation of *tests*, let alone unilateral nuclear disarmament.[28] Their demand was 'international agreement to stop tests'.[29] Through the unions the party pressed for a three-power agreement for a temporary cessation of testing.[30] In

July the Daily Worker called a 'March for Life' which amounted to little more than moral denunciation of the bomb. And in the lead-up to Labour Party conference the CP was demanding that the (Conservative) government be forced to take up the latest Soviet offer of talks aimed towards an agreement on nuclear weapons, even though it was precisely the lack of confidence in such talks leading anywhere that was swelling the ranks of the unilateralists. World News's analysis of the Labour Party conference resolutions contained not a mention of unilateralism despite the fact that this was the overwhelming theme.[31] This cannot have been because the CPGB did not understand the difference of the two approaches. It was much more likely that they wished to swim in the unilateralist current in the hope that they might influence its course[32] towards the (Soviet) policy of great power talks. When the CPGB protested after the Norwood debate that they had not changed their line,[33] they were being perfectly truthful. Indeed, after the vote they boasted that the AEU resolution, which was closest to their own line, had been described as 'the most important' of the resolutions before the conference in the H-bomb debate. The AEU resolution was anti-unilateralist.

After the Norwood vote the Communist Party leaders combined their support for the Bevan-NEC position on the H-bomb with denunciation of the Left's alleged betrayal on the *Industry and Society* document.[34]

The CP were making political capital both out of the victory of the Labour Party right on defence, *and* the disarray of the left that had been brought about partly by Bevan and the unions adopting the position they themselves supported! The aftermath of Bevan's defection produced bitter exchanges between Tribune and the Communist Party. Leading Bevanite, Tom Driberg, wrote that Bevan's closest associates considered the Russians were anxious that Britain should *not* unilaterally give up nuclear weapons since that might *increase* tensions and the prospect of war. He noted that since the crucial vote at conference the Daily Worker had made 'no attack on Bevan and the NEC on this issue' but had, instead concentrated its fire on the nationalisation policy contained in *Industry and Society*. The Daily Worker editorials of 4th and 5th October, he further noted, managed to make no mention of the H-bomb issue on which the rest of the press were concentrating. There were only passing references, which Driberg felt 'seemed to imply support for the NEC's attitude', i.e. 'the banning of nuclear weapons by international agreement' rather than through unilateral action.[35]

The Monday following conference, the Daily Worker replied to Driberg's 'insinuation' that the Daily Worker might have been influenced to change its policy as a result of what Mr Khrushchev was alleged to have said to Mr Bevan. The paper declared it had always striven to get the maximum number of British citizens fighting for 'a policy that will force the existing British government to change its attitude on the bomb'. 'It had always stood for international agreement to stop H-tests . . .' 'That was substantially the policy adopted at the Labour Party conference'.[36] In other words, Driberg was right. The Communist Party did support the line of Bevan and the NEC against the rank and file unilateralist Bevanites, but they had not had to change their policy to achieve this. The CPGB's old line that the 'real' left were to be found in the ranks whilst the left leaders were barely distinguishable from the right was backfiring on them. For on this occasion, they supported Bevan and the NEC against the constituency ranks. The Communist Party now argued the left's unilateralism was divisive.

The Daily Express was so intrigued by the whole affair that it attempted a reconstruction of Bevan's East European itinerary and the events that led up to his *volte face*. It noted that Bevan and Jennie Lee's visit to Russia began on September 11th; that on September 17th they were received by Khrushchev at Yalta for 'long friendly conversations' and that back in Moscow on the 18th, Bevan found Khrushchev 'exceedingly anxious to establish friendly relations with the US'. On October 1st at Brighton, Express men, Evans and Aitken (formerly of Tribune) revealed Bevan was changing his mind on the H-bomb,

> 'Mr Bevan has been telling his friends that Mr K. said to him, "Do not create a vacuum in Europe by giving up the bomb".'[37]

Newsweek took up the story when it reported,

> 'Labour Party insiders reveal that Khrushchev tipped Aneurin Bevan . . . that the Red Moon would be launched . . . They say this tip plus the Soviet intercontinental ballistic missile helped to influence Bevan's turnabout speech against banning the bomb'.[38]

In its post-conference issue, Tribune returned to the attack on the Daily Worker, which had 'hailed Labour's decision, condoled with Aneurin Bevan on his difficult hour at the microphone and toned down its reporting of the attacks on him'.[39] Subsequently Tribune alleged that the Political Committee of the Communist Party had referred benevolently to 'the important resolutions adopted on the suspension of nuclear tests and the banning of nuclear weapons by international agreement'. Tribune believed it had unmasked 'the strangest red plot of all' when it pointed out that the 'strangest aspect of the voting on the H-bomb resolutions at the Labour Party conference was the behaviour of the trade unions whose leadership is responsive to the Communist Party line'. Tribune was referring, above all, to the ETU which had opted for Bevan and the NEC against unilateralism.

> 'The Communist attitude may well have had an influence too, on the decision of other unions whose delegates include people frequently sympathetic to Communist thinking—notably the Boilermakers, the AEU and the NUR.'[40]

The Bevanite journal said that in Brighton, on the evening after the vote had been taken 'many distrustful fellow travellers were heard flatly refusing to believe that the Communist Party favoured Britain keeping the bomb'. It was rather like the days of the Soviet-Nazi pact Tribune mused, 'Mr J. R. Campbell is probably unaware that he has joined the bourgeoisie'.[41]

The Daily Worker's editor was stung to reply that Tribune had joined the Daily Express, for had not the Express 'produced the remarkable theory that Mr Khrushchev told Mr Bevan that Britain should make the H-bomb and that therefore the Communist Party has changed its policy'.[42] In a section headed 'When Left Helps Right' the Daily Worker said not a single major trade union had voted for unilateralism and that 'some people' had put forward the unilateralist motion which went further than the unions had so far shown themselves prepared to go.[43]

Unilateralism was 'divisive'; it diverted attention from the main question; it produced profound disagreement; 'the most "left" sounding demand has in practice helped the right wing'.[44] J. R. Campbell put flesh on the spectre behind the unilateralist manoeuvre in his 'Spotlight on Politics' column. He asked 'What is happening in the ranks of the former Bevanites, Trotskyites and what have you, gathered around Tribune?' They were 'creating diversions' over the H-bomb issue whilst the Bevanite members of the NEC refused to take a firm line against *Industry and Society* thereby giving Gaitskell 'a walkover for his fundamentally reactionary right wing policy'. The Bevanites had voted for *Industry and Society* on the NEC and none of them, he alleged, had spoken against it at the conference. Thus the CPGB falsely dismissed the unilateralist's campaign as a means of diverting attention away from the left's role in supporting the right over domestic industrial policy.[45]

John Gollan addressed a meeting called 'After Bevanism?'[46] in which he alleged 'It is Bevanism that has collapsed not the genuine left'. All previous left currents had 'failed' to build a comprehensive alternative—the ILP, Socialist League, Keep Left and now Bevanism. Whether Gollan made clear to his audience that CP backed Bevan on the very issue on which he deserted his followers is not recorded. And if they supported him on the issue and denounced his followers for merely creating diversions, it is difficult to see exactly who was left to claim the title 'genuine left', unless by this Gollan meant his own party. Indeed he appeared to be playing a double role here—deriding Bevanism's collapse (due to the defection of Bevan himself) whilst supporting the Bevan-Khrushchev position on international agreement to secure nuclear disarmament. No doubt the CP was grateful, after two years on the receiving end of Tribune's barbs, for the opportunity to hit back.[47] And so the Communist Party's conformity with Moscow's requirements in the field of nuclear disarmament had brought them finally to support for Bevan and Gaitskell. The 'right' turn which began after 1952 and the 19th congress of the CPSU carried them, in Britain, not to an alignment with the Labour left, but on the contrary, to the new Gaitskell-Bevan leadership. Late in the year a declaration of the twelve ruling Communist Parties formally dropped the use of the term 'Social Democrats'. Henceforth they were to be called 'Socialists'![48]

Accordingly Khrushchev personally wrote to the Labour Party and to six other European Socialist parties, urging them to act to save peace in the Middle East crisis.[49] Bevan, commenting on the letter, revealed that Khrushchev had warned of the crisis before it broke and added that 'I suspect that (he) intended that I should be a purveyor of his warning to the western world'.[50]

In the event the NEC rejected 'out of hand' Khrushchev's proposal of joint talks between the CPSU and the Labour Party, since Labour could not negotiate with what was, in effect, the government of another country. The NEC's vote was unanimous and the CPGB remarked that this reflected no credit 'on those who used to call themselves Bevanites'.[51] And so, for the time being, the CPGB got little comfort from the Kremlin's new orientation towards the social democratic parties. In the aftermath of the Norwood vote Bevan was full of praise for the Russian achievement in space. He was over-generous to the point where he conceded too much to the undertakers of the Hungarian revolution. He argued that the people of the west had confused freedom of expression with freedom of self-expression and that the Russian revolution had opened up new horizons and that 'millions of workers have a feeling of liberation'.[52] Bevan neglected to add that counter revolution in the thirties had buried not only the Bolshevik leaders but the society for which they strove. Even as he wrote those words Imre Nagy and Pal Maleter, (who undoubtedly had the support of millions of Hungarian workers seeking such liberation) were being held incommunicado before their secret trial and execution in May 1958. And this was merely the surface of the repressions. The November 1957 conference of Communist parties reaffirmed a tough centralist line. Khrushchev and Mao re-opened the campaign against Titoism.[53] Collectivisation of agriculture was reimposed (except in Poland). Industrial production targets were raised in some buffer states by as much as 100 per cent.[54] The outlook for workers' freedoms in Eastern Europe could hardly inspire the optimism of Bevan's words.

In view of this sad indulgence on Bevan's part it was perhaps poetic justice that the Trotskyists were beginning to make some headway on the left. Whilst they justified the Warsaw Pact as a necessity for Soviet defence, they were in other respects, the sternest critics of the Kremlin and had reaped considerable advantage from the Hungarian events. They had by now recovered from the loss of Socialist Outlook and, gathering around themselves some important CPGB defectors, launched The Newsletter.[55] Indeed the mover of the very Norwood resolution which split Bevan from Bevanism, was the well-known Trotskyist Vivienne Mendelson.

But even if the Trotskyists had been able to counter Bevan's indulgence towards the Kremlin, and even if they had been able to enrich the debate in Tribune, they allowed their attention to be diverted from the Tribune arena, which was still the clearing house of the left, towards the milieu of disaffected Communists. And the irony was that many of these found in the Trotskyist movement the centralised, dogmatic sectarianism of the early Cominform. For these Communists, whilst the Hungarian events were the catalyst in their break with King Street, the latter's drift towards collaboration with social democracy since the dissolution of the Cominform was at least as great a consideration. Within a very short space of time the Trotskyists founded the Socialist Labour League and, after some initial hesitation, took the path of the open party, ready to do battle with social democracy from the sidelines as the CPGB had done before it.

There were many other flourishing debating circles at the time. The break-up of Bevanism caused a hundred flowers to bloom. There were the International Socialists, the Universities and Left Review, the Socialist Forum movement and the Workers League, to name the more important. For the Communist Party the lean years had arrived. From the Bevanites they had learned nothing and gained nothing. They had opposed Bevanism when it was in the ascendant, added to its confusion of German Rearmament at its apogee, and joined its defecting leader in the last period of its decline. And yet there was sufficient a fund of goodwill and short memory on the part of the parliamentary left for the CPGB to take heart that all was not lost. The period of the Cominform had depleted the ranks of their sympathisers in the PLP. They would spend the next ten years building bridges to the Tribune left. Unlike the Trotskyists, they never gave up.

NOTES

1. The division of the world into spheres of influence at Yalta and Potsdam was concluded on 1st August 1945. Five days later Hiroshima was bombed. In the same week of September 1949 that Mao proclaimed the Peoples Republic of China, Russia broke the West's monopoly of nuclear weapons. Thus the division of the world through agreement of allies was superseded by the division of the world by allies turned enemies and armed with nuclear weapons. In 1952 the USA exploded its first Hydrogen bomb, followed a year later by Russia. This breakthrough in destructive technology led on to the year of Geneva when the nuclear powers foisted an agreement on to Vietnam. But London disarmament talks in 1954 were abortive despite Russian concessions on conventional armaments. The disarmament talks of 1956 and 1957 really got nowhere. Then, after the launching of the Sputnik with its clear implications of intercontinental nuclear missiles Russia promptly withdrew from the talks.
2. Foot, *Vol II, op. cit.* (p. 563). The plan had recently been approved by the Second International meeting in Vienna in Bevan's presence.
3. It was suggested in some quarters that Bevan had prior knowledge of this. See below.
4. Foot, *Vol II, op. cit.* (p. 564).
5. Khrushchev wrote to the NEC asking for talks with the Labour Party after the Brighton conference. See below.
6. Tribune, 27.9.57.
7. See Daily Worker, 11.9.57 and 17.10.57.
8. Tribune, 20.12.57.
9. Tribune, 29.3.57 and 22.3.57.
10. The Times, 22.4.57.
11. Tribune, 29.3.57.
12. Tribune, 12.4.57. Manchester Guardian, 15.4.57.

13. Foot, *Vol II, op. cit.* (p. 551).
14. as above.
15. Tribune, 5.4.57.
16. Foot, *Vol II, op. cit.* (p. 552).
17. as above.
18. Foot, *Vol II, op. cit.* (p. 554).
19. Foot, *Vol II, op. cit.* (p. 554).
20. as above. Tribune, 20.9.57 advertised an H-bomb campaign committee demonstration in Trafalgar Square with Castle, Greenwood, Zilliacus and Soper as speakers. In the Tribune of 27.9.57, 5,000 were reported to have taken part.
21. Foot, *Vol II, op. cit.* (p. 553).
22. Tribune, 26.7.57. Unlike the World News which did not comment in its LP conference preview on the unilateralist resolutions, Tribune noted 'several resolutions which in calling for a cessation of nuclear tests, leave it unclear whether Britain should lead in default of world agreement'.
23. Tribune, 30.8.57. The Editorial was clearly unilateralist.
24. It was held on September 22nd.
25. See below Tom Driberg's allegation that the CPGB had changed its line.
26. World News, 26.1.57.
27. World News, 12.1.57.
28. The PLP went further than this.
29. World News, 23.3.57, Claire Yuille.
30. World News, 15.6.57. AEU South London District Committee.
31. *Aneurin Bevan, Vol II*, by M. Foot, *op. cit.*
32. Later when CND had become popular the CPGB dramatically changed course and participated in the Aldermaston unilateralist demonstration. Its slogan was . . . 'Summit Talks'.
33. See Driberg dispute below.
34. It was overwhelmingly carried by 5,383,000 to 1,442,000. See Foot, *Vol. II, op. cit.* (p. 572).
35. Reynolds News, Sunday, 6.10.57.
36. Daily Worker, 7.10.57.
37. Bevan denied this in a television interview.
38. Tribune, 11.10.57 quoting Newsweek, 4.10.57 Eldon Griffiths, chief European correspondent said the story was obtained by one of his staff.
39. Tribune, 11.10.57.
40. Tribune, 11.10.57. The pro-unilateralists were ASSET, FBU, Draughtsmen and something less than half the Constituency Parties.
41. Tribune, 11.10.57.
42. Daily Worker, 12.10.57, editorial.
43. Daily Worker, 12.10.57. The paper also said, 'No Communist is allowed to represent his union at the Labour Party conference. The union delegates who voted were all Labour Party

members. Whilst this is true it does not contradict Tribune's allegation that those who voted for the NEC were 'unions whose leadership *is responsive* to the Communist Party line'. In the same issue Tribune had spoken of 'fellow travellers'. It had never alleged that Communist Party members were involved.

44. Daily Worker, 12.10.57. The paper also said about the moving of the unilateralist motion, 'We consider that this was an utterly wrong action. It merely had the effect of diverting attention from the main question'. History subsequently recorded that unilateralism was the main question, for within three years, at Scarborough, in 1960 the unilateralists carried the day at the Labour Party conference, with the support of many big unions. The editorial of the Daily Worker, 12.10.57 denied there had ever been any ambiguity in the Communist Party's line on the H-bomb.
45. Daily Worker, 12.10.57.
46. Daily Worker, 16.10.57.
47. Indeed even Tribune's old flame, Yugoslavia, turned on Bevan. The paper *Borba* dismissed his remarks about wanting to do away with the H-bomb as intended to satisfy the more radical delegates, whilst Cousins had won their applause. (Tribune, 18.10.57). Tribune retaliated with a sharp attack on despotism in Yugoslavia, and noted that, even in China, the 'hundred flowers' campaign was terminating amid demands for use of the death penalty against dissenters.
48. Tribune, 29.11.57.
49. For the CPGB's view on this see the Daily Worker, 16.10.57.
50. Tribune, 18.10.57.
51. Daily Worker, 24.10.57.
52. Tribune, 11.10.57.
53. Fetjo, *op. cit.* (pp. 138–144).
54. Fetjo, *op. cit.* (pp. 144–5).
55. Its first editor was the greatly respected Peter Fryer who left the Trotskyists shortly after.

Chapter Twelve

The Politics of Bevanism

To what extent was there continuity of personnel and programme in the Bevanite movement? Did it indeed have sufficient, distinguishing programmatic characteristics to warrant the suffix 'ism'? We may put aside the now proven contention that, at the base, at the level of party-union ranks, Bevanism constituted a powerful mood or current of revolt against the direction taken by the Labour Cabinet between 1949–51, and against the direction of the Attlee-Deakin leadership in both foreign and domestic policy after the election defeat of 1951. This was a movement of the ranks to begin to take hold of its executive bodies and organisations to effect a return to radical policies. But because parliamentary Bevanism, inevitably, expressed this mass current indirectly, and in muted fashion, and because Bevan gave his name to it, some commentators have wrongly concluded that Bevanism was nothing more than a parliamentary group.

This view was certainly not shared by Bevan's opponents in the Labour Party, organised around the journal Socialist Commentary. An editorial which appeared shortly after the Morecambe conference observed,

> 'What, after all, is Bevanism? The extraordinary fact is that there is *no* distinct policy which can be attached, like a placard, to this name'.

It concluded that there were 'really two Bevanisms',

> 'The first is what Aneurin and his leading adjutants actually stand for in terms of concrete policies; what statements they put their names to; what, as practical politicians they know to be possible and impossible. This Bevanism is, as we have said, all but indistinguishable from the remainder

of the party's policy. It is therefore little more than a myth. But the second is entirely different—it is what their followers have been led to believe is Bevanism'.[1]

However, even at parliamentary level the term 'Bevanite' was ambiguous and no clear guide to voting behaviour on different issues. The most reliable point of reference available is the actual Bevanite membership list of 47 MPs and four others, supplied by Jo Richardson who was secretary to both the Keep Left and Bevanite Groups.[2]

In addition we may consider, with due care, such factors as membership of 'Peace' and East European 'Friendship' Societies, set up as front organisations after 1947. Also helpful is a knowledge of contributions to Communist or Trotskyist influenced journals like Labour Monthly and Socialist Outlook. Though this may on occasions merely indicate a desire to participate in debate with opponents, it might, taken with other factors and voting behaviour, indicate a certain political alignment or sympathy.

Finally there is the record of voting and abstention behaviour in a series of parliamentary divisions between 1947 and 1955, which may indicate recruits and defectors from the Bevanite ranks, as well as members. For comparative purposes the Keep Left, 'Nennist' and Bevanite ranks are arranged in blocs.* The final bloc consists of people who were neither Keep Lefters nor Bevanite members, nor Nennists, but who took part in some revolts alongside the Bevanites.

First, in relation to Keep Left, thirteen out of the twenty associated with the group and its manifestos became full members of the Bevanite group after it was formed in the Spring of 1951. Six of them contributed to Labour Monthly, although most of these contributions predate the Cold War, and three associated with front organisations even after the Cold War period had begun. Two were associated with Socialist Outlook. In the case of Harold Davies this was a firm commitment to a regular parliamentary column. Nine Keep Lefters voted for NATO ratification, the rest abstaining or absent when the vote was taken. The only other votes relevant to the Keep Left group reveal nine participants in revolt on the Northern

* See Appendix.

Ireland Bill[3] and Ian Mikardo the sole Keep Left rebel over conscription in 1947.

Scrutiny of the 'Nennist' bloc reveals some quite distinct patterns. To begin with very few were ever associated with the Bevanites at all. Emrys Hughes, Maurice Orbach and Julius Silverman, were the only three out of the eighteen listed to become group members. Seven contributed to Labour Monthly, three of these—Zilliacus, Hutchinson and S. O. Davies—on a number of occasions; three contributed to the Trotskyist influenced Socialist Outlook especially S. O. Davies and Thomas Braddock who had a close working relationship with the management of the paper, some of whom later joined the Communist Party. Three of the Nennist group were expelled from the Labour Party and stood, with Communist support, against Labour in the 1950 election as 'Labour Independents'.[4] Five were associated with Communist front organisations and one, P. Barstow, openly joined the Communist Party in 1952. Three Nennists voted with the Communists against NATO in the May 1949 vote. All the others abstained, with the exception of W. G. Cove. Taken together these events suggest that something more than a single-issue group thrown together accidentally over the Nenni telegram issue. In the opinion of the National Executive the Nennists were 'acting as a group in organised opposition to party policy' and that 'among the signatories were also the names of some of those who signed the message to the Communist controlled German Unity Congress,' which was later repudiated by the Parliamentary Labour Party. With the exception of Emrys Hughes, Maurice Orbach and Julius Silverman the Nennist group played no constructive part in the evolution of the Bevanite left, and it is fair to say that the majority of them represented a political outlook, that was, on the whole, alien to the traditons of British social democracy and incapable of developing its left wing.

Examination of the political and voting behaviour of the Bevanite group proper, produced a very different picture. Of the forty-seven listed MP members, eight contributed to Labour Monthly, five of these contributed only once, and rather early on. Four contributed to Socialist Outlook, Harold Davies and Ellis Smith being deeply involved. Five were members of front organisations—this was a much smaller proportion than the Nennists. Nine Bevanites rebelled on the National Service vote, fourteen on the Northern Ireland Bill, 27 abstained on NATO (eleven voting for NATO, one against) and 42 were involved in the Defence White Paper revolt in 1952. The Bevanites agreed to abstain in the November 1954 European Defence Community vote due to fear of mass expulsions, but three of them did vote *against*, as the Communist Party had advised Labour to, (two of these were Nennists turned Bevanites). The last two votes—on the atomic energy Bill in April 1954 and the Labour opposition's amendment in March 1955 saw Bevanite rebellions of 24 and 28 massively augmented by a rebellion from the non-Bevanite left listed in bloc four. On these, the last two Bevanite rebellions, the number of non-Bevanite votes were 39 and 34 respectively, which indicated that a new broader left was already in the process of formation by 1954 to 1955 just as the centre left Bevanites were taking their distance from their old colleagues.[5] It is perhaps significant too that both these votes were intimately connected with the issue of nuclear defence.

What the voting pattern indicates is a gradual escalation of the Bevanite current in the late forties and early fifties, followed by the broadening out of the left in 1954–55, so that the Bevanite group proper were in a minority in the ranks of the rebels in the votes of those years, though undoubtedly still the recognised leadership of the left. There is no evidence of a Bevanite whip. If it had existed it would have produced greater conformity in voting patterns, and the rebellions of 1954 and 1955 might have been bigger by about 13 and 17 respectively.

The picture of a broad, organised, but not tightly disciplined group containing within it divergent views, is confirmed by a review of the Bevanite attitude to policy matters as such. The Bevanites were careful not to allow themselves to be portrayed as usurpers of the democratic process of policy making within the party. In this respect they were clearer than their Keep Left forbears.

Both Keep Left and Keeping Left contained a large element of policy formulation, and Keep Left, in particular, went further when it advised the government of 'twenty things to do now',[6] which were presented as a shopping list. But it also made reference to the manifesto on which Labour had been elected in 1945 as the touchstone for its proposals,

> '*Let Us Face the Future*—the document that inspired Great Britain to discard the Tories—described how the Government was going to tackle, and has in fact tackled, this . . . task . . .
>
> This nationalisation programme has been carried out vigorously and needs to be continued to embrace every industry which has a hold over our national economy or which cannot be made efficient in private hands'.[7]

Keep Left considered its aim was 'to provide some ideas for the Margate conference and after', once more genuflecting in the direction of the proper procedure for policy formulation. Later, Keeping Left could boast that some of the proposals of Keep Left had in fact been embraced by the government. But the 1950 pamphlet was at pains to point out,

> 'We have omitted in this chapter discussion of certain proposals—for instance, the Party's specific nationalisation plans—because they are fully discussed in *Labour Believes in Britain.* Moreover many of the suggestions we have made are elaborations of ideas contained in the official party policy'.[8]

Furthermore we find in Keeping Left the beginnings of an awareness that Labour's problem was less to do with the need to outline and propose new policies, so much as *to ensure the carrying out of policies already agreed upon and to which the party was committed.* For it was the party leadership's *own drift away* from such policies which underlay the growing revolt in the ranks. As Keeping Left noted on the back sleeve

> 'Since 1954 we have moved so far and so fast that the ideas of the rank and file and the actions of the Government are sometimes a long way apart. Very often this is because changed conditions have demanded changes in method and it is the rank and file who are lagging behind; but sometimes principles have been overriden by expediency, and here it is the attitude of the leadership that is rightly questioned'.[9]

The Bevanites were far more explicit and far clearer on their attitude towards party policy. They never made the mistake of counterposing their own programmatic demands to those of conference, but on the contrary, often underlined that their proposals *were* party policy which the leadership of the party was deserting. This is a most important aspect of Labour revolts. The most serious left wing revolts encompass this element of *preserving what is in the party programme*, against those leaders who seek to *change* the direction of party policy from what has been mutually agreed upon.

This was expressed in Keep Left as opposition to the Government's abandonment of the Grand Alliance and its acceptance of the 'two blocs' with Britain in the American bloc. It was expressed again in the Bevanite revolt which originated specifically in the Government's attack on the free Health Service to which the labour movement was committed. The theme recurrs throughout the Bevanite parliamentary revolts between 1951–55. The Bevanites repeatedly took up policies and standpoints of the movement being discarded by the party leadership. We find it again in the Clause Four campaign, and in the campaign for the Scarborough conference decision on the H-bomb later in 1960. *This approach spills over automatically into demands for the democratisation of the party, the democratisation of procedure for the election of the leadership, to render it more directly accountable to the ranks and the policies decided at conference.*

So the Bevanites stood to gain nothing by putting forward 'an alternative policy'. Accordingly they made their position very plain.

> 'We would like to make one thing clear at the outset. The pamphlet is not intended to be a statement of policy for the Labour Party. The function of policy-making lies with the Annual Conference of the Party, acting on the guidance and advice of the National Executive Committee of the Party. What is here intended is in no sense a challenge to these authorities'.[10]

The message was repeated in the main text of *One Way Only*, and the approach embellished in such a way that there could be no ambiguity.

'What then is the alternative? What sort of policy ought the government to pursue in order to deal with this domestic situation?"

'It is not our purpose to put forward a programme for the Government or for the Labour Party. The only body competent to make policy for the Labour Party, as the authors of the Foreword have said, is the party's annual conference. And in any event the Party already has a programme which is contained in a document called *Let Us Win Through Together.* That document lays down a large number of proposals for dealing with Britain's economy which are as valid now as they were when they were written.'[11]

The Bevanites at this point catalogued the uncompleted tasks of the party manifesto. It was an unassailable political position. No one could seriously charge them with disregard for due process of policy making. This largely explains why the party leadership had to resort to personal vilification, bureaucratic manoeuvres and petty tyranny.

One Way Only was a powerful and immensely popular piece of political pamphleteering. It listed the policies agreed upon at the Margate conference and examined the leadership's performance in every case.

'Last year, at Margate, Conference enthusiastically endorsed the World Plan for Mutual Aid as its constructive peace policy. Since then both there and in the USA rearmament has been given an overriding priority and has begun to swallow up the labour and resources which should have been available for such schemes'.[12]

This example was followed by a string of 'Last year . . . this year' comparisons which underlined that it was the party leadership and not the rebels who were inventing new policies. The approach was further developed in *Going Our Way*. Here the issue of accountability was introduced. Not only was there a retreat from policy but those responsible were defying democratic procedure . . .

'. . . there can be no justification, in a democratic organisation, for the authority given by a mass membership to be used *against* the known feelings of those members. Yet that

> is precisely what has been happening during the past few months. During the past few months, most of the twelve trade union members of the National Executive have been casting their votes *against* the wishes of the people who elected them'.[13]

The pamphlet then cited how, on the occasion of the NEC's endorsement of the Gaitskell budget, seven trade union leaders were responsible for supporting a budget which was at direct variance with the decisions of their union conferences and policy statements. The pamphlet then quoted from the conference resolutions of the unions concerned, and named the union leaders who had violated them. It concluded,

> 'The men who did it may have been speaking for themselves; they were assuredly speaking for nobody else . . . When the Government called for a bang of the rubber stamp, these trade union leaders rushed to give it'.[14]

Is it any wonder that the trade union bureaucracy were the most enthusiastic supporters of the Gaitskell wing of the party when their misdemeanours were so devastatingly catalogued by the Bevanites? From the very outset the Bevan group set their sights on the bureaucratic targets.

Even in *It Need Not Happen*, the last of the big-scale Bevanite pamphlets and, arguably, the weakest, the main thrust of their case was that Labour had been united in its opposition to German Rearmament until September, 1950, and that,

> 'the support now being given by the Parliamentary Party and the National Executive for the immediate rearmament of Western Germany is in direct contravention of the policy unanimously agreed at Margate'.[15]

Any attempt to delineate a Bevanite programme ought therefore to be set in the context of the movement's commitment to the *Labour Party and its programme.* This did not weaken, but *strengthened* the Bevanite movement. For the party programme represented the real, concrete steps taken by the mass movement in the direction of establishing socialism. By contrast 'alternative programmes' are generally offered by those who do not begin from the reality of the Labour movement, who imagine themselves policy makers, and who therefore have more in common with the utopian socialists of the nineteenth century. The proliferation of fringe parties, each with their separate programme to replace the programme which the Labour movement itself works out, is a good example of utopian socialism in contemporary Britain. None-theless there are certain key policy issues to which the Bevanites and their predecessors in Keep Left gave prominence and which are worthy of review and comparison with party pronouncements.

Labour's post-war election manifestos did not give foreign policy its due importance in the movement's programme. *Let Us Face The Future* (1945) gave foreign affairs one page out of twelve, and grudgingly conceded 'We cannot cut ourselves off from the rest of the world—and we ought not to try'. It argued for a continued wartime association of the USSR, USA, and British Commonwealth; the establishment of a United Nations organisation; publicised and reducing expenditure on armaments and self government for India. Considering the huge scale of Britain's empire there was remarkably little about the future of the Crown's colonial subjects—one sentence promising 'planned progress for our Colonial Dependencies'. *Let Us Win Through Together* (1950) was similarly neglectful even though by this time Germany was effectively divided and conflict had erupted in Malaya, Greece and Palestine. This manifesto also devoted one page out of twelve to foreign affairs. The innovation was the commitment to strengthening the Atlantic Community and Western Europe and the declara-tion that Labour would 'stand firm against any attempt to intimidate us or to undermine our position in the world'. Even so Labour remained 'ready at any moment to co-operate fully with Russia' if she were ready to work for peace and friend-ship. But Labour now spoke of a 'strengthening' of the Com-monwealth. India's independence was celebrated but Labour spoke only of 'creating the economic and social basis' for democratic self government with regard to the rest of the dependencies. By 1951 however, the hurriedly produced two-page manifesto opened with a foreign policy priority. 'Our first aim is to save the peace of the world'. Labour expressed 'grievous disappointments' at the frustration of its 1945 hopes for post-war co-operation 'particularly with the Soviet Union'.

> 'The Labour government decided without hesitation that Britain must play her full part in the strengthening of collective defence. Britain must be strong; so must the Commonwealth'.[16]

The manifesto was especially concerned that if the Conservatives should win 'there would be no major power in the Councils of Western Europe represented by Labour', and it was vital that Labour's voice should be heard for the 'fate of civilisation'. The new priority of foreign over domestic policy was confirmed in the 1955 manifesto 'Forward With Labour'. One and a half of its four pages were devoted to peace and foreign affairs. And it opened with the greatest priority of all, the preoccupation of the epoch,

> 'As we in Britain prepare to go to the poll, the Hydrogen bomb looms over all mankind. What can we do to meet that menace?'[17]

It called for summit talks; multilateral disarmament under international control; relaxation of tension in Europe through negotiated German unification; the admission of Mao's China to UNO and the neutralisation of Formosa and a huge third world aid programme combined with gradual preparation for self government in the Commonwealth.

This growing emphasis on foreign policy, evident in the Labour manifestos found expression in the Bevanites' own increasing preoccupation with international affairs. Keep Left's ten points on foreign policy really contain the essential Bevanite approach—fear the 'Collective security against Communism' could become the formula for the division of Europe and the world into Soviet and American spheres of influence. This was further elaborated in *Keeping Left* which expressly cited Titoism as an example of a nation seeking to break out of the two blocs straitjacket.[18] Both the Keep Left manifestos were committed to a united Germany and a united Europe. Both saw Social Democracy as the only force capable of achieving this, and *Keeping Left* expressly called for Labour to produce a socialist policy for Europe.

The Bevanite view was also evident in the Keep Left manifestos' reiteration of the theme of world mutual aid. This was how they envisaged Kremlin totalitarianism, to which they were totally opposed, might be halted—not only in Europe but in the third world, through economic development to forestall unrest and revolt.

The authors of the pamphlets *One Way Only* and *Going Our Way* embrace many of the presuppositions of the Keep Left manifestos but *not*, it should be noted, Keep Left's firm statement on the renunciation of manufacture of atomic bombs by Britain. The Bevanite pamphlets deal at great length with the international war on poverty—especially in Asia, and they express anger and frustration at the Labour government's failure to breathe life into the World Plan for Mutual Aid. They reveal a concern with these matters totally out of keeping with the tenor of contemporary left-wing Labour politics. At the same time the Bevanites were firmly committed to the NATO alliance, notwithstanding the high level of abstention in the 1949 Commons vote. They were equally committed to a certain, possibly quite substantial, level of rearmament, even quoting Yugoslavia's experience as justification,

> 'Tito survives today because he had arms and the will to defend his country. The Russians, who imposed upon him the most savage blockade in modern history would not have stopped short of more forceful measures if they had thought they could employ them with impunity'.[19]

They wanted to deter the Russians, restrain the Americans, and allow the peaceful evolution of a social democratic Europe in alliance with third world saved from Communism by the provision of a massive aid programme, which would establish the 'principle of fair shares between nations'. Whilst much of what the Bevanites wrote to this effect may, to the modern reader, smack of social-democratic colonial paternalism, it ought not to obscure the fact that the authors had an appreciation of the dangers of world economic imbalance and that their concern was absolutely genuine. It was a challenging view to address to a nation weaned on imperialist greed and arrogance, and there is every reason to assume that it expressed a widespread sentiment in the mass Labour movement.

The commitment to world mutual aid is to be found in

both Keep Left manifestos, *One Way Only, Going Our Way* and even in the last pamphlet *It Need Not Happen* where it was suggested that projected West German rearmament expenditure might be diverted into the fund for such aid. But the naïvety of Bevanism was its 'leaders' belief that a social democratic Europe in allegiance with an aid-assisted third world might be ensured by a Labour movement *firmly committed to the American alliance*, and with the ultimate consent of the Kremlin through international negotiation. In other words Bevanism subjected itself to the very two camps it had begun by renouncing.

Nonetheless the preoccupation with world mutual aid contains the germ of an appreciation of the essential unity of the world economy and this carried over into their discussions on domestic policy. These discussions always took place within the context of world problems, and always, within the bounds of the party's programme. The following excerpt from *One Way Only* expresses the Bevanite approach to great effect by quoting from the direct experience of factory workers at the time,

> 'Until recently there were many people in Great Britain who thought that political problems were divided into two hermetically sealed compartments, called respectively "home affairs" and "foreign affairs" which had no connection with one another. We all know better now . . . We have seen how the materials we need for our work disappear off the floor of the workshop because of something that's happened on the other side of Asia, and we have seen how the prices of goods in the shops are forced up by raw material scrambles thousands of miles from our shores'.[20]

One Way Only saw in Britain's internal economic and social problems the 'microcosm of the economic and social problems of the whole world'—the disparity between rich and poor—and the prevention of capital development sufficient to eradicate it through stockpiling, rearmament and war preparation. Basically the argument of the Bevanite pamphlets was that a mistaken foreign policy was making impossible both the realisation of Labour's domestic socialist reforms and the improvement of the lot of the colonial peoples of South East Asia simultaneously. In this manner the Bevanites established an identity of interests between the British working class and the mass movements of the third world determined upon radical change in their conditions of life.

If the main, Bevanite pamphlets exhibit a lack of concrete proposals for domestic reform it is due solely to their commitment to the party programme, which they believed could not be implemented without a major shift in the emphasis of Labour's foreign policy.

In addition to the main Bevanite publications there was an entire series of Tribune monthly pamphlets, which were produced between Autumn 1950 and the resumption of the weekly Tribune in 1952. But these were informative, discursive and critical rather than exercises in policy formulation. They covered everything from Zionism to taxation; and gambling to the state of Northern Ireland. This latter pamphlet *John Bull's Other Ireland* ran into four editions and sold almost 200,000 copies—a striking illustration of the scale of the popularity of the more successful Bevanite pamphlets. Worthy of special mention was Bevan's own book, *In Place of Fear*. Completed whilst on holiday in Yugoslavia, shortly after the Cabinet resignations, it was published in April 1952 by William Heinemann.[21] It was translated into French, Italian, German and Spanish, an honour not bestowed on many volumes produced by British Labour politicians. Michael Foot says of the book 'it was an instantaneous publishing success',[22] and remarks that it was 'packed with striking aphorisms and original reflections'.[23] It dealt with the political topics of the day 'always in unexpected contexts and often with tentative, unexpected conclusions'.[24]

Bevan's book certainly was remarkable and it is not difficult to see why it generated such huge controversy after the press conference on publication day. It is the work of a social democrat greatly influenced by Marxism, and considering Bevan's leadership chances, this fact alone was likely to produce alarm. Unlike Labour candidates for the leadership before and since, who boasted that they had never got further than page one of *Capital*, Bevan acknowledged his debt to Marxism.

> 'Marx and the school which he founded, put into the hands of the working class movement of the late nineteenth and the first part of the twentieth century, the most complete blueprints for political action the world has ever seen.'[25]

Bevan confided,

> 'In so far as I can be said to have had a political training at all, it has been in Marxism'.[26]

but he stopped short of describing himself as a Marxist because he did not accept the exclusive necessity for revolution in the establishment of socialism. He was scathing towards the opponents of Marxism. They were,

> 'usually so deeply prejudiced that they are shut off from reality by a wall of their own making. Their unscholarly bias renders them as unfit guides to political conduct as the Marxist dogmatists. A sympathetic understanding of what Marxists are trying to say to the world is a prerequisite to learning where the Marxist practitioners are liable to go wrong'.[27]

Bevan claims his experience with Marxism was shared by thousands of British working class men and women.

> 'The relevance of what we were reading to our industrial and political experience had all the impact of a divine revelation. Everything fell into place. The dark places were lighted up and the difficult ways made easy.'[28]

Yet he combined this enthusiasm towards Marxism with emphatic rejection of what many would regard as its central tenets, and he was, at the same time, hostile to those who reduced Marxism to the level of a dogma. He was frank about what he regarded as the weaknesses of Marxism,

> 'Quite early in my studies it seemed to me that classic Marxism consistently understated the role of a political democracy with a fully developed franchise'.[29]

He was also,

> 'deeply conscious of the failure to take into account . . . the subjective attitude of peoples'.[30]

Yet the entire book centres on the question that is central to Marxism, and Bevan raises it on the very first page,

> 'Where does power lie in this particular state of Great Britain and how can it be attained by the workers?'[31]

In pursuit of the answer to this question, he related, for the first time, the story of the confrontation between Robert Smillie and the leaders of the Triple Alliance with Lloyd George in 1919. He quoted at length from Smillie's account of Lloyd George's speech to the union leaders,

> 'For if a force arises in the state which is stronger than the state itself, then it must be ready to take on the functions of the state or withdraw and accept the authority of the state. "Gentlemen," asked the Prime Minister, "have you considered, and, if you have, are you ready?" "From that moment on," said Robert Smillie, "we were beaten and we knew we were".'[32]

Bevan claims this is a classic example of subjective attitudes overriding objective circumstance. 'The workers and their leaders paused even when their coercive power was greater than that of the state',[33] he concludes, taking issue with those who would argue that it was not the workers but only the leaders, who hesitated and lacked the will to seize power. Yet Bevan did not glamorise democracy, nor did he identify it with parliament. He speaks unambiguously about 'capitalist democracy'.

> 'the issue, therefore, in a capitalist democracy, resolves itself into this; either poverty will use democracy to win the struggle against property, or property, in fear of poverty, will destroy democracy'.[34]

The art of Conservative politics, he maintained, lay in persuading poverty to use its political freedom to keep wealth in power. As long as political democracy ('capitalist democracy') existed, the welfare of working class people was on 'the agenda of political discussion' and demanded its consideration. By contrast 'fascism and all forms of authoritarian government take it off the agenda again'.[35]

Here Bevan puts a high value on 'capitalist democracy',

seeing it as of little use or even an obstacle to the Establishment, but indispensable to the working class in the transition to socialism. He counterposes it to *all* forms of authoritarianism, including, that is, the Soviet state.

Whilst conceding the impressiveness of Soviet economic achievements he appears, at first sight, to entertain no illusions as to the reactionary nature of the political regime in the USSR. He regarded 'Soviet Communism' as the 'running mate' of fascism.[36] It was, he believed, one of the tragedies of history that the first experiments in socialism took place in economically backward countries,[37] and that this fact had compounded the problems of western socialists.

> 'It is probable that Western Europe would have gone socialist after the war if Soviet behaviour had not given it too grim a visage'.[38]

Yet, quite inconsistently, Bevan also argued 'the picture of the Russian worker held down by a ruthless dictatorship is false'.[39]

Bevan did not elaborate or develop an analysis of the Soviet or Eastern European States and his comments, whilst often brilliant and penetrating, reveal little evidence of familiarity with established theorists, Marxist or otherwise, in this field. But he did venture some remarks on possible future developments in the East European and Stalinist arena. He was of the opinion that since the machinery of oppression had a power and universality 'without parallel in the whole of history' and since communication was a monopoly of the state, Soviet citizens were totally atomised. Yet despite this he concludes that the Soviet state would eventually face the need to ensure the co-operation of the Soviet workforce. This however would not come about 'until they are conscious of constriction of their material wants'. Until that happened the Soviet workers would not protest, he asserted. There is more than a hint of behaviourism in this remark and Bevan undoubtedly permitted himself an economic-determinist view of the future course of developments in Eastern Europe which he certainly would not have entertained in a British context, where he always stressed worker participation and the development of political consciousness in industry. But, perhaps more important, Bevan here applies the same gradualist approach to political developments in a totalitarian state that he believed best for a democratic one. And whilst Bevan's fascination with the Yugoslav 'mutation'[40] (the choice of noun is instructive) led him correctly to predict that 'China will be next',[41] he did not project that China and Yugoslavia might merely develop more novel forms of totalitarian oppression. He assumed that they would inevitably develop in the direction of greater democracy. This is surprising considering the importance that Bevan attached to democratic liberties. Without them Bevan believed socialism could neither be established nor maintained. And it would be a mistake, in this respect, to consider that Bevan necessarily equated democracy with parliament, even though he held parliament paramount in the achievement of socialism.

> 'Parliament in Britain is centuries old. Democracy has only just come of age',[42]

he remarked in a reference to the achievement of the full adult franchise of 1929. He believed that the House of Commons was,

> 'an elaborate conspiracy to prevent the real clash of opinion which exists outside from finding an appropriate echo within its walls. It is a shock absorber between privilege and the pressure of popular discontent'.[43]

In many respects Bevan exhibited far greater breadth of mind and depth of insight than his Marxist contemporaries—specifically in the last two chapters of his book, where he deals prophetically with problems of ecology, energy, world resources, atomic weapons, imbalances in the world economy and the development of opposition of Soviet rule in Eastern Europe. It has to be borne in mind that his book appeared when Stalinism was at its height—four years after the iron curtain had descended on the working class and nation states of Eastern Europe, and one year before the first modern revolutions against Soviet reaction, the East German rising. Bevan had no reason to suppose that Marxist orthodoxy was anything other than that which the leaders of world Stalinism and their servants in the West European Communist parties asserted at any given time. Considering the 'unacceptable face' that this presented and considering it was the middle of the cold war period it is remarkable that Bevan publicly acknowledged his debt to Marxism to the extent that he did.

There were no Eurocommunists; no polycentrists; no dissidents to speak of. The forces of critical Trotskyism were tiny, theoretically puny and of little consequence in Britain. But Bevan who never professed Marxism, did try for a time to differentiate between Marxism and 'Soviet Communism', to project the possible future course of its development and to relate the evolution of socialism to the fulfilment of human needs on a global scale. Bevan did not profess to have all the answers, but he certainly addressed himself to the key questions which many 'new thinkers'[44] appeared to be studiously avoiding. The book is curiously inconsistent at times, but never prosaic. It is always shedding new light. *In Place of Fear* expresses all the energetic ambiguity of the early Bevanite years. It expresses considerable scepticism towards parliament, yet embraces it as the means of achieving socialism. It respects Marxism but rejects much of its essence. It abhors Soviet totalitarianism but believes it is necessary to live with it (a concession Bevan would never have made to the fascist regimes to which he likened it). Its greatest strength is that the experience and ambition of the British working class movement, personalised in Bevan's own political journey, finds clear and passionate expression in its pages. One can well appreciate why the Bevanite generation of British Labour, saw in this book their past struggles, their present banner and their future hopes.

It is hardly surprising that in the sixties it was chiefly from the ranks of the Bevanites that the main forces of the leadership of the Labour party derived.[45] The forces of the Left of the party today are infinitely better placed than they were in the fifties. The manifestos of the seventies become ever more far-reaching in their proposals. The party increasingly asserts its will over the leadership at conference, and important changes in the method of election of leader, selection of the Cabinet and representation on the NEC are currently on the agenda. Whatever controversy may surround the record of the Wilson governments of the sixties and seventies, it was a period of steady advance for the left within the unions and the party, the kind of development which Aneurin Bevan himself projected and worked for.

Of what value is a study of the Bevanite movement for Labour today? Many of the problems to which the Bevanites addressed themselves remain on the agenda for resolution but in a different context. One aspect of this changed context is the different life experience of present generations. Mass movements cannot be generated by the oratory or will power of 'leaderships'. Mass movements arise spontaneously out of objective historical circumstance.

Labour Party members need to recognise squarely that they represent a smaller percentage of the working population than their counterparts in Bevanite days. On the other hand trade union membership has virtually doubled and embraces layers who owe no 'natural allegiance' to Labour. It is here Labour's case will have to be fought—within the unions and the non-party mass of the people.

But democratic questions are far from simple. Enhanced accountability and democratisation within the Labour Party is negated if not pursued *as an integral part of the process of subjugating the party itself to the aspirations of the working class as a whole.* Otherwise it becomes *a sophisticated form of apparatism—of substituting the party for the class,* and we shall end up with a leadership and policy accountable to a party which is becoming more remote from the mass of the people.

Secondly Labour must convince the younger generation that ecological survival especially in relation to nuclear energy is an essential part, even a priority, in its programme. The Bevanite movement, let us recall, was engulfed and swept along by the tidal wave of CND after 1957, this in turn defeated the Gaitskellite leadership in 1960. All the signs are that a mass movement of world proportions is in the process of formation on the nuclear issue.

Finally the Bevanite experience exposed mercilessly the shortcomings of those of its leaders who looked to the gradual emergence of a more liberal Communist hierarchy in Eastern Europe. Even Bevan, whose democratic credentials were widely recognised, fell foul of this perspective. The present volume contains a solemn warning in this respect. The revolution in Hungary disrupted Bevan's relationship with the Khrushchev leadership. But the greater the social tensions in Eastern Europe, the more tenaciously he oriented towards 'detente' with the undertakers of the Hungarian revolution. Within months Bevan was in Yalta being wooed from unilateralism in the tragic run up to the Brighton conference.

For their part the British Communists contributed absolutely nothing to the Bevanite current except to assist in its final dissolution. These are harsh words but incontrovertible in the light of the evidence assembled. If the left today continues (with some honourable exceptions) to place its relations with the Communists in the quaintly named 'broad left' above the principle of defence of dissident trade unionists and the right of parties of the Second International to be formed in the Soviet bloc, it will prepare for itself a new 'Brighton' and will fail to win the new generation.

There was some excuse for the Bevanites. The dissidents had not yet arrived. But there will be no excuse if Labour fails to aid the people to whom this book is dedicated.

NOTES

1. Socialist Commentary, Column 16, November, 1952. Editorial 'The Month After Morecambe'. On the editorial Board were Rita Hinden, Allan Flanders, Lucjan Blit, Frank Horrabin, W. Arthur Lewis, and Fred Mulley MP.
2. See Appendix to this volume: grid and List of Bevanite members supplied to the author by Miss Richardson.
3. When Ireland left the Commonwealth Labour moved a Bill outlining the status of North and South. The 'revolt' was over a clause which gave to Stormont rather than to the people of Northern Ireland, the right to the final say in whether to remain part of the UK.
4. Labour Party Annual Conference Report 1948 (p. 17).
5. The Bevanites who deserted the cause on this occasion—Crossman, Hale, Swingler, Delargy, Irvine and Wilson.
6. *Keep Left* (p. 45) published by the New Statesman and Nation, London, May 1947.

7. *Keep Left, op. cit.* (p. 11).
8. *Keeping Left* (p. 43) published by the New Statesman and Nation, London, January 1950.
9. *Keeping Left, op. cit.*, back cover.
10. *One Way Only* (foreword), published by Tribune, London 1951.
11. *One Way Only, op. cit.* (p. 60). The Bevanites presented a list of uncompleted tasks agreed upon by the movement, included in the manifesto, and therefore morally binding on the party leadership.
    'The control of "financial forces"; a Development Council for ship-building and ship-repairing; the rate for the job; the abolition of price rings and rigged markets; more industrial democracy; more efficiency and social responsibility in the nationalised industries; the creation, by compulsion if need be, of Development Councils; the provision of buildings and equipment to approved manufacturers; public competition in privately-owned industries; the nationalisation of some monopoly concerns; the public ownership of sugar, cement and possibly some chemicals; the full use of statutory powers against inefficient farmers; nationalisation of food-producing land which is not fully used; the reform of fruit and vegetable marketing; the public ownership of some mineral workings; the "mutualisation" of industrial assurance; reconsideration of the problem of the tied cottage; public responsibility for all water supplies; the reduction of excessive prices; publicly-owned markets; the rationalisation of cold stores; public ownership of meat wholesaling; Government bulk buying of consumer goods; the establishment of a Consumer Advice Centre—all that, though some people would like to forget it, is Labour Party policy. Some of those measures may now be susceptible to some modification and improvement; *they all remain to be carried out.* There is, in fact, no need whatever for the Government and the Party to engage in a frantic search for new ideas and new policies to deal with the present situation. All that *is needed is the resolute implementation of the ideas which the Party has already worked out* and the policies which it has already adopted. Within the framework of those ideas and policies there is ample scope for a "combined operation" against inflation.' (*My emphasis*—MJ).
12. *One Way Only, op. cit.* (p. 4). It sold 100,000 copies. See p. 137.
13. *Going Our Way* (p. 6–7) published by Tribune, London 1951.
14. *Going Our Way, op. cit.* (p. 7).
15. *It Need Not Happen* (p. 17) published by Tribune, London 1954.
16. *Labour Party Election Manifesto*, 1951.
17. *Forward With Labour*, Labour Party Election manifesto, 1955.
18. *One Way Only, op. cit.* (p. 9).
19. *One Way Only, op. cit.* (p. 9).
20. *One Way Only, op. cit.* (p. 13).
21. *In Place of Fear* by Aneurin Bevan, Wm. Heinemann, London, April 1952. All quotations however taken from the later 1961

edition published by MacGibbon and Kee, London.

22. Foot, *Vol. II op. cit.* (p.368). Wm. Heinemann records show two editions in 1952—12,500 copies of the 10/6 (52p) edition and 25,000 copies of the 6/- (30p) edition.
23. Foot, *Vol II, op. cit.* (p. 369).
24. *ibid.*
25. *In Place of Fear* (p. 37) by Aneurin Bevan, MacGibbon & Kee, London 1961.
26. Bevan, *op. cit.* (p. 38).
27. Bevan, *op. cit.* (p. 38).
28. Bevan, *op. cit.* (p. 38).
29. Bevan, *op. cit.* (p. 39).
30. Bevan, *op. cit.* (p. 42).
31. Bevan, *op. cit.* (p. 29).
32. Bevan, *op. cit.* (p. 41).
33. Bevan, *op. cit.* (p. 41).
34. Bevan, *op. cit.* (p. 23).
35. Bevan, *op. cit.* (p. 25).
36. Bevan, *op. cit.* (p. 201).
37. Bevan, *op. cit.* (p. 180).
38. Bevan, *op. cit.* (p. 91).
39. Bevan, *op. cit.* (p. 167).
40. Bevan, *op. cit.* (p. 36).
41. Bevan, *op. cit.* (p. 37).
42. Bevan, *op. cit.* (p. 28).
43. Bevan, *op. cit.* (p. 27).
44. The phrase used to describe the Gaitskellite intellectuals—Roy Jenkins, Tony Crosland and others.
45. It is also worth noting that Richard Crossman in his diaries has provided Labour with an encyclopaedic dossier on the workings of the state machine, and how this might frustrate the achievement of Labour's programme. These diaries themselves deserve a doctoral thesis investigation.

Appendix

Voting Grid on Crucial Rebellions or Abstentions

Index to Columns

- B Listed by Miss Jo Richardson, MP, former secretary to the Bevanite and Keep Left group, as members of the Bevanite Group (* = former Commonwealth party; B = known Bevanite).
- L Contributor to Labour Monthly, controlled by CPGB. Whilst this may mean nothing, taken with other factors it could indicate a significant orientation. Figures indicate number of contributions 1947–57.
- S Contributor to Socialist Outlook, controlled by Trotskyists. Whilst no MPs were known to be Trotskyists, willingness to contribute again indicates a certain approach to left politics (* denotes more than a few contributions).
- F This broad category indicates membership of one or more of the various 'front' organisations—'Peace Committees', or East European 'Friendship Societies'.
- KL 'Keep Left' Manifesto signatories 1947.
- KK 'Keeping Left' signatory 1950.
- N Nenni Telegram signatories 1947.
- 1 Rebellion of 72 Labour MPs March 1947 over National Service Bill, (March 1947).
- 2 63 vote against government on N. Ireland Bill 16.5.49.
- 3 6 vote against NATO 12.5.49. The six were Pritt, Platts Mills, and Zilliacus, later expelled; Chamberlain, Tom Braddock and Harold Davies all closely working alongside 'Socialist Outlook' at the time. (P = pro NATO, voted FOR) (A = abstained or no record of vote) Not one of the later Morecambe six were to be found listed in the 'Aye' or 'No' lobby.
- 4 Rebellion of 57 Labour MPs on government defeats. White Paper 5.3.52.
- 5 6 vote against EDC nine-power agreement November 1954, (Bevanites abstained).
- 6 63 Labour MPs rebellion over atomic energy Bill arguing no H-Bombs should be manufactured by UK without parliamentary agreement 29.4.54.

7 62 abstain on Labour opposition's amendment (2.3.55) to Government Defence White Paper immediately prior to the Bevan expulsion crisis. Note the desertion of the centre left marked with an asterisk.

N.B.

One event not recorded here, worthy of mention was an amendment to a government resolution moved by S. O. Davies and seconded by Emrys Hughes calling for withdrawal of British Forces from Korea on 5th July 1950. It was defeated without a division.

N.B.

The Northern Ireland revolt: When Ireland left the Commonwealth the government moved a resolution outlining the new status of Ireland and declared that N. Ireland would remain part of the U.K., and that *in no event would it cease to do so without Stormont's consent.* One Labour MP, Mr Beattie (West Belfast) moved deletion of this latter clause, this was defeated 345–21. Leslie Hale then proposed the people of N. Ireland rather than Stormont would be consulted. This was the 'revolt' alluded to. 45 Labour MPs supported him. It was defeated—54 voting for Hale's motion.

Group	Name	B	L	S	F	KL	KK	N	1	2	3	4	5	6	7
Keeping Left	Geoffrey Bing	B			F	KL		N		2	A	4		6	
Keeping Left	Donald Bruce	[B]	L1			KL	KK				P				
Keeping Left	Richard Crossman	B	L2			KL	KK				A	4		6	*
Keeping Left	Harold Davies	B	L2	S*	F	KL	KK	N			A	4		6	7
Keeping Left	Michael Foot	B				KL					P	4			7
Keeping Left	Leslie Hale	B				KL	KK			2	P	4			*
Keeping Left	Fred Lee					KL					A				
Keeping Left	Benn Levy		L1			KL					P				
Keeping Left	R. W. G. Mackay					KL				2	P				
Keeping Left	J. P. W. Mallalieu	B	L1			KL				2	P	4			7
Keeping Left	Ian Mikardo	B				KL	KK		1	2	A	4		6	
Keeping Left	Ernest Millington*					KL					A				
Keeping Left	Stephen Swingler	B	L1	S	F	KL	KK	N			A	4		6	*
Keeping Left	George Wigg					KL	KK				A				
Keeping Left	Woodrow Wyatt					KL				2	P				
Keep Left	Richard Acland*	B					KK				P	4			7
Keep Left	Barbara Castle	B					KK				A	4			7
Keep Left	Tom Horabin						KK			2	A				
Keep Left	Marcus Lipton	B					KK			2	A	4		6	
Keep Left	Thomas Williams	B					KK		1	2	P	4		6	7
"Nennists"	H. L. Austin							N		2	A				
"Nennists"	P. Barstow							N	1		A	Joined CPGB 1952			
"Nennists"	Thomas Braddock		L1	S*				N	1		3				
"Nennists"	W. G. Cove							N	1		P	4		6	
"Nennists"	S. O. Davies		L4	S*	F			N		2	A	4	5		
"Nennists"	W. Dobbie							N			A				
"Nennists"	Emrys Hughes	B	L1		F			N			3	4	5	6	7
"Nennists"	Lester Hutchinson		L3		F			N			A	Expelled from LP			
"Nennists"	H. Lever							N			A	4			
"Nennists"	J. D. Mack							N			A				
"Nennists"	Maurice Orbach	B						N			A	4		6	7
"Nennists"	C. Royle							N	1	2	A			6	7
"Nennists"	Julius Silverman	B	L1		F			N	1	2	A	4		6	7
"Nennists"	Sidney Silverman		L1		F			N	1		A	4	5	6	7
"Nennists"	L. J. Solley							N	1		A				
"Nennists"	William Warbey							N			A			6	7
"Nennists"	Konni Zilliacus		L9	S				N	1		3	Expelled from LP—readmitted			

Bevanite Group not included in other categories

	B	L	S	F	N	1	2	3	4	5	6	7
John Baird	B							P	4		6	7
C. R. Bence	B								4			7
Aneurin Bevan	B							A	4		6	7
F. G. Bowles	B							A	4		6	7
Fenner Brockway	B	L2	S						4			7
J. Carmichael	B					1		A	4			7
George Craddock	B								4	5	6	7
Hugh Delargy	B						2	P	4		6	*
Desmond Donnelly	B								4		6	
Tom Driberg	B						2	A	4			7
Edward Evans	B							A	4		6	
Ernest Fernyhough	B			F			2	A	4	5	6	7
John Freeman	B							A	4			
Will Griffiths	B							A	4			7
Arthur Irvine	B							P	4			*
F. E. Jones	B							A	4			7
Jennie Lee	B							A	4			7
Malcolm McMillan	B						2	P	4			
Archie Manuel	B								4		6	7
Cecil Poole	B							A	4			
John Rankin	B					1	2	A	4		6	7
Ellis Smith	B		S*					A	4			
Julian Snow	B							P	4		6	7
Barnett Stross	B			F				A	4			
John Timmons	B					1	2	P	4			
Harold Wilson	B							A	4			*
Walter Monslow	B					1		A	4		6	7
Tudor Watkins	B					1		A	4			
David Weitzman	B							A			6	7
T. W. Jones	B										6	7
Goronwy Roberts	B					1		A			6	7

Other Left, or Bevanite Associates or Temporary Allies

	B	L	S	F	NL	KK	N	1	2	3	4	5	6	7
D. R. Grenfell								1		P	4			7
H. Usborne				F				1		A	4			7
Arthur Lewis										P	4			7
Fred Longden								1	2	A	4			
J. McGovern								1	2	P	4			
Walter Padley											4		6	
George Thomas								1		A	4			
Victor Yates								1	2	A	4	5	6	7
Frank Beswick			S						2	P			6	7
T. Clune													6	7
J. Forman								1		P			6	7
J. Hudson								1	2	A			6	7
H. G. McGhee								1	2	A			6	
W. Paling										P			6	7
G. Pargiter										P			6	7
Ben Parkin		L1								A			6	7
Sir Leslie Plummer													6	7
J. Reeves										P			6	7
Kenneth Robinson										A			6	7
H. Slater													6	7
P. Wells								1		P			6	
Anthony Greenwood										P			6	7
Allan Scholefield													6	
A. Wedgewood-Benn													6	
A. Blenkinsop										P			6	
M. Cullen										A			6	7
Maurice Edelman										P			6	7
John Edwards										P			6	7
J. Harrison										A			6	7
J. Hubbard										P			6	7
Lena Jeger													6	7
W. Reed													6	7
Harvey Rhodes										A			6	7
P. L. Shurmer													6	7
H. Slater													6	
Bernard Taylor													6	7
Reginald Sorenson		L1						1		A			6	7
Thomas Brown								1		P			6	7

Other Left or Bevanite Associates or Temporary Allies

	B	L	S	F	NL	KK	N	1	2	3	4	5	6	7
G. Darling													6	
Ernest Davies										A			6	7
Alber Evans										P			6	
Eric Fletcher										P			6	
W. J. Irving										P			6	
Dr. Horace King													6	
J. E. McColl													6	
J. McKay										P			6	
Percy Morris													6	
J. Parker									2	P			6	
N. Smith										P			6	
J. Palmer													6	
E. G. Willis										P			6	
F. T. Willey										P			6	
T. Brown										P			6	

Index